THE AMERICAN LAW INSTITUTE

A Concise Restatement
of
TORTS

Compiled
by
KENNETH S. ABRAHAM
Class of 1962 Professor
and
Albert Clark Tate, Jr. Research Professor
University of Virginia
School of Law

·A·L·I·

ST. PAUL, MN
AMERICAN LAW INSTITUTE PUBLISHERS
2000

ISBN 0–314–24760–2

FOREWORD

Work on the original Restatement of Torts began in 1923, shortly after the establishment of The American Law Institute earlier that year. Together with the Restatements of Agency and Contracts, it was thus one of the very first undertakings of the Institute. The Reporter with overall responsibility for this work in the ensuing years was Francis H. Bohlen of the University of Pennsylvania, although there were no fewer than seven subsidiary Reporters who drafted various portions of the Restatement, the fourth and final volume of which was published in 1939.

After another 16 years, in 1955, the Institute returned to the subject of torts, revisiting and reconsidering every aspect of the original Restatement, reformulating and frequently expanding its provisions in light of subsequent legal developments. The Restatement Second of Torts, which took 24 years to complete, eventually superseded and entirely replaced its predecessor, no portion of which, therefore, is included in this volume. The Reporters for Torts Second were two of the most eminent torts scholars of the 20th century, William L. Prosser of the University of California's Hastings College of the Law and John W. Wade of Vanderbilt University. The initial drafting was almost entirely the work of Prosser, and the first 19 chapters were approved by the Institute and published while he was still the Reporter. After Prosser's resignation in 1970, Wade assumed the responsibility of revising Prosser's drafts of the remaining chapters, presenting them for approval, and overseeing their publication.

By 1991 additional major developments in the law of torts had convinced the Institute that the time had come to begin a Third Restatement of the subject. This time, however, it was decided to concentrate at the outset on the specific areas of tort law most immediately in need of revision or expansion and to proceed by way of specific integrated projects within the broader framework of a complete Restatement of Torts. The initial project, a reexamination of products-liability law, was a particularly appropriate one for the Institute to undertake in light of the extraordinary influence of its previous treatment of this topic, in particular that of § 402A of Torts Second, which by 1990 had itself been cited nearly 3000 times by the courts. Because of the broad development of the case law in the intervening years, Restatement Third, Torts: Products Liability, which was approved in 1997 and published in 1998, was able to present a far more expansive, nuanced, and sophisticated analysis of this complex and challenging subject than had been possible for the previous Restatement to achieve three decades earlier. Its Reporters were James A. Henderson of Cornell University and Aaron D. Twerski of Brooklyn Law School.

The second segment of Torts Third to be undertaken was an analysis of the apportionment of liability in cases in which multiple tortfeasors may be responsible in varying degrees for a single injury, a problem that has become particularly acute and difficult to resolve in comparative-negligence regimes, which may require that the plaintiff's own degree of fault be entered into the equation. The Reporters for Restatement Third, Torts: Apportionment of Liability, which was approved in 1999 and published in 2000, were William C. Powers, Jr., of the University of Texas and Michael D. Green of the University of Iowa.

Now in early development is an extensive reexamination of the general principles underlying tort law, including those of negligence. The Reporters for this major component of Torts Third are Gary T. Schwartz of the University of California at Los Angeles and Harvey S. Perlman of the University of Nebraska. Other segments of the new Restatement are expected to follow in due course.

In all, the various Torts Restatements have been cited more than 60,000 times by the state and federal courts and have contributed immeasurably to the clarification of tort law throughout the United States. In compiling this Concise Restatement, Professor Kenneth S. Abraham of the University of Virginia has assembled in a compact, convenient, and readily accessible format those portions of these Restatements that an experienced teacher of torts regards as especially pertinent and helpful to an introductory study of the subject. Most of this compilation necessarily derives from Torts Second, but it also draws upon the Institute's Restatement Third reformulations of products liability and apportionment of liability. Regarding products liability, the influential and still-relevant § 402A has been retained as well, enabling the reader to conveniently compare the Institute's earlier formulation with its current one.

While assembly of a most manageable study aid entailed the cutting of many relevant sections, as well as the omission or paring of commentary to many sections whose black-letter provisions have been included, the material ultimately retained has not been rewritten or changed in substance; its language is precisely that which has been relied upon (and quoted extensively) by the courts throughout the past several decades of tort law development. To facilitate additional research, cross-references to sections that are not included in

FOREWORD

this volume, as well to those that are, have been retained. Appendices A-C contain the complete tables of contents for each of the three Restatements excerpted here. By reference to these appendices, interested students may see the full extent of what is included in these volumes, all of which can be accessed in most law-school libraries as well as online. Also on the shelves and online, specially-prepared Institute summaries of all cases citing the particular provisions of these Restatements are housed in adjacent "Appendix" volumes, showing the extent to which the Restatements have influenced tort law in jurisdictions throughout the United States.

The Institute is grateful to Professor Abraham for assembling this excellent compilation and hopeful that it will prove useful both as a supplement to the study of torts and as an introduction to the perennially evolving Torts Restatements.

LANCE LIEBMAN
DIRECTOR
THE AMERICAN LAW INSTITUTE

March, 2000

*

THE AMERICAN LAW INSTITUTE

The American Law Institute was created in 1923 as a private organization of judges, lawyers, and legal scholars seeking to respond to "general dissatisfaction with the administration of justice" by working for improvement of the law. The Institute's primary goal, as stated in its charter, was to "promote the clarification and simplification of the law and its better adaptation to social needs." The incorporators included William Howard Taft and Charles Evans Hughes; Benjamin Cardozo and Learned Hand were among the early leaders.

From the beginning, the ALI worked on "Restatements" of the common law with the goal of helping the systematic development of the law and the pursuit of consistent legal doctrine among the states. The first Restatements were on the subjects of Agency, Conflict of Laws, Contracts, Judgments, Property, Restitution, Security, Torts, and Trusts. Subsequent Restatement projects have included The Foreign Relations Law of the United States, Unfair Competition, and The Law Governing Lawyers. Other major ALI projects have included the Uniform Commercial Code (for which the ALI has a partner, the National Conference of Commissioners on Uniform State Laws), the Model Penal Code, Principles of Corporate Governance, and Principles of the Law of Family Dissolution.

The ALI's working method is to choose for each project one or more experts, usually law professors, as "Reporters" and to subject each of their successive drafts to detailed review by "Advisers" consisting of judges, lawyers, and academics and by a special consultative group of interested Institute members. After appropriate revision, a draft is next submitted for review to the Institute's Council, a governing body of some 60 members drawn widely from the various branches of the legal profession, and then, as a "Tentative Draft," to the membership as a whole at the Institute's Annual Meeting, during which time it is also made generally available for public comment and review. When the project in its entirety has been approved by both the Council and the membership, a process that can take many years, the final, official text is prepared for publication.

The Institute's membership includes judges, practitioners, and law teachers from all areas of the United States as well as many foreign countries, selected on the basis of professional achievement and demonstrated interest in the improvement of the law. Ex officio members include the Chief Justice and Associate Justices of the

NOTE

Supreme Court of the United States, the Chief Judges of the federal courts of appeals and the highest courts of the states, law school Deans, and the Presidents of the American Bar Association, state bar associations, and other prominent legal organizations.

SUMMARY OF CONTENTS

TORTS 2D

DIVISION ONE

INTENTIONAL HARMS TO PERSONS, LAND, AND CHATTELS

DIVISION TWO

NEGLIGENCE

*

TABLE OF CONTENTS

TORTS 2D

DIVISION ONE

INTENTIONAL HARMS TO PERSONS, LAND, AND CHATTELS

CHAPTER 1. MEANING OF TERMS USED THROUGHOUT THE RESTATEMENT OF TORTS

CHAPTER 2. INTENTIONAL INVASIONS OF INTERESTS IN PERSONALITY

TOPIC 1. THE INTEREST IN FREEDOM FROM HARMFUL BODILY CONTACT

TOPIC 2. THE INTEREST IN FREEDOM FROM OFFENSIVE BODILY CONTACT

TABLE OF CONTENTS

TABLE OF CONTENTS

TABLE OF CONTENTS

TABLE OF CONTENTS

TABLE OF CONTENTS

DIVISION THREE

STRICT LIABILITY

CHAPTER 20. LIABILITY OF POSSESSORS AND HARBORERS OF ANIMALS

TOPIC 1. TRESPASS BY LIVESTOCK

TOPIC 2. HARM CAUSED BY ANIMALS OTHERWISE THAN BY TRESPASS BY LIVESTOCK

CHAPTER 21. ABNORMALLY DANGEROUS ACTIVITIES

DIVISION FOUR

MISREPRESENTATION

CHAPTER 22. MISREPRESENTATION AND NONDISCLOSURE CAUSING PECUNIARY LOSS

TOPIC 1. FRAUDULENT MISREPRESENTATION (DECEIT)

TITLE A. FRAUDULENT CHARACTER OF MISREPRESENTATION

TITLE B. EXPECTATION OF INFLUENCING CONDUCT

TITLE C. JUSTIFIABLE RELIANCE

TITLE D. CAUSATION

TITLE E. DAMAGES FOR FRAUDULENT MISREPRESENTATION

TOPIC 2. CONCEALMENT AND NONDISCLOSURE

DIVISION FIVE

DEFAMATION

CHAPTER 24. INVASION OF INTEREST IN REPUTATION

TOPIC 1. ELEMENTS OF A CAUSE OF ACTION FOR DEFAMATION

TOPIC 2. DEFAMATORY COMMUNICATIONS

TOPIC 3. TYPES OF DEFAMATORY COMMUNICATION

TOPIC 4. FORMS OF DEFAMATORY COMMUNICATIONS

TOPIC 5. DEFAMATION ACTIONABLE IRRESPECTIVE OF SPECIAL HARM (DEFAMATION ACTIONABLE PER SE)

TABLE OF CONTENTS

DIVISION SIX–A

PRIVACY

CHAPTER 28A. INVASION OF PRIVACY

DIVISION NINE

INTERFERENCE WITH ADVANTAGEOUS ECONOMIC RELATIONS

CHAPTER 37. INTERFERENCE WITH CONTRACT OR PROSPECTIVE CONTRACTUAL RELATION

DIVISION TEN

INVASIONS OF INTERESTS IN LAND OTHER THAN BY TRESPASS

CHAPTER 40. NUISANCE

TOPIC 1. TYPES OF NUISANCE

TOPIC 2. PRIVATE NUISANCE: ELEMENTS OF LIABILITY

TOPIC 5. DEFENSES

TABLE OF CONTENTS

DIVISION THIRTEEN

REMEDIES

CHAPTER 47. DAMAGES

TOPIC 1. GENERAL STATEMENTS

TOPIC 2. DIMINUTION OF DAMAGES

TORTS 3D

PRODUCTS LIABILITY

CHAPTER 1. LIABILITY OF COMMERCIAL PRODUCT SELLERS BASED ON PRODUCT DEFECTS AT TIME OF SALE

TOPIC 1. LIABILITY RULES APPLICABLE TO PRODUCTS GENERALLY

TORTS 3D

APPORTIONMENT OF LIABILITY

TABLE OF CONTENTS

*

RESTATEMENT OF THE LAW SECOND

TORTS

DIVISION ONE

INTENTIONAL HARMS TO PERSONS, LAND, AND CHATTELS

Chapter 1

MEANING OF TERMS USED THROUGHOUT THE RESTATEMENT OF TORTS

§ 1. Interest

The word "interest" is used throughout the Restatement of this Subject to denote the object of any human desire.

Comment:

d. Legally protected interests. If society recognizes a desire as so far legitimate as to make one who interferes with its realization civilly liable, the interest is given legal protection, generally against all the world, so that everyone is under a duty not to invade the interest by interfering with the realization of the desire by certain forms of conduct. Thus the interest in bodily security is protected against not only intentional invasion but against negligent invasion or invasion by the mischances inseparable from an abnormally dangerous activity. Every man has a right, as against every other, not to have his interest in bodily security invaded in any of these manners. On the other hand, the interest in freedom from merely offensive bodily contacts is protected only against acts done with the intention stated as necessary in that part of the Restatement which deals with liability for such contacts. (See § 18.) Therefore, there is a right to freedom from only such contacts as are so caused, and there is no duty other than a duty not to cause offensive touchings by acts done with the intention there described.

§ 4. Duty

The word "duty" is used throughout the Restatement of this Subject to denote the fact that the actor is required to conduct himself in a particular manner at the risk that if he does not do so he becomes subject to liability to another to whom the duty is owed for any injury sustained by such other, of which that actor's conduct is a legal cause.

§ 6. Tortious Conduct

The word "tortious" is used throughout the Restatement of this Subject to denote the fact that conduct whether of act or omission is of such a character as to subject the actor to liability under the principles of the law of Torts.

§ 7. Injury and Harm

(1) The word "injury" is used throughout the Restatement of this Subject to denote the invasion of any legally protected interest of another.

(2) The word "harm" is used throughout the Restatement of this Subject to denote the existence of loss or detriment in fact of any kind to a person resulting from any cause.

(3) The words "physical harm" are used throughout the Restatement of this Subject to denote the physical impairment of the human body, or of land or chattels.

§ 8A. Intent

The word "intent" is used throughout the Restatement of this Subject to denote that the actor desires to cause consequences of his act, or that he believes that the consequences are substantially certain to result from it.

Comment:

a. "Intent," as it is used throughout the Restatement of Torts, has reference to the consequences of an act rather than the act itself. When an actor fires a gun in the midst of the Mojave Desert, he intends to pull the trigger; but when the bullet hits a person who is present in the desert without the actor's knowledge, he does not intend that result. "Intent" is limited, wherever it is used, to the consequences of the act.

b. All consequences which the actor desires to bring about are intended, as the word is used in this Restatement. Intent is not, however, limited to consequences which are desired. If the actor knows that the consequences are certain, or substantially certain, to result from his act, and still goes ahead, he is treated by the law as if he had in fact desired to produce the result. As the probability that the consequences will follow decreases, and becomes less than substantial certainty, the actor's conduct loses the character of intent, and becomes mere recklessness, as defined in § 500. As the probability decreases further, and amounts only to a risk that the result will follow, it becomes ordinary negligence, as defined in § 282. All three have their important place in the law of torts, but the liability attached to them will differ.

Illustrations:

1. A throws a bomb into B's office for the purpose of killing B. A knows that C, B's stenographer, is in the office. A has no desire to injure C, but knows that his act is substantially certain to do so. C is injured by the explosion. A is subject to liability to C for an intentional tort.

2. On a curve in a narrow highway A, without any desire to injure B, or belief that he is substantially certain to do so, recklessly drives his automobile in an attempt to pass B's car. As a result of this recklessness, A crashes into B's car, injuring B. A is subject to liability to B for his reckless conduct, but is not liable to B for any intentional tort.

§ 9. Legal Cause

The words "legal cause" are used throughout the Restatement of this Subject to denote the fact that the causal sequence by which the actor's tortious conduct has resulted in an invasion of some legally protected interest of another is such that the law holds the actor responsible for such harm unless there is some defense to liability.

§ 10. Privilege

(1) The word "privilege" is used throughout the Restatement of this Subject to denote the fact that conduct which, under ordinary circumstances, would subject the actor to liability, under particular circumstances does not subject him to such liability.

(2) A privilege may be based upon

(a) the consent of the other affected by the actor's conduct, or

(b) the fact that its exercise is necessary for the protection of some interest of the actor or of the public which is of such importance as to justify the harm caused or threatened by its exercise, or

(c) the fact that the actor is performing a function for the proper performance of which freedom of action is essential.

§ 10A. Consent

The word "consent" is used throughout the Restatement of this Subject to denote willingness in fact that an act or an invasion of an interest shall take place.

§ 12. Reason to Know; Should Know

(1) The words "reason to know" are used throughout the Restatement of this Subject to denote the fact that the actor has information from which a person of reasonable intelligence or of the superior intelligence of the actor would infer that the fact in question exists, or that such person would govern his conduct upon the assumption that such fact exists.

(2) The words "should know" are used throughout the Restatement of this Subject to denote the fact that a person of reasonable prudence and intelligence or of the superior intelligence of the actor would ascertain the fact in question in the performance of his duty to another, or would govern his conduct upon the assumption that such fact exists.

Chapter 2

INTENTIONAL INVASIONS OF INTERESTS IN PERSONALITY

TOPIC 1. THE INTEREST IN FREEDOM FROM HARMFUL BODILY CONTACT

§ 13. Battery: Harmful Contact

An actor is subject to liability to another for battery if

(a) he acts intending to cause a harmful or offensive contact with the person of the other or a third person, or an imminent apprehension of such a contact, and

(b) a harmful contact with the person of the other directly or indirectly results.

§ 16.   Character of Intent Necessary

(1) If an act is done with the intention of inflicting upon another an offensive but not a harmful bodily contact, or of putting another in apprehension of either a harmful or offensive bodily contact, and such act causes a bodily contact to the other, the actor is liable to the other for a battery although the act was not done with the intention of bringing about the resulting bodily harm.

(2) If an act is done with the intention of affecting a third person in the manner stated in Subsection (1), but causes a harmful bodily contact to another, the actor is liable to such other as fully as though he intended so to affect him.

Comment on Subsection (1):

a. In order that the actor shall be liable under the rule stated in this Section, it is not necessary that he intend to bring about the harmful contact which results from his act. It is enough that he intends to bring about an offensive contact or an apprehension of either a harmful or offensive contact, and that the bodily harm results as a legal consequence from such offensive contact or from such apprehension. The interest in freedom from either form of contact or from the apprehension of it is so far a part of the other's interest in his bodily security that the intention to inflict an offensive contact or to create an apprehension of either a harmful or offensive contact is sufficient to make the actor liable for a harmful contact resulting therefrom, even though such harmful contact was not intended.

Illustrations:

1.   Intending an offensive contact, A lightly kicks B on the shin. The blow, although offensive, is so slight that it would normally cause no bodily harm. B is suffering from a diseased leg, of which A neither knows nor has reason to know. The slight blow so aggravates the diseased condition as to result in a prolonged and expensive illness, which finally leads to permanent harm to the leg. A is subject to liability to B for the bodily harm caused by his act.

2.   A is playing golf. B, his caddie, is inattentive and A becomes angry. Intending to frighten but not to harm B, A aims a blow at him with a golf club which he stops some eight inches from B's head. Owing to the negligence of the club maker from whom A has just bought the club, the rivet which should have secured the head is defective, though A could not have discovered the defect without removing the head. The head of the club flies

off and strikes B in the eye, putting it out. A is subject to liability to B for the loss of his eye.

Comment on Subsection (2):

b. The intention which is necessary to make the actor liable under the rule stated in this Section is not necessarily an intention to cause a harmful or offensive contact or an apprehension of such contact to the plaintiff himself or otherwise to cause him bodily harm. It is enough that the actor intends to produce such an effect upon some other person and that his act so intended is the legal cause of a harmful contact to the other. It is not necessary that the actor know or have reason even to suspect that the other is in the vicinity of the third person whom the actor intends to affect and, therefore, that he should recognize that his act, though directed against the third person, involves a risk of causing bodily harm to the other so that the act would be negligent toward him.

Illustration:

3. A and B are trespassers upon C's land. C sees A but does not see B, nor does he know that B is in the neighborhood. C throws a stone at A. Immediately after C has done so, B raises his head above a wall behind which he has been hiding. The stone misses A but strikes B, putting out his eye. C is subject to liability to B.

TOPIC 2. THE INTEREST IN FREEDOM FROM OFFENSIVE BODILY CONTACT

§ 18. Battery: Offensive Contact

(1) An actor is subject to liability to another for battery if

(a) he acts intending to cause a harmful or offensive contact with the person of the other or a third person, or an imminent apprehension of such a contact, and

(b) an offensive contact with the person of the other directly or indirectly results.

(2) An act which is not done with the intention stated in Subsection (1, a) does not make the actor liable to the other for a mere offensive contact with the other's person although the act involves an unreasonable risk of inflicting it and, therefore, would be negligent or reckless if the risk threatened bodily harm.

Comment:

    c. Meaning of "contact with another's person." In order to make the actor liable under the rule stated in this Section, it is not necessary that he should bring any part of his own body in contact with another's person. It is enough that he intentionally cause his clothing or anything held or attached to him to come into such contact. So too, he is liable under the rule stated in this Section if he throws a substance, such as water, upon the other or if he sets a dog upon him. It is not necessary that the contact with the other's person be directly caused by some act of the actor. All that is necessary is that the actor intend to cause the other, directly or indirectly, to come in contact with a foreign substance in a manner which the other will reasonably regard as offensive. Thus, if the actor daubs with filth a towel which he expects another to use in wiping his face with the expectation that the other will smear his face with it and the other does so, the actor is liable as fully as though he had directly thrown the filth in the other's face or had otherwise smeared his face with it. So too, if the actor at a dignified social function, and for the purpose of making another appear ridiculous, pulls from under him a chair upon which he is about to sit, the actor is liable to the other under the rule stated in this Section.

    Since the essence of the plaintiff's grievance consists in the offense to the dignity involved in the unpermitted and intentional invasion of the inviolability of his person and not in any physical harm done to his body, it is not necessary that the plaintiff's actual body be disturbed. Unpermitted and intentional contacts with anything so connected with the body as to be customarily regarded as part of the other's person and therefore as partaking of its inviolability is actionable as an offensive contact with his person. There are some things such as clothing or a cane or, indeed, anything directly grasped by the hand which are so intimately connected with one's body as to be universally regarded as part of the person. On the other hand, there may be things which are attached to one's body with a connection so slight that they are not so regarded. The line of distinction is very difficult to draw. It is a thing which is felt rather than one to be defined, since it depends upon an emotional reaction. Thus, the ordinary man might well regard a horse upon which he is riding as part of his personality but, a passenger in a public omnibus or other conveyance would clearly not be entitled so to regard the vehicle merely because he was seated in it. If the actor recognizes any object, however slightly or remotely attached to the other's person, as being so far a part of the other's personality that he can accomplish his purpose of offending the other by some contact with it, it is not unreasonable to regard the object in the same light and, therefore, to make the actor liable under the rule stated in this Section. This may well be so although the connection with the plaintiff's body is so slight that if the actor had dealt with the object as a thing and not as a means through which he could reach and offend the other's dignity, the other as a reasonable man should not regard the integrity of his person as violated. Thus, if a plaintiff is taking his dog on a leash for an airing and the defendant, during an altercation kicks the dog, saying "That's what I think of your master," it may be that the defendant is liable. On the other hand, if the dog snaps at the defendant's heels, the defendant, if he kicks and harms it, while he may possibly make himself liable for any harm done to the plaintiff's possessory interest in the dog, does not thereby make himself liable for an offensive contact with the plaintiff's person.

d. Knowledge of contact. In order that the actor may be liable under the statement in this Subsection, it is not necessary that the other should know of the offensive contact which is inflicted upon him at the time when it is inflicted. The actor's liability is based upon his intentional invasion of the other's dignitary interest in the inviolability of his person and the affront to the other's dignity involved therein. This affront is as keenly felt by one who only knows after the event that an indignity has been perpetrated upon him as by one who is conscious of it while it is being perpetrated.

Illustrations:

1. A, a surgeon, while B is under anesthesia, makes an examination of her person to which she has not given her consent. A is subject to liability to B.

2. A kisses B while asleep but does not waken or harm her. A is subject to liability to B.

§ 19. What Constitutes Offensive Contact

A bodily contact is offensive if it offends a reasonable sense of personal dignity.

Caveat:

The Institute expresses no opinion as to whether the actor is liable if he inflicts upon another a contact which he knows will be offensive to another's known but abnormally acute sense of personal dignity.

Comment:

a. In order that a contact be offensive to a reasonable sense of personal dignity, it must be one which would offend the ordinary person and as such one not unduly sensitive as to his personal dignity.

9

It must, therefore, be a contact which is unwarranted by the social usages prevalent at the time and place at which it is inflicted.

Illustrations:

1. A flicks a glove in B's face. This is an offensive touching of B.

2. A, while walking in a densely crowded street, deliberately but not discourteously pushes against B in order to pass him. This is not an offensive touching of B.

3. A, who is suffering from a contagious skin disease, touches B's hands, thus putting B in reasonable apprehension of contagion. This is an offensive touching of B.

4. A, a child, becomes sick while riding in B's taxicab. B takes hold of A in order to help her. This is not an offensive touching.

§ 20. Character of Intent Necessary

(1) If an act is done with the intention of inflicting upon another a harmful bodily contact or of putting the other in apprehension of either a harmful or offensive bodily contact, and if it causes an offensive bodily contact to the other, the actor is subject to liability to the other although the act was not done with the intention of bringing about the resulting offensive contact.

(2) If an act is done with the intention of affecting a third person in the manner stated in Subsection (1) but causes an offensive bodily contact to another, the actor is subject to liability to such other as fully as though he intended so to affect him.

TOPIC 3. THE INTEREST IN FREEDOM FROM APPREHENSION OF A HARMFUL OR OFFENSIVE CONTACT

§ 21. Assault

(1) An actor is subject to liability to another for assault if

    (a) he acts intending to cause a harmful or offensive contact with the person of the other or a third person, or an imminent apprehension of such a contact, and

    (b) the other is thereby put in such imminent apprehension.

(2) An action which is not done with the intention stated in Subsection (1, a) does not make the actor liable to the other for an apprehension caused thereby although the act involves an unreasonable risk of causing it and, therefore, would be negligent or reckless if the risk threatened bodily harm.

§ 22. Attempt Unknown to Other

An attempt to inflict a harmful or offensive contact or to cause an apprehension of such contact does not make the actor liable for an assault if the other does not become aware of the attempt before it is terminated.

§ 30. Conditional Threat

If the actor intentionally puts another in apprehension of an imminent and harmful or offensive contact, he is subject to liability for an assault although he gives to the other the option to escape the contact by obedience to a command given by the actor, unless the command is one which the actor is privileged to enforce by the infliction of the threatened contact or by a threat to inflict it.

§ 31. Threat by Words

Words do not make the actor liable for assault unless together with other acts or circumstances they put the other in reasonable apprehension of an imminent harmful or offensive contact with his person.

TOPIC 4. THE INTEREST IN FREEDOM FROM CONFINEMENT

§ 35. False Imprisonment

(1) An actor is subject to liability to another for false imprisonment if

(a) he acts intending to confine the other or a third person within boundaries fixed by the actor, and

(b) his act directly or indirectly results in such a confinement of the other, and

(c) the other is conscious of the confinement or is harmed by it.

(2) An act which is not done with the intention stated in Subsection (1, a) does not make the actor liable to the

other for a merely transitory or otherwise harmless confinement, although the act involves an unreasonable risk
of imposing it and therefore would be negligent or reckless if the risk threatened bodily harm.

Illustration:

2. Just before closing time, A, a shopkeeper, sends B into a
cold storage vault to take inventory of the articles therein. For-
getting that he has done so, he locks the door of the vault on
leaving the premises. If in a few moments thereafter, he remem-
bers that B is in the vault and immediately goes back and releases
B, he is not liable to B for the momentary confinement to which B
has been subjected. On the other hand, if he does not remember
that B is in the vault until he reaches home and, therefore,
although he acts immediately, he cannot release B until B has
been confined in the cold vault for so long a time as to bring on a
heavy cold which develops into pneumonia, he is subject to
liability to B for the illness so caused.

§ 36. What Constitutes Confinement

(1) To make the actor liable for false imprisonment, the
other's confinement within the boundaries fixed by the
actor must be complete.

(2) The confinement is complete although there is a reasonable means of escape, unless the other knows of it.

(3) The actor does not become liable for false imprisonment by intentionally preventing another from going in a
particular direction in which he has a right or privilege to
go.

Comment:

a. *Means of escape.* If the actor knows of an avenue of escape,
he cannot intend to imprison the other by closing all the other exits
unless he believes that the other is unaware of the available avenue of
escape. Since the actor has intended to imprison the other, the other is
not required to run any risk of harm to his person or to his chattels or
of subjecting himself to any substantial liability to a third person in
order to relieve the actor from a liability to which his intentional
misconduct has subjected him. So too, even though there may be a
perfectly safe avenue of escape, the other is not required to take it if
the circumstances are such as to make it offensive to a reasonable
sense of decency or personal dignity.

On the other hand, it is unreasonable for one whom the actor intends to imprison to refuse to utilize a means of escape of which he is himself aware merely because it entails a slight inconvenience or requires him to commit a technical invasion of another's possessory interest in land or chattels which subjects him at most to the risk of an action for nominal damages which in practice is seldom if ever brought.

b. *Confinement and exclusion.* The area within which another is completely confined may be large and need not be stationary. Whether the area from which the actor prevents the other from going is so large that it ceases to be a confinement within the area and becomes an exclusion from some other area may depend upon the circumstances of the particular case and be a matter for the judgment of the court or jury.

§ 39. Confinement by Physical Force

The confinement may be by overpowering physical force, or by submission to physical force.

§ 40. Confinement by Threats of Physical Force

The confinement may be by submission to a threat to apply physical force to the other's person immediately upon the other's going or attempting to go beyond the area in which the actor intends to confine him.

§ 40A. Confinement by Other Duress

The confinement may be by submission to duress other than threats of physical force, where such duress is sufficient to make the consent given ineffective to bar the action.

§ 41. Confinement by Asserted Legal Authority

(1) The confinement may be by taking a person into custody under an asserted legal authority.

(2) The custody is complete if the person against whom and in whose presence the authority is asserted believes it to be valid, or is in doubt as to its validity, and submits to it.

Comment:

a. *Arrest.* The person asserting the authority may do so under some process which he represents as valid and sufficient to authorize him to take the other into custody or under an asserted privilege to do so without process. The taking of another into custody under such an authority is an arrest whether the authority be valid or invalid.

Illustrations:

    1. A has in his possession an invalid warrant of arrest. He serves it upon B who, believing it to be valid, submits to it. A has confined B.

    2. A, a private citizen, obtains a policeman's uniform and badge. While wearing both, he says to B, "I arrest you," the circumstances being such that a policeman, but not a private citizen, would be privileged to make the arrest. B, believing A to be a policeman, submits. A has confined B.

§ 42. Knowledge of Confinement

Under the rule stated in § 35, there is no liability for intentionally confining another unless the person physically restrained knows of the confinement or is harmed by it.

TOPIC 5. THE INTEREST IN FREEDOM FROM EMOTIONAL DISTRESS

§ 46. Outrageous Conduct Causing Severe Emotional Distress

(1) One who by extreme and outrageous conduct intentionally or recklessly causes severe emotional distress to another is subject to liability for such emotional distress, and if bodily harm to the other results from it, for such bodily harm.

(2) Where such conduct is directed at a third person, the actor is subject to liability if he intentionally or recklessly causes severe emotional distress

    (a) to a member of such person's immediate family who is present at the time, whether or not such distress results in bodily harm, or

    (b) to any other person who is present at the time, if such distress results in bodily harm.

Caveat:

    The Institute expresses no opinion as to whether there may not be other circumstances under which the actor may be subject to liability for the intentional or reckless infliction of emotional distress.

Comment:

a. This Section is concerned only with emotional distress which is inflicted intentionally or recklessly. As to the negligent infliction of emotional distress, see §§ 312, 313, 436, and 436 A.

b. As indicated in Chapter 47, emotional distress may be an element of damages in many cases where other interests have been invaded, and tort liability has arisen apart from the emotional distress. Because of the fear of fictitious or trivial claims, distrust of the proof offered, and the difficulty of setting up any satisfactory boundaries to liability, the law has been slow to afford independent protection to the interest in freedom from emotional distress standing alone. It is only within recent years that the rule stated in this Section has been fully recognized as a separate and distinct basis of tort liability, without the presence of the elements necessary to any other tort, such as assault, battery, false imprisonment, trespass to land, or the like. This Section may be regarded as an extension of the principle involved in the rules stated in §§ 21–34 as to the tort of assault.

c. The law is still in a stage of development, and the ultimate limits of this tort are not yet determined. This Section states the extent of the liability thus far accepted generally by the courts. The Caveat is intended to leave fully open the possibility of further development of the law, and the recognition of other situations in which liability may be imposed.

d. Extreme and outrageous conduct. The cases thus far decided have found liability only where the defendant's conduct has been extreme and outrageous. It has not been enough that the defendant has acted with an intent which is tortious or even criminal, or that he has intended to inflict emotional distress, or even that his conduct has been characterized by "malice," or a degree of aggravation which would entitle the plaintiff to punitive damages for another tort. Liability has been found only where the conduct has been so outrageous in character, and so extreme in degree, as to go beyond all possible bounds of decency, and to be regarded as atrocious, and utterly intolerable in a civilized community. Generally, the case is one in which the recitation of the facts to an average member of the community would arouse his resentment against the actor, and lead him to exclaim, "Outrageous!"

The liability clearly does not extend to mere insults, indignities, threats, annoyances, petty oppressions, or other trivialities. The rough edges of our society are still in need of a good deal of filing down, and in the meantime plaintiffs must necessarily be expected and required to be hardened to a certain amount of rough language, and to occasional acts that are definitely inconsiderate and unkind. There is no occasion for the law to intervene in every case where some one's feelings are hurt. There must still be freedom to express an unflattering opinion, and some safety valve must be left through which irascible tempers may blow off relatively harmless steam. See Magruder, Mental and Emotional Disturbance in the Law of Torts, 47 Harvard Law Review 1033, 1053 (1936). It is only where there is a special relation between the parties, as stated in § 48, that there may be recovery for insults not amounting to extreme outrage.

Illustrations:

    1. As a practical joke, A falsely tells B that her husband has been badly injured in an accident, and is in the hospital with both legs broken. B suffers severe emotional distress. A is subject to liability to B for her emotional distress. If it causes nervous shock and resulting illness, A is subject to liability to B for her illness.

    2. A, the president of an association of rubbish collectors, summons B to a meeting of the association, and in the presence of an intimidating group of associates tells B that B has been collecting rubbish in territory which the association regards as exclusively allocated to one of its members. A demands that B pay over the proceeds of his rubbish collection, and tells B that if he does not do so the association will beat him up, destroy his truck, and put him out of business. B is badly frightened, and suffers severe emotional distress. A is subject to liability to B for his emotional distress, and if it results in illness, A is also subject to liability to B for his illness.

    3. A is invited to a swimming party at an exclusive resort. B gives her a bathing suit which he knows will dissolve in water. It does dissolve while she is swimming, leaving her naked in the presence of men and women whom she has just met. A suffers extreme embarrassment, shame, and humiliation. B is subject to liability to A for her emotional distress.

    4. A makes a telephone call but is unable to get his number. In the course of an altercation with the telephone operator, A calls her a God damned woman, a God damned liar, and says that if he were there he would break her God damned neck. B suffers severe emotional distress, broods over the incident, is unable to sleep, and is made ill. A's conduct, although insulting, is not so outrageous or extreme as to make A liable to B.

    e. The extreme and outrageous character of the conduct may arise from an abuse by the actor of a position, or a relation with the other, which gives him actual or apparent authority over the other, or power to affect his interests. Thus an attempt to extort money by a threat of arrest may make the actor liable even where the arrest, or the threat alone, would not do so. In particular police officers, school authorities, landlords, and collecting creditors have been held liable for extreme abuse of their position. Even in such cases, however, the actor has not been held liable for mere insults, indignities, or annoyances that are not extreme or outrageous.

Illustrations:

5. A, a private detective, calls on B and represents himself to be a police officer. He threatens to arrest B on a charge of espionage unless B surrenders letters of a third person which are in her possession. B suffers severe emotional distress and resulting illness. A is subject to liability to B for both.

f. The extreme and outrageous character of the conduct may arise from the actor's knowledge that the other is peculiarly susceptible to emotional distress, by reason of some physical or mental condition or peculiarity. The conduct may become heartless, flagrant, and outrageous when the actor proceeds in the face of such knowledge, where it would not be so if he did not know. It must be emphasized again, however, that major outrage is essential to the tort; and the mere fact that the actor knows that the other will regard the conduct as insulting, or will have his feelings hurt, is not enough.

h. Court and jury. It is for the court to determine, in the first instance, whether the defendant's conduct may reasonably be regarded as so extreme and outrageous as to permit recovery, or whether it is necessarily so. Where reasonable men may differ, it is for the jury, subject to the control of the court, to determine whether, in the particular case, the conduct has been sufficiently extreme and outrageous to result in liability.

Chapter 4

DEFENSES OF PERSON, LAND, AND CHATTELS—RECAPTION

TOPIC 1. SELF–DEFENSE AND DEFENSE OF THIRD PERSONS

TOPIC 2. DEFENSE OF ACTOR'S INTEREST IN HIS EXCLUSIVE POSSESSION OF LAND AND CHATTELS

TOPIC 1. SELF–DEFENSE AND DEFENSE OF THIRD PERSONS

§ 63. Self–Defense by Force Not Threatening Death or Serious Bodily Harm

(1) An actor is privileged to use reasonable force, not intended or likely to cause death or serious bodily harm, to defend himself against unprivileged harmful or offensive contact or other bodily harm which he reasonably believes that another is about to inflict intentionally upon him.

(2) Self-defense is privileged under the conditions stated in Subsection (1), although the actor correctly or reasonably believes that he can avoid the necessity of so defending himself,

(a) by retreating or otherwise giving up a right or privilege, or

(b) by complying with a command with which the actor is under no duty to comply or which the other is not privileged to enforce by the means threatened.

Illustrations:

3. A strikes B with a whip. B by reasonable force disarms A. B is not privileged thereafter to inflict a similar beating upon A.

4. A, a small boy, throws a snowball at B, hitting B in the eye and causing him severe pain. B is not privileged to inflict a beating upon A either as a punishment or as a warning against similar misconduct in the future.

i. Reasonableness of actor's belief. In determining whether the actor's apprehension of the intentional infliction of bodily harm or an offensive contact is reasonable, the circumstances which are known, or should be known, to the actor must be such as would lead a reasonable man to entertain such an apprehension. In this connection, the qualities which primarily characterize a "reasonable man" are ordinary firmness and courage. The other's conduct may put the actor in a reasonable apprehension of bodily harm or an offensive contact, although it is not the sole cause of such apprehension. The acts or statements of third persons may give to the other's conduct so threatening an appearance as to make it capable of causing such an apprehension, though standing by itself, the conduct would not be capable of so doing.

The privilege stated in this Section is conditioned upon the actor's reasonable belief that the other's conduct is both intended and likely to inflict an offensive contact or bodily harm upon him. But it is not necessary that the contact or harm which he apprehends shall be the same as that intended by the other. The actor may know, or reasonably believe in the existence of facts which are unknown to the other, which lead him reasonably to apprehend consequences from the other's threatened conduct not realized by the other. Thus, the actor may be privileged to use force to prevent the other from continuing a course of conduct which is obviously intended only to inflict an offensive contact, but which the actor reasonably believes, because of circumstances unknown to the other, to be likely to go beyond the other's intention and to cause serious bodily harm to the actor.

j. Reasonableness of means employed in self-defense. The contact or other bodily harm which the actor is privileged to inflict in self-defense must be reasonable; that is, it must not be disproportionate in extent to the harm from which the actor is seeking to protect himself. A degree of force may be privileged to ward off a blow which threatens substantial harm, where the same degree of force would not be privileged merely to prevent touching in an insulting manner.

Since the means used must be proportionate to the danger threatened, it is obvious that one is not privileged to protect one's self even from a blow which is likely to cause some fairly substantial injury by means which are intended or likely to cause death or serious bodily harm. (See § 65.) The reasonable character of the means which the actor uses is determined by what a reasonable man, under the circumstances which the actor knows or has reason to know to exist at the time, would regard as permissible in view of the danger threatening him. In determining this, account must be taken of the fact that the other's conduct has put the actor in a position in which he must make a rapid decision. The test is what a reasonable man in such an emergency would believe permissible and not that which, after the event and when the emergency is past, a reasonable man would so recognize as having been sufficient.

Comment on Subsection (2):

m. Actor's duty to retreat. The actor, if he reasonably believes that he is threatened with the intentional imposition of bodily harm, or even of an offensive contact, may stand his ground and repel the attack by the use of reasonable force, which does not threaten serious harm or death, even though he might with absolute certainty of safety avoid the threatened bodily harm or offensive contact by retreating. If one so threatened is privileged to use force in self-defense, although the necessity of so doing can be avoided by relinquishing his privilege to choose his own location, it follows that reasonable force may be used to repel a threatened attack, although the necessity of so doing can be avoided by relinquishing the exercise of any other right or privilege. It also follows that there is a privilege to use force to repel such an attack although the threat to make it is conditioned upon noncompliance with a demand with which the actor is under no legal duty to comply, or which the other is not privileged to enforce by the means which he threatens to employ for that purpose.

On the other hand, if the threatened attack is conditioned upon the actor's non-compliance with the demand made upon him, the actor is not privileged to use force to protect himself against the attack so threatened, if the demand is one with which the actor knows or should know that he is under a legal duty to comply, and the force which the other threatens to apply to him is no greater than the other is privileged to apply for the purpose of securing compliance with his demand.

§ 64. Self–Defense Against Negligent Conduct

(1) **Except as stated in Subsection (2), an actor is privileged to use reasonable force, not intended or likely to cause death or serious bodily harm, to defend himself against harmful or offensive contact or bodily harm which he reasonably believes to be threatened by the conduct of another, although he recognizes such conduct to be negligent.**

(2) **The actor is not privileged so to defend himself if he knows or should know that he can escape the necessity of doing so by retreating, or by giving up the exercise of a right or privilege which, under the circumstances, it is reasonable to require him to relinquish.**

§ 65. Self–Defense by Force Threatening Death or Serious Bodily Harm

(1) **Subject to the statement in Subsection (3), an actor is privileged to defend himself against another by force intended or likely to cause death or serious bodily harm, when he reasonably believes that**

(a) the other is about to inflict upon him an intentional contact or other bodily harm, and that

(b) he is thereby put in peril of death or serious bodily harm or ravishment, which can safely be prevented only by the immediate use of such force.

(2) The privilege stated in Subsection (1) exists although the actor correctly or reasonably believes that he can safely avoid the necessity of so defending himself by

(a) retreating if he is attacked within his dwelling place, which is not also the dwelling place of the other, or

(b) permitting the other to intrude upon or dispossess him of his dwelling place, or

(c) abandoning an attempt to effect a lawful arrest.

(3) The privilege stated in Subsection (1) does not exist if the actor correctly or reasonably believes that he can with complete safety avoid the necessity of so defending himself by

(a) retreating if attacked in any place other than his dwelling place, or in a place which is also the dwelling of the other, or

(b) relinquishing the exercise of any right or privilege other than his privilege to prevent intrusion upon or dispossession of his dwelling place or to effect a lawful arrest.

Comment on Subsections (2) and (3):

g. *Standing one's ground.* As stated in § 63, one whom another threatens to attack may stand his ground and repel the attack with any reasonable force which does not threaten death or serious bodily harm, although he realizes that he can safely retreat and so avoid the necessity of using self-defensive force. But the interest of society in the life and efficiency of its members and in the prevention of the serious breaches of the peace involved in bloody affrays requires one attacked with a deadly weapon, except within his own dwelling place, to retreat before using force intended or likely to inflict death or serious bodily harm upon his assailant, unless he reasonably believes that there is any chance that retreat cannot be safely made. But even the slightest doubt, if reasonable, is enough to justify his standing his ground, and in determining whether his doubt is reasonable every allowance must be made for the predicament in which his assailant has placed him.

Illustrations:

4. A is standing upon a public highway. B points a revolver at him and threatens to shoot him. If A cannot prevent B from shooting him by any other means than by shooting B, he is privileged to do so.

5. A is standing upon a public highway. B, while still some distance away, starts towards A brandishing a razor and threatening to kill him. B is lame, and A knows that he can with perfect safety avoid B's attack by running away. A is not privileged to stand his ground, await B's attack and shoot or stab B to defend himself against it.

§ 76. Defense of Third Person

The actor is privileged to defend a third person from a harmful or offensive contact or other invasion of his interests of personality under the same conditions and by the same means as those under and by which he is privileged to defend himself if the actor correctly or reasonably believes that

(a) the circumstances are such as to give the third person a privilege of self-defense, and

(b) his intervention is necessary for the protection of the third person.

TOPIC 2. DEFENSE OF ACTOR'S INTEREST IN HIS EXCLUSIVE POSSESSION OF LAND AND CHATTELS

§ 77. Defense of Possession by Force Not Threatening Death or Serious Bodily Harm

An actor is privileged to use reasonable force, not intended or likely to cause death or serious bodily harm, to prevent or terminate another's intrusion upon the actor's land or chattels, if

(a) the intrusion is not privileged or the other intentionally or negligently causes the actor to believe that it is not privileged, and

(b) the actor reasonably believes that the intrusion can be prevented or terminated only by the force used, and

(c) the actor has first requested the other to desist and the other has disregarded the request, or the actor reasonably believes that a request will be useless or that substantial harm will be done before it can be made.

Illustrations:

1. A's boat gets adrift and grounds upon B's beach. A storm arises which threatens to carry the boat out to sea. A, being privileged to enter B's land for the purpose of saving his boat, attempts to do so. B is not privileged to use any force to prevent his entry.

2. A finds a highway impassable. He makes a detour over B's field around the obstruction. While so doing, he stops his car for the purpose of taking luncheon. B tells him to move on. A refuses to do so. B may use such force as is reasonable to compel him to obey.

3. A enters B's land under the facts stated in Illustration 1. As he passes B's orchard, he stops to gather fruit growing in it. B is privileged to use such force as is reasonable to expel A from his premises.

e. *Other's incomplete privilege.* Clause (a) applies not only to the exclusion or expulsion of another whose intrusion is fully privileged, but also to the expulsion of one whose privilege to intrude protects him from liability for the mere invasion of the possessor's dignitary interest in the exclusiveness of his possession, but does not protect him from liability for material harm done to its physical condition, no matter how unintentionally and unavoidably. Thus, one entering another's premises to preserve his chattel from destruction is not liable for his mere intrusion, but is liable for the damage done to the premises by the exercise of his privilege to enter, no matter how carefully the privilege is exercised. So too, one who uses another's premises as a haven of refuge when his life is threatened by some force of nature is subject to liability for any material harm which he does, although he is not liable for his harmless intrusion. In neither case is the possessor privileged to prevent the intrusion unless he has reasonable grounds to believe that it is likely to cause substantial bodily harm to him or third persons, whether upon the premises or not. Even the certainty that it will cause material harm to the physical condition of the premises is not enough to give him the privilege to exclude the intruder and so sacrifice the intruder's life to save his possession from even material harm.

Illustrations:

4. A, while out sailing with his family in a catboat upon a lake, is overtaken by a sudden squall, and his boat is in danger of being swamped. A puts into B's dock for shelter. B is not

23

privileged to use force to prevent A from taking shelter there, whether A's use of the dock for this purpose does or does not appear likely to cause harm to the dock. But if A harms the dock while taking shelter there, he is subject to liability to B for the harm done to it.

5. A's vessel is moored to B's dock. A violent storm arises which causes the vessel to pound against the dock, threatening to do it substantial harm. A, being confronted with the necessity of putting to sea and imperiling both ship and crew, or securing it to the dock by additional hawsers, adopts the latter alternative. B is not privileged to cast the boat adrift, but A is subject to liability for the damage the boat does to the dock.

§ 84. Use of Mechanical Device Not Threatening Death or Serious Bodily Harm

The actor is so far privileged to employ, for the purpose of protecting his possession of land or chattels from intrusion, a device not intended or likely to cause death or serious bodily harm that he is not liable for bodily harm done thereby to a deliberate intruder, if

(a) the use of such a device is reasonably necessary to protect the land or chattels from intrusion, and

(b) the use of the particular device is reasonable under the circumstances, and

(c) the device is one customarily used for such a purpose, or reasonable care is taken to make its use known to probable intruders.

Comment:

c. Barbed wires and spiked walls. A barbed wire fence or spiked railing may be so constructed, located and maintained as to be a reasonable means of protecting the actor's possession of land or chattels from intrusion, and may therefore be privileged in so far as to give immunity from liability to a deliberate intruder; but it may involve an unreasonable risk of harm to persons coming upon, or using or touching his land or chattels with his consent, or in the enjoyment of a privilege, or while lawfully using the highway, none of whom the actor intends the device to affect. The rule stated in this Section does not purport to give the conditions under which there will be liability for the use of a device which, while a legitimate means of protecting land or chattels, creates an unreasonable risk of harm to such persons. These conditions are stated in that part of the Restatement of this Subject which deals with the liability of a possessor of land or chattels, for harm unintentionally caused by its physical condition. (See §§ 328 E–379 A.)

d. The use of such devices as spring guns or mantraps, which are likely to cause death or serious harm, is considered in § 85. This Section deals only with the privilege to protect land or chattels from intrusion by the use of devices which are not likely to cause death or serious bodily harm to intruders, such as barbed wire fences or spiked railings. While these devices are intended to harm one who deliberately persists in intruding, their purpose is not so much to harm intruders, as to protect the actor's possession of land or chattels from intrusion by the deterrent effect which the knowledge of their use, whether derived from observation or the fact that they are customarily used or from a warning, is likely to have upon those who would otherwise intrude. The use of watch dogs or other animals to prevent intrusions upon land or chattels is dealt with in that part of the Restatement of this Subject which states the liability of one who harbors or maintains on his premises animals, wild or domesticated (see § 516).

f. Necessity of warning. The use of an undiscriminating device is justifiable only because of its probable effectiveness in preventing intrusions. This effect is attained not so much by the harm which is inflicted upon the individuals who are hurt by it while intruding as by the deterrent force exerted upon those who otherwise might intrude by their knowledge that if they do so they will run the risk of harm. Therefore, there is no privilege to use such a device if the fact of its use is concealed from possible intruders or is not reasonably likely to be known by them. Thus, the use of a barbed wire fence or spiked railing, except in localities in which the use is so customary as to be expected by all those who are likely to be in the neighborhood, is privileged only if it is so constructed as to carry on its face in the daytime a warning of its presence. Even in such a locality, a possessor of land is not privileged to erect a barbed wire fence or spiked railing concealed by hedge or trees. If, as is often the case, the use of such device is notoriously customary in the particular neighborhood, the possessor is entitled to assume that the existence of the custom and its notoriety will even on a dark night be sufficient to apprise intending trespassers that such a means of protection may have been installed.

§ 85. Use of Mechanical Device Threatening Death or Serious Bodily Harm

The actor is so far privileged to use a device intended or likely to cause serious bodily harm or death for the purpose of protecting his land or chattels from intrusion that he is not liable for the serious bodily harm or death

thereby caused to an intruder whose intrusion is, in fact, such that the actor, were he present, would be privileged to prevent or terminate it by the intentional infliction of such harm.

Illustration:

   1.   A, who owns a field adjacent to a golf course, is constantly annoyed by caddies coming into his field for balls driven out of bounds. To prevent these intrusions A installs spring guns upon his land. B, a caddy entering in search of a ball, is shot by one of these guns and has his eye put out. A is subject to liability to B whether he has or has not posted warnings or personally warned the caddy who was injured.

Chapter 7

INVASIONS OF THE INTEREST IN THE EXCLUSIVE POSSESSION OF LAND AND ITS PHYSICAL CONDITION (TRESPASS ON LAND)

TOPIC 1. INTENTIONAL ENTRIES ON LAND

TOPIC 1. INTENTIONAL ENTRIES ON LAND

§ 158. Liability for Intentional Intrusions on Land

One is subject to liability to another for trespass, irrespective of whether he thereby causes harm to any legally protected interest of the other, if he intentionally

   (a) enters land in the possession of the other, or causes a thing or a third person to do so, or

   (b) remains on the land, or

   (c) fails to remove from the land a thing which he is under a duty to remove.

§ 163. Intended Intrusions Causing No Harm

One who intentionally enters land in the possession of another is subject to liability to the possessor for a trespass, although his presence on the land causes no harm to the land, its possessor, or to any thing or person in whose security the possessor has a legally protected interest.

§ 164. Intrusions Under Mistake

One who intentionally enters land in the possession of another is subject to liability to the possessor of the land as a trespasser, although he acts under a mistaken belief of law or fact, however reasonable, not induced by the conduct of the possessor, that he

(a) is in possession of the land or entitled to it, or

(b) has the consent of the possessor or of a third person who has the power to give consent on the possessor's behalf, or

(c) has some other privilege to enter or remain on the land.

Chapter 8

PRIVILEGED ENTRIES ON LAND

TOPIC 2. PRIVILEGES ARISING IRRESPECTIVE OF ANY TRANSACTION BETWEEN THE PARTIES

TOPIC 2. PRIVILEGES ARISING IRRESPECTIVE OF ANY TRANSACTION BETWEEN THE PARTIES

§ 196. Public Necessity

One is privileged to enter land in the possession of another if it is, or if the actor reasonably believes it to be, necessary for the purpose of averting an imminent public disaster.

Comment:

a. The privilege stated in this Section is conferred upon the actor for the protection of the public. It is essential therefore that the entry be made in order to protect against or repel a public enemy, or to prevent or mitigate the effects of an impending public disaster such as a conflagration, flood, earthquake, or pestilence.

As to entries made solely to protect the actor's own life or property or the life or property of other private persons, see § 197.

b. Since the privilege stated in this Section is given for the benefit of the public, the actor in the exercise of the privilege may break and enter a dwelling or other structure as well as a fence or other enclosure, and he may use reasonable force against the person, if it reasonably appears to the actor to be necessary to do so in order to accomplish the purpose for which the privilege exists. (Compare Comments *f* and *i.*)

Although the actor is subject to liability for harm done in the unreasonable exercise of the privilege stated in this Section (see § 214), in so far as his original entry was privileged, he is not liable for such entry and for acts done prior to such unreasonable conduct. Nor does such misconduct terminate the actor's privilege to be on the land and do acts thereon for the accomplishment of the privilege. (See § 215.)

§ 197. Private Necessity

(1) One is privileged to enter or remain on land in the possession of another if it is or reasonably appears to be necessary to prevent serious harm to

(a) the actor, or his land or chattels, or

(b) the other or a third person, or the land or chattels of either, unless the actor knows or has reason to know that the one for whose benefit he enters is unwilling that he shall take such action.

(2) Where the entry is for the benefit of the actor or a third person, he is subject to liability for any harm done in the exercise of the privilege stated in Subsection (1) to any legally protected interest of the possessor in the land or connected with it, except where the threat of harm to avert which the entry is made is caused by the tortious conduct or contributory negligence of the possessor.

Comment on Subsection (1):

a. The privilege stated in this Subsection exists only where in an emergency the actor enters land for the purpose of protecting himself or the possessor of the land or a third person or the land or chattels of any such persons. Furthermore, the privilege must be exercised at a reasonable time and in a reasonable manner. Although the actor is subject to liability for harm done in the unreasonable exercise of the privilege stated in this Section (see § 214), in so far as his original entry was privileged, he is not liable for such entry, or for acts done prior to such unreasonable conduct, except as stated in Comment *i.*

k. The important difference between the status of one who is a trespasser on land and one who is on the land pursuant to an incomplete privilege is that the latter is entitled to be on the land and therefore the possessor of the land is under a duty to permit him to come and remain there and hence is not privileged to resist his entry. Consequently, where the possessor of the land resists such a privileged entry, the actor's use of reasonable force to overcome such resistance to his entry or remaining on the land so long as the necessity continues is completely privileged. Therefore he is not liable for harm so occasioned. (Compare § 77(a) and the Comments there.)

Illustration:

15.   While A is canoeing on a navigable river he is suddenly overtaken by a violent storm. To save himself and his canoe from destruction, A seeks to land at B's dock and pull his canoe up on the dock. B by force attempts to prevent A from so doing, whereupon A uses reasonable force to B's person to effect his entry. A is not liable to B for the harm so occasioned.

Chapter 9

INTENTIONAL INVASIONS OF INTERESTS IN THE PRESENT AND FUTURE POSSESSION OF CHATTELS

TOPIC 1. TRESPASS TO CHATTELS

TOPIC 1. TRESPASS TO CHATTELS

§ **217.   Ways of Committing Trespass to Chattel**

A trespass to a chattel may be committed by intentionally

(a) **dispossessing another of the chattel, or**

(b) **using or intermeddling with a chattel in the possession of another.**

§ **218.   Liability to Person in Possession**

One who commits a trespass to a chattel is subject to liability to the possessor of the chattel if, but only if,

   (a) he dispossesses the other of the chattel, or

   (b) the chattel is impaired as to its condition, quality, or value, or

   (c) the possessor is deprived of the use of the chattel for a substantial time, or

   (d) bodily harm is caused to the possessor, or harm is caused to some person or thing in which the possessor has a legally protected interest.

TOPIC 2. CONVERSION

§ 222A. What Constitutes Conversion

(1) Conversion is an intentional exercise of dominion or control over a chattel which so seriously interferes with the right of another to control it that the actor may justly be required to pay the other the full value of the chattel.

(2) In determining the seriousness of the interference and the justice of requiring the actor to pay the full value, the following factors are important:

   (a) the extent and duration of the actor's exercise of dominion or control;

   (b) the actor's intent to assert a right in fact inconsistent with the other's right of control;

   (c) the actor's good faith;

   (d) the extent and duration of the resulting interference with the other's right of control;

   (e) the harm done to the chattel;

   (f) the inconvenience and expense caused to the other.

§ 229. Conversion by Receiving Possession in Consummation of Transaction

One who receives possession of a chattel from another with the intent to acquire for himself or for a third person a proprietary interest in the chattel which the other has not the power to transfer is subject to liability for conversion to a third person then entitled to the immediate possession of the chattel.

DIVISION TWO

NEGLIGENCE

Chapter 12

GENERAL PRINCIPLES

TOPIC 1. THE ELEMENTS OF A CAUSE OF ACTION FOR NEGLIGENCE

TOPIC 2. THE STANDARD BY WHICH NEGLIGENCE IS DETERMINED

TOPIC 3. DETERMINATION OF STANDARD OF CONDUCT

TITLE A. FUNCTION OF LEGISLATION

TITLE B. FACTORS IMPORTANT IN DETERMINATION OF STANDARD OF REASONABLE CONDUCT

TOPIC 4. TYPES OF NEGLIGENT ACTS

TOPIC 1. THE ELEMENTS OF A CAUSE
OF ACTION FOR NEGLIGENCE

§ 281. Statement of the Elements of a Cause of Action for
Negligence

The actor is liable for an invasion of an interest of
another, if:

(a) the interest invaded is protected against unintentional invasion, and

(b) the conduct of the actor is negligent with respect
to the other, or a class of persons within which he is
included, and

(c) the actor's conduct is a legal cause of the invasion, and

(d) the other has not so conducted himself as to
disable himself from bringing an action for such invasion.

TOPIC 2. THE STANDARD BY WHICH
NEGLIGENCE IS DETERMINED

§ 283. Conduct of a Reasonable Man: the Standard

Unless the actor is a child, the standard of conduct to which he must conform to avoid being negligent is that of a reasonable man under like circumstances.

Comment:

c. Standard of the "reasonable man." Negligence is a departure from a standard of conduct demanded by the community for the protection of others against unreasonable risk. The standard which the community demands must be an objective and external one, rather than that of the individual judgment, good or bad, of the particular individual. It must be the same for all persons, since the law can have no favorites; and yet allowance must be made for some of the differences between individuals, the risk apparent to the actor, his capacity to meet it, and the circumstances under which he must act.

In dealing with this problem the law has made use of the standard of a hypothetical "reasonable man." Sometimes this person is called a reasonable man of ordinary prudence, or an ordinarily prudent man, or a man of average prudence, or a man of reasonable sense exercising ordinary care. It is evident that all such phrases are intended to mean very much the same thing. The actor is required to do what this ideal individual would do in his place. The reasonable man is a fictitious person, who is never negligent, and whose conduct is always up to standard. He is not to be identified with any real person; and in particular he is not to be identified with the members of the jury, individually or collectively. It is therefore error to instruct the jury that the conduct of a reasonable man is to be determined by what they would themselves have done.

The chief advantage of this standard of the reasonable man is that it enables the triers of fact who are to decide whether the actor's conduct is such as to subject him to liability for negligence, to look to a community standard rather than an individual one, and at the same time to express their judgment of what that standard is in terms of the conduct of a human being. The standard provides sufficient flexibility, and leeway, to permit due allowance to be made for such differences between individuals as the law permits to be taken into account, and for all of the particular circumstances of the case which may reasonably affect the conduct required, and at the same time affords a formula by which, so far as possible, a uniform standard may be maintained.

§ 283A. Children

If the actor is a child, the standard of conduct to which he must conform to avoid being negligent is that of a reasonable person of like age, intelligence, and experience under like circumstances.

Comment:

    c. Child engaging in adult activity. An exception to the rule stated in this Section may arise where the child engages in an activity which is normally undertaken only by adults, and for which adult qualifications are required. As in the case of one entering upon a professional activity which requires special skill (see § 299A), he may be held to the standard of adult skill, knowledge, and competence, and no allowance may be made for his immaturity. Thus, for example, if a boy of fourteen were to attempt to fly an airplane, his age and inexperience would not excuse him from liability for flying it in a negligent manner. The same may be true where the child drives an automobile. In this connection licensing statutes, and the examinations given to drivers, may be important in determining the qualifications required; but even if the child succeeds in obtaining a license he may thereafter be required to meet the standard established primarily for adults.

§ 283B. Mental Deficiency

Unless the actor is a child, his insanity or other mental deficiency does not relieve the actor from liability for conduct which does not conform to the standard of a reasonable man under like circumstances.

Comment:

    a. If the actor is a child, his mental deficiency is taken into account. See § 283A.

    b. The rule that a mentally deficient adult is liable for his torts is an old one, dating back at least to 1616, at a time when the action for trespass rested upon the older basis of strict liability, without regard to any fault of the individual. Apart from mere historical survival, its persistence in modern law has been explained on a number of different grounds. These are as follows:

    1. The difficulty of drawing any satisfactory line between mental deficiency and those variations of temperament, intellect, and emotional balance which cannot, as a practical matter, be taken into account in imposing liability for damage done.

2. The unsatisfactory character of the evidence of mental deficiency in many cases, together with the ease with which it can be feigned, the difficulties which the triers of fact must encounter in determining its existence, nature, degree, and effect; and some fear of introducing into the law of torts the confusion which has surrounded such a defense in the criminal law. Although this factor may be of decreasing importance with the continued development of medical and psychiatric science, it remains at the present time a major obstacle to any allowance for mental deficiency.

3. The feeling that if mental defectives are to live in the world they should pay for the damage they do, and that it is better that their wealth, if any, should be used to compensate innocent victims than that it should remain in their hands.

4. The belief that their liability will mean that those who have charge of them or their estates will be stimulated to look after them, keep them in order, and see that they do not do harm.

c. Insane persons are commonly held liable for their intentional torts. While there are very few cases, the same rule has been applied to their negligence. As to mental deficiency falling short of insanity, as in the case of stupidity, lack of intelligence, excitability, or proneness to accident, no allowance is made, and the actor is held to the standard of conduct of a reasonable man who is not mentally deficient, even though it is in fact beyond his capacity to conform to it.

§ 283C. Physical Disability

If the actor is ill or otherwise physically disabled, the standard of conduct to which he must conform to avoid being negligent is that of a reasonable man under like disability.

Comment:

a. So far as physical characteristics are concerned, the hypothetical reasonable man may be said to be identical with the actor. Physical handicaps and infirmities, such as blindness, deafness, short stature, or a club foot, or the weaknesses of age or sex, are treated merely as part of the "circumstances "under which a reasonable man must act. Thus the standard of conduct for a blind man becomes that of a reasonable man who is blind. This is not a different standard from that of the reasonable man stated in § 283, but an application of it to the special circumstances of the case.

b. The same allowance is made for physical, as distinguished from mental, illness. Thus a heart attack, or a temporary dizziness due to fever or nausea, as well as a transitory delirium, are regarded merely as circumstances to be taken into account in determining what the reasonable man would do. The explanation for the distinction between such physical illness and the mental illness dealt with in § 283B probably lies in the greater public familiarity with the former, and the comparative ease and certainty with which it can be proved.

c. A person under such temporary or permanent physical disability may be required, under particular circumstances, to take more precautions than one who is not so disabled, while under other circumstances he may be required to take less. Thus an automobile driver who suddenly and quite unexpectedly suffers a heart attack does not become negligent when he loses control of his car and drives it in a manner which would otherwise be unreasonable; but one who knows that he is subject to such attacks may be negligent in driving at all.

§ 284. Negligent Conduct; Act or Failure to Act

Negligent conduct may be either:

(a) an act which the actor as a reasonable man should recognize as involving an unreasonable risk of causing an invasion of an interest of another, or

(b) a failure to do an act which is necessary for the protection or assistance of another and which the actor is under a duty to do.

TOPIC 3. DETERMINATION OF STANDARD OF CONDUCT

§ 285. How Standard of Conduct Is Determined

The standard of conduct of a reasonable man may be

(a) established by a legislative enactment or administrative regulation which so provides, or

(b) adopted by the court from a legislative enactment or an administrative regulation which does not so provide, or

(c) established by judicial decision, or

(d) applied to the facts of the case by the trial judge or the jury, if there is no such enactment, regulation, or decision.

Comment:

g. Function of jury. If no standard of obligatory conduct has been established by a legislative enactment and there is no ruling of an appellate court upon substantially identical situations and the trial court has not withdrawn the case from the jury, the jury must itself define the standard of the reasonable man with such particularity as is necessary to make it applicable to the facts of the case before it.

In so defining the standard of conduct, the jury must act within the instructions given it by the court. See Comment *f*.

TITLE A. FUNCTION OF LEGISLATION

§ 286. **When Standard of Conduct Defined by Legislation or Regulation Will Be Adopted**

The court may adopt as the standard of conduct of a reasonable man the requirements of a legislative enactment or an administrative regulation whose purpose is found to be exclusively or in part

(a) to protect a class of persons which includes the one whose interest is invaded, and

(b) to protect the particular interest which is invaded, and

(c) to protect that interest against the kind of harm which has resulted, and

(d) to protect that interest against the particular hazard from which the harm results.

Comment on Clause (a):

f. When purpose is to protect particular class. A statute, ordinance, or administrative regulation may, because of its title, preamble, detailed provisions, history, or other reasons, be found to be intended for the protection of the interests of only a particular class of persons. If so, a violation of the provision will be held to be negligence toward persons who are included within the particular class, but not toward those who do not fall within it.

§ 288A. **Excused Violations**

(1) An excused violation of a legislative enactment or an administrative regulation is not negligence.

(2) Unless the enactment or regulation is construed not to permit such excuse, its violation is excused when

(a) the violation is reasonable because of the actor's incapacity;

(b) he neither knows nor should know of the occasion for compliance;

(c) he is unable after reasonable diligence or care to comply;

(d) he is confronted by an emergency not due to his own misconduct;

(e) compliance would involve a greater risk of harm to the actor or to others.

§ 288B. Effect of Violation

(1) The unexcused violation of a legislative enactment or an administrative regulation which is adopted by the court as defining the standard of conduct of a reasonable man, is negligence in itself.

(2) The unexcused violation of an enactment or regulation which is not so adopted may be relevant evidence bearing on the issue of negligent conduct.

Comment on Subsection (1):

a. Where a statute or ordinance is adopted by the court as defining the standard of conduct of a reasonable man under the particular circumstances, as stated in §§ 285 and 286, the unexcused violation of the provision is a clear departure from that standard, and is conclusive on the issue of an actor's negligence. Usually it is said that such a violation is negligence "per se," or in itself. The same is true where the standard defined by an administrative regulation is adopted by the court as that of a reasonable man. The courts have tended less frequently to adopt the standard of such a regulation, but where it is adopted, the violation becomes negligence in itself.

b. This means that the violation becomes conclusive on the issue of the actor's departure from the standard of conduct required of a reasonable man, and so, without more, is negligence. Such negligence makes the actor subject to liability, as that phrase is defined in § 5, but it does not necessarily make him liable. His conduct must still be a legal cause of the harm to the plaintiff, and there remain the possibilities of defenses, such as contributory negligence and assumption of risk, as to which see Chapters 17 and 17A.

Illustration:

1. A statute, which is found to define a standard of conduct for the protection of persons on the highway against the risk of collision, provides that after sunset no person shall drive an

unlighted vehicle on the highway. Without excuse, A drives an unlighted vehicle on the highway after sunset. As a result of the absence of lights, he collides with B's automobile and injures B. A's violation of the statute is negligence, which makes him subject to liability to B.

§ 288C. Compliance With Legislation or Regulation

Compliance with a legislative enactment or an administrative regulation does not prevent a finding of negligence where a reasonable man would take additional precautions.

TITLE B. FACTORS IMPORTANT IN DETERMINATION OF STANDARD OF REASONABLE CONDUCT

§ 289. Recognizing Existence of Risk

The actor is required to recognize that his conduct involves a risk of causing an invasion of another's interest if a reasonable man would do so while exercising

(a) such attention, perception of the circumstances, memory, knowledge of other pertinent matters, intelligence, and judgment as a reasonable man would have; and

(b) such superior attention, perception, memory, knowledge, intelligence, and judgment as the actor himself has.

§ 291. Unreasonableness; How Determined; Magnitude of Risk and Utility of Conduct

Where an act is one which a reasonable man would recognize as involving a risk of harm to another, the risk is unreasonable and the act is negligent if the risk is of such magnitude as to outweigh what the law regards as the utility of the act or of the particular manner in which it is done.

Comment:

   a. The problem involved may be expressed in homely terms by asking whether "the game is worth the candle."

   b. Burden of proof. Conduct is not negligent unless the magnitude of the risk involved therein so outweighs its utility as to make the risk unreasonable. Therefore, one relying upon negligence as a cause of action or defense must convince the court and jury that this is the case.

c. Standardized judgment. In determining whether the actor should realize the unreasonable character of a known or recognizable risk, the judgment of the actor, unless he be a child, must conform to the standard of a reasonable man, neither more nor less. He is not excused because he is peculiarly inconsiderate of others or reckless of his own safety, nor is he negligent if his moral or social conscience is so sensitive that he regards as improper conduct which a reasonable man would regard as proper. In this respect the problem differs somewhat from that of determining whether the actor should recognize the risk which his conduct involves and its magnitude, in which allowance is made for certain physical infirmities and in which the actor is required to utilize such superior qualities as he may possess. As to the standard to which the judgment of a child must conform, see § 283 A.

d. Weighing risk against utility of conduct which creates it. The magnitude of the risk is to be compared with what the law regards as the utility of the act. If legal and popular opinion differ, it is the legal opinion which prevails. The point upon which there is likely to be such divergence between the two is usually in respect to the social value of the respective interests concerned. If the legal valuation differs from that attached to the respective interests by a persistent and long-continued course of public conviction, as distinguished from a novel and possibly ephemeral opinion, courts should and often do re-examine their valuation and make it conform to the settled popular opinion. In so far as the legal valuation depends upon the settled public conviction at the time and place, there is often a necessary difference of decision on a particular question, not only between England and America, but even between different States of the United States.

e. The law attaches utility to general types or classes of acts as appropriate to the advancement of certain interests rather than to the purpose for which a particular act is done, except in the case in which the purpose is of itself of such public utility as to justify an otherwise impermissible risk. Thus, the law regards the free use of the highway for travel as of sufficient utility to outweigh the risk of carefully conducted traffic, and does not ordinarily concern itself with the good, bad, or indifferent purpose of a particular journey. It may, however, permit a particular method of travel which is normally not permitted if it is necessary to protect some interest to which the law attaches a preeminent value, as where the legal rate of speed is exceeded in the pursuit of a felon or in conveying a desperately wounded patient to a hospital.

§ 292. Factors Considered in Determining Utility of Actor's Conduct

In determining what the law regards as the utility of the actor's conduct for the purpose of determining whether the actor is negligent, the following factors are important:

(a) the social value which the law attaches to the interest which is to be advanced or protected by the conduct;

(b) the extent of the chance that this interest will be advanced or protected by the particular course of conduct;

(c) the extent of the chance that such interest can be adequately advanced or protected by another and less dangerous course of conduct.

§ 293. Factors Considered in Determining Magnitude of Risk

In determining the magnitude of the risk for the purpose of determining whether the actor is negligent, the following factors are important:

(a) the social value which the law attaches to the interests which are imperiled;

(b) the extent of the chance that the actor's conduct will cause an invasion of any interest of the other or of one of a class of which the other is a member;

(c) the extent of the harm likely to be caused to the interests imperiled;

(d) the number of persons whose interests are likely to be invaded if the risk takes effect in harm.

§ 295A. Custom

In determining whether conduct is negligent, the customs of the community, or of others under like circumstances, are factors to be taken into account, but are not controlling where a reasonable man would not follow them.

Comment:

a. Customs and common practices. A custom or usage may be common to the community in general, as in the case of the custom of shaking hands with the right hand, or it may consist of and be limited to the common practices of a relatively small group of persons who engage in particular activities, as in the case of the methods followed in maritime navigation. For a custom or such common practices to be relevant on the issue of negligence, they must be reasonably brought home to the actor's locality, and must be so general, or so well known, that the actor must be charged with knowledge of them, or with negligence in remaining ignorant.

b. *Relevance of custom.* Any such custom of the community in general, or of other persons under like circumstances, is always a factor to be taken into account in determining whether the actor has been negligent. Evidence of the custom is admissible, and is relevant, as indicating a composite judgment as to the risks of the situation and the precautions required to meet them, as well as the feasibility of such precautions, the difficulty of any change in accepted methods, the actor's opportunity to learn what is called for, and the justifiable expectation of others that he will do what is usual, as well as the justifiable expectation of the actor that others will do the same. If the actor does what others do under like circumstances, there is at least a possible inference that he is conforming to the community standard of reasonable conduct; and if he does not do what others do, there is a possible inference that he is not so conforming. In particular instances, where there is nothing in the situation or in common experience to lead to the contrary conclusion, this inference may be so strong as to call for a directed verdict, one way or the other, on the issue of negligence. Thus, even in the absence of any applicable traffic statute, one who drives on the right side of a private way is under ordinary circumstances clearly not negligent in doing so, and one who drives on the left side is under ordinary circumstances clearly negligent.

On the same basis, evidence of the past practices of the parties to the action in dealing with each other is admissible, and relevant, as indicating an understood standard of conduct, or the reasonable expectation of each party as to what the other will do.

c. *When custom not controlling.* Any such custom is, however, not necessarily conclusive as to whether the actor, by conforming to it, has exercised the care of a reasonable man under the circumstances, or by departing from it has failed to exercise such care. Customs which are entirely reasonable under the ordinary circumstances which give rise to them may become quite unreasonable in the light of a single fact in the particular case. It may be negligence to drive on the right side of the road, and it may not be negligence to drive on the left side when the right side is blocked by a dangerous ditch. Beyond this, customs and usages themselves are many and various. Some of them are the result of careful thought and decision, while others arise from the kind of inadvertence, neglect, or deliberate disregard of a known risk which is associated with negligence. No group of individuals and no industry or trade can be permitted, by adopting careless and slipshod methods to save time, effort, or money, to set its own uncontrolled standard at the expense of the rest of the community. If the only test is to be what has always been done, no one will ever have any great incentive to make any progress in the direction of safety. It follows, therefore, that whenever the particular circumstances, the risk, or other elements in the case are such that a reasonable man would not conform to the custom, the actor may be found negligent in conforming to it; and whenever a reasonable man would depart from the custom, the actor may be found not to be negligent in so departing.

Illustrations:

1. It is the usual custom of railroads to couple cars by bumping them together. On a day when the tops of the cars are covered with ice, and brakemen are required to stand on top of them, the A Railroad follows this custom. When the cars are bumped B, a brakeman, loses his footing on top of one of the cars, falls off, and is injured. A Railroad may be found to be negligent toward B.

2. In the year 1932 A was engaged in towing barges between cities on the open Atlantic Ocean. A's tugs were not equipped with radio sets with which storm warnings could be received. Although the existence of such radio sets was generally known, and they could be installed with little trouble or expense, other coastwise carriers had not equipped their tugs with them. A received no warning of a storm which overtook one of his tugs, and sank a barge towed by him, which was the property of B. Notwithstanding the general custom not to carry radio sets, A may be found to be negligent toward B.

§ 296. Emergency

(1) In determining whether conduct is negligent toward another, the fact that the actor is confronted with a sudden emergency which requires rapid decision is a factor in determining the reasonable character of his choice of action.

(2) The fact that the actor is not negligent after the emergency has arisen does not preclude his liability for his tortious conduct which has produced the emergency.

TOPIC 4. TYPES OF NEGLIGENT ACTS

§ 299A. Undertaking in Profession or Trade

Unless he represents that he has greater or less skill or knowledge, one who undertakes to render services in the

practice of a profession or trade is required to exercise the skill and knowledge normally possessed by members of that profession or trade in good standing in similar communities.

Comment:

a. Skill, as the word is used in this Section, is something more than the mere minimum competence required of any person who does an act, under the rule stated in § 299. It is that special form of competence which is not part of the ordinary equipment of the reasonable man, but which is the result of acquired learning, and aptitude developed by special training and experience. All professions, and most trades, are necessarily skilled, and the word is used to refer to the special competence which they require.

b. Profession or trade. This Section is thus a special application of the rule stated in § 299. It applies to any person who undertakes to render services to another in the practice of a profession, such as that of physician or surgeon, dentist, pharmacist, oculist, attorney, accountant, or engineer. It applies also to any person who undertakes to render services to others in the practice of a skilled trade, such as that of airplane pilot, precision machinist, electrician, carpenter, blacksmith, or plumber. This Section states the minimum skill and knowledge which the actor undertakes to exercise, and therefore to have. If he has in fact greater skill than that common to the profession or trade, he is required to exercise that skill, as stated in § 299, Comment *e.*

f. Schools of thought. Where there are different schools of thought in a profession, or different methods are followed by different groups engaged in a trade, the actor is to be judged by the professional standards of the group to which he belongs. The law cannot undertake to decide technical questions of proper practice over which experts reasonably disagree, or to declare that those who do not accept particular controversial doctrines are necessarily negligent in failing to do so. There may be, however, minimum requirements of skill applicable to all persons, of whatever school of thought, who engage in any profession or trade. Thus any person who holds himself out as competent to treat human ailments must have a minimum skill in diagnosis, and a minimum knowledge of possible methods of treatment. Licensing statutes, or those requiring a basic knowledge of science for the practice of a profession, may provide such a minimum standard.

§ 301. Effect of Warning

(1) **Except as stated in Subsection (2), a warning given by the actor of his intention to do an act which involves a risk of harm to others does not prevent the actor from being negligent.**

(2) **The exercise of reasonable care to give reasonably adequate warning prevents the doing of an act from being negligent, if**

(a) **the law regards the actor's interest in doing the act as paramount to the other's interest in entering or remaining on the area endangered thereby, or**

(b) **the risk involved in the act, or its unreasonable character, arises out of the absence of warning.**

§ 302A. Risk of Negligence or Recklessness of Others

An act or an omission may be negligent if the actor realizes or should realize that it involves an unreasonable risk of harm to another through the negligent or reckless conduct of the other or a third person.

Illustrations:

1. A leaves a hole in the street, which would be quite obvious to an attentive automobile driver, but might easily not be discovered by an inattentive driver. B, a driver who is not keeping a proper lookout, drives into the hole and is injured. A may be found to be negligent toward B.

2. The same facts as in Illustration 1, except that the person injured is C, a guest in B's automobile. A may be found to be negligent toward C.

§ 302B. Risk of Intentional or Criminal Conduct

An act or an omission may be negligent if the actor realizes or should realize that it involves an unreasonable risk of harm to another through the conduct of the other or a third person which is intended to cause harm, even though such conduct is criminal.

Comment:

d. Normally the actor has much less reason to anticipate intentional misconduct than he has to anticipate negligence. In the ordinary case he may reasonably proceed upon the assumption that others will not interfere in a manner intended to cause harm to anyone. This is

45

true particularly where the intentional conduct is a crime, since under ordinary circumstances it may reasonably be assumed that no one will violate the criminal law. Even where there is a recognizable possibility of the intentional interference, the possibility may be so slight, or there may be so slight a risk of foreseeable harm to another as a result of the interference, that a reasonable man in the position of the actor would disregard it.

Illustration:

2. A leaves his automobile unlocked, with the key in the ignition switch, while he steps into a drugstore to buy a pack of cigarettes. The time is noon, the neighborhood peaceable and respectable, and no suspicious persons are about. B, a thief, steals the car while A is in the drugstore, and in his haste to get away drives it in a negligent manner and injures C. A is not negligent toward C.

With this illustration, compare Illustration 14 below.

e. There are, however, situations in which the actor, as a reasonable man, is required to anticipate and guard against the intentional, or even criminal, misconduct of others. In general, these situations arise where the actor is under a special responsibility toward the one who suffers the harm, which includes the duty to protect him against such intentional misconduct; or where the actor's own affirmative act has created or exposed the other to a recognizable high degree of risk of harm through such misconduct, which a reasonable man would take into account. The following are examples of such situations. The list is not an exclusive one, and there may be other situations in which the actor is required to take precautions.

A. Where, by contract or otherwise, the actor has undertaken a duty to protect the other against such misconduct. Normally such a duty arises out of a contract between the parties, in which such protection is an express or an implied term of the agreement.

Illustration:

3. The A Company makes a business of conducting tourists through the slums of the city. It employs guards to accompany all parties to protect them during such tours. B goes upon such a tour. While in a particularly dangerous part of the slums the guards abandon the party. B is attacked and robbed. The A Company may be found to be negligent toward B.

TOPIC 5. MISREPRESENTATIONS THREATENING PHYSICAL HARM

§ **311.** Negligent Misrepresentation Involving Risk of Physical Harm

(1) One who negligently gives false information to another is subject to liability for physical harm caused by action taken by the other in reasonable reliance upon such information, where such harm results

(a) to the other, or

(b) to such third persons as the actor should expect to be put in peril by the action taken.

(2) Such negligence may consist of failure to exercise reasonable care

(a) in ascertaining the accuracy of the information, or

(b) in the manner in which it is communicated.

Comment:

a. The rule stated in this Section represents a somewhat broader liability than the rules stated as to liability for pecuniary loss resulting from negligent misrepresentation, stated in § 552, to which reference should be made for comparison.

b. The rule stated in this Section finds particular application where it is a part of the actor's business or profession to give information upon which the safety of the recipient or a third person depends. Thus it is as much a part of the professional duty of a physician to give correct information as to the character of the disease from which his patient is suffering, where such knowledge is necessary to the safety of the patient or others, as it is to make a correct diagnosis or to prescribe the appropriate medicine. The rule is not, however, limited to information given in a business or professional capacity, or to those engaged in a business or profession. It extends to any person who, in the course of an activity which is in furtherance of his own interests, undertakes to give information to another, and knows or should realize that the safety of the person of others may depend upon the accuracy of the information.

Illustrations:

1. A train of the A Railroad is approaching a grade crossing. An employee of the Railroad negligently raises the crossing gates, and so informs approaching automobile drivers that no train is

coming. B sees the gates raised, drives onto the crossing, and is struck by the train. A Railroad is subject to liability to B.

2. The A Company is conducting blasting operations near a railroad. B, an employee of the railroad, comes to inquire as to the progress of the work. As he arrives a blast is being set off, and he is advised to take cover. Immediately after the blast the foreman of A Company negligently informs B that all danger is over and he can safely come into the open. A delayed explosion occurs, and B is struck and injured by a rock. A Company is subject to liability to B.

3. A has charge of B, a lunatic of violent tendencies. A advertises for a servant, and C applies for the employment. A informs C that B is insane, but negligently gives C the impression that B is not violent or dangerous. C accepts the employment, and is attacked and injured by B. A is subject to liability to C.

TOPIC 7. DUTIES OF AFFIRMATIVE ACTION

§ 314. Duty to Act for Protection of Others

The fact that the actor realizes or should realize that action on his part is necessary for another's aid or protection does not of itself impose upon him a duty to take such action.

Comment:

c. The rule stated in this Section is applicable irrespective of the gravity of the danger to which the other is subjected and the insignificance of the trouble, effort, or expense of giving him aid or protection.

The origin of the rule lay in the early common law distinction between action and inaction, or "misfeasance" and "non-feasance." In the early law one who injured another by a positive affirmative act was held liable without any great regard even for his fault. But the courts were far too much occupied with the more flagrant forms of misbehavior to be greatly concerned with one who merely did nothing, even though another might suffer serious harm because of his omission to act. Hence liability for non-feasance was slow to receive any recognition in the law. It appeared first in, and is still largely confined to, situations in which there was some special relation between the parties, on the basis of which the defendant was found to have a duty to take action for the aid or protection of the plaintiff.

The result of the rule has been a series of older decisions to the effect that one human being, seeing a fellow man in dire peril, is under no legal obligation to aid him, but may sit on the dock, smoke his cigar, and watch the other drown. Such decisions have been condemned by legal writers as revolting to any moral sense, but thus far they remain the law. It appears inevitable that, sooner or later such extreme cases of morally outrageous and indefensible conduct will arise that there will be further inroads upon the older rule.

Illustration:

> 1. A sees B, a blind man, about to step into the street in front of an approaching automobile. A could prevent B from so doing by a word or touch without delaying his own progress. A does not do so, and B is run over and hurt. A is under no duty to prevent B from stepping into the street, and is not liable to B.

d. The rule stated in this Section applies only where the peril in which the actor knows that the other is placed is not due to any active force which is under the actor's control. If a force is within the actor's control, his failure to control it is treated as though he were actively directing it and not as a breach of duty to take affirmative steps to prevent its continuance (see § 302, Comments *a* and *c*).

Illustrations:

> 2. A, a factory owner, sees B, a young child or a blind man who has wandered into his factory, about to approach a piece of moving machinery. A is negligent if he permits the machinery to continue in motion when by the exercise of reasonable care he could stop it before B comes in contact with it.

§ 314A. Special Relations Giving Rise to Duty to Aid or Protect

(1) A common carrier is under a duty to its passengers to take reasonable action

> **(a) to protect them against unreasonable risk of physical harm, and**

> **(b) to give them first aid after it knows or has reason to know that they are ill or injured, and to care for them until they can be cared for by others.**

(2) An innkeeper is under a similar duty to his guests.

(3) A possessor of land who holds it open to the public is under a similar duty to members of the public who enter in response to his invitation.

(4) One who is required by law to take or who voluntarily takes the custody of another under circumstances such as to deprive the other of his normal opportunities for protection is under a similar duty to the other.

TITLE A. DUTY TO CONTROL CONDUCT
OF THIRD PERSONS

§ 315. General Principle

There is no duty so to control the conduct of a third person as to prevent him from causing physical harm to another unless

(a) a special relation exists between the actor and the third person which imposes a duty upon the actor to control the third person's conduct, or

(b) a special relation exists between the actor and the other which gives to the other a right to protection.

§ 316. Duty of Parent to Control Conduct of Child

A parent is under a duty to exercise reasonable care so to control his minor child as to prevent it from intentionally harming others or from so conducting itself as to create an unreasonable risk of bodily harm to them, if the parent

(a) knows or has reason to know that he has the ability to control his child, and

(b) knows or should know of the necessity and opportunity for exercising such control.

Comment:

a. While the father as head of the family group is no longer responsible for the actions of all the members of his household or even for those of his minor child, he is responsible for their conduct in so far as he has the ability to control it. This duty is not peculiar to a father. It extends to the mother also in so far as her position as mother gives her an ability to control her child.

§ 319. Duty of Those in Charge of Person Having Dangerous Propensities

One who takes charge of a third person whom he knows or should know to be likely to cause bodily harm to others if not controlled is under a duty to exercise reasonable care to control the third person to prevent him from doing such harm.

TITLE B. DUTY TO AID OTHERS AND SERVICES GRATUITOUSLY RENDERED OR UNDERTAKEN

§ 321. Duty to Act When Prior Conduct Is Found to Be Dangerous

(1) If the actor does an act, and subsequently realizes or should realize that it has created an unreasonable risk of causing physical harm to another, he is under a duty to exercise reasonable care to prevent the risk from taking effect.

(2) The rule stated in Subsection (1) applies even though at the time of the act the actor has no reason to believe that it will involve such a risk.

Comment:

a. The rule stated in Subsection (1) applies whenever the actor realizes or should realize that his act has created a condition which involves an unreasonable risk of harm to another, or is leading to consequences which involve such a risk. The rule applies whether the original act is tortious or innocent. If the act is negligent, the actor's responsibility continues in the form of a duty to exercise reasonable care to avert the consequences which he recognizes or should recognize as likely to follow. But even where he has had no reason to believe, at the time of the act, that it would involve any unreasonable risk of physical harm to another, he is under a duty to exercise reasonable care when, because of a change of circumstances, or further knowledge of the situation which he has acquired, he realizes or should realize that he has created such a risk.

Illustrations:

1. A is playing golf. He sees no one on or near a putting green and drives to it. While the ball is in the air, B, another player, suddenly appears from a bunker directly in the line of A's drive. A is under a duty to shout a warning to B.

§ 322. Duty to Aid Another Harmed by Actor's Conduct

If the actor knows or has reason to know that by his conduct, whether tortious or innocent, he has caused such bodily harm to another as to make him helpless and in danger of further harm, the actor is under a duty to exercise reasonable care to prevent such further harm.

Comment:

a. The rule stated in this Section applies not only where the actor's original conduct is tortious, but also where it is entirely innocent. If his act, or an instrumentality within his control, has inflicted upon another such harm that the other is helpless and in danger, and a reasonable man would recognize the necessity of aiding or protecting him to avert further harm, the actor is under a duty to take such action even though he may not have been originally at fault. This is true even though the contributory negligence of the person injured would disable him from maintaining any action for the original harm resulting from the actor's original conduct.

b. The words "further harm" include not only an entirely new harm due to the dangerous position in which the other has been placed by the actor's tortious act (Illustration 1), but also any increase in the original harm caused by the failure to give assistance (Illustration 2), and any protraction of the harm which prompt attention would have prevented (Illustration 3).

Illustrations:

1. A negligently or innocently runs down B on an unlighted country road. B is unconscious. A leaves B lying in the middle of the highway, where another car subsequently runs over him. This is an entirely new harm from which A should have protected him and for which A is subject to liability to B, whether or not A would have been liable for the original harm.

2. A, a "hit and run driver," negligently or innocently runs over B, inflicting serious wounds. Although A knows B's condition, he drives away and leaves B lying in the road. The weather is exceedingly cold, and B, unable to move, contracts pneumonia from the exposure. A is subject to liability to B for the illness, whether or not he would have been liable for the original wounds.

3. A negligently or innocently runs down B on a little-frequented highway, rendering B helpless. A does not take B to a nearby hospital. In consequence, B receives no medical attention for twelve hours. Had B's wounds been immediately taken care of and properly disinfected, they would have healed immediately. The delay retards the process of healing for several weeks. A is subject to liability to B for the additional period of healing, whether or not A would have been liable for the original harm.

§ 323. Negligent Performance of Undertaking to Render Services

One who undertakes, gratuitously or for consideration, to render services to another which he should recognize as necessary for the protection of the other's person or things, is subject to liability to the other for physical harm resulting from his failure to exercise reasonable care to perform his undertaking, if

(a) his failure to exercise such care increases the risk of such harm, or

(b) the harm is suffered because of the other's reliance upon the undertaking.

Caveat:

The Institute expresses no opinion as to whether:

(1) the making of a contract, or a gratuitous promise, without in any way entering upon performance, is a sufficient undertaking to result in liability under the rule stated in this Section, or

(2) there may not be other situations in which one may be liable where he has entered upon performance, and cannot withdraw from his undertaking without leaving an unreasonable risk of serious harm to the other.

TOPIC 9. PROOF OF NEGLIGENCE AND FUNCTIONS OF COURT AND JURY

§ 328A. Burden of Proof

In an action for negligence the plaintiff has the burden of proving

(a) facts which give rise to a legal duty on the part of the defendant to conform to the standard of conduct established by law for the protection of the plaintiff,

(b) failure of the defendant to conform to the standard of conduct,

(c) that such failure is a legal cause of the harm suffered by the plaintiff, and

(d) that the plaintiff has in fact suffered harm of a kind legally compensable by damages.

Comment:

a. Meaning of burden of proof. The phrase "burden of proof," as used in the Restatement of this Subject, includes both the burden of introducing sufficient evidence to justify a jury in finding for the party having the burden, and the burden of persuading the jury to find for that party upon the matter in issue. This burden of proof, which concerns the ultimate burden of producing a preponderance of the evidence, is to be distinguished from the burden of going forward with evidence, at a particular point in the proceeding, which may shift from one party to the other according to the proof introduced.

§ 328B. Functions of Court

In an action for negligence the court determines

(a) whether the evidence as to the facts makes an issue upon which the jury may reasonably find the existence or non-existence of such facts;

(b) whether such facts give rise to any legal duty on the part of the defendant;

(c) the standard of conduct required of the defendant by his legal duty;

(d) whether the defendant has conformed to that standard, in any case in which the jury may not reasonably come to a different conclusion;

(e) the applicability of any rules of law determining whether the defendant's conduct is a legal cause of harm to the plaintiff; and

(f) whether the harm claimed to be suffered by the plaintiff is legally compensable.

Comment:

b. Liability for negligence is often said to be a mixed question of law and fact. By this it is meant, not only that both the court and the jury have an important part to play in the determination of the liability, and that separate functions are assigned to each, but, further, that these functions to some extent overlap and are interdependent. In general, the court must decide questions of law, and the jury questions of fact. But since a question of law may involve a ruling upon a question of fact, and a question of fact may involve the application of a rule of law, the two are often interwoven, and it becomes impossible to state the function of the court without reference to that of the jury, and vice versa. The division of functions between court and jury is in part a matter of historical origins, in part a matter of present ideas of policy as to proper procedure in the trial of a case.

Comment on Clause (d):

g. Normally the determination of the question whether the defendant has conformed to the standard of conduct required of him by the law is for the jury. Although it involves an application of the legal standard, and to a considerable extent a decision as to its content and meaning (see § 328C), it is customarily regarded as a question of fact. As in the case of other questions of fact, however (see Comment *d* above), the court reserves a power of determination of the preliminary question whether the evidence will permit the jury reasonably to come to more than one conclusion. Where it is clear upon the evidence that the defendant has or has not conformed to what the standard of the law requires, and that no reasonable man could reach a contrary conclusion, the court must withdraw the issue from the jury and direct a verdict, or give binding instructions if there are still other issues in the case. Thus the court may rule that it is necessarily negligence to drive across a railway track without stopping to look and listen, or that it is not negligence to fail to take precautions which no reasonable man would consider to be necessary under the circumstances.

§ 328C. Functions of Jury

In an action for negligence the jury determines, in any case in which different conclusions may be reached on the issue:

(a) the facts,

(b) whether the defendant has conformed to the standard of conduct required by the law,

(c) whether the defendant's conduct is a legal cause of the harm to the plaintiff, and

(d) the amount of compensation for legally compensable harm.

Comment:

a. This Section supplements § 328B, dealing with the function of the court in actions for negligence, and should be read together with it. See also, as to the functions of the court and jury as to the issue of contributory negligence, § 476.

As stated in Comment *d* on § 328B, the court in the first instance has the power and duty to decide whether the evidence as to facts is such that the jury may reasonably come to more than one conclusion; and where only one conclusion may reasonably be drawn, the issue is withdrawn from the jury. In any case where the jury may reasonably arrive at either conclusion as to the existence or non-existence of facts, the issue is for the jury to decide.

Comment on Clause (b):

b. In any case where there may be such reasonable disagreement, it is the function of the jury to apply to the facts in evidence the standard of conduct required by the law in the performance of the defendant's legal duty. This standard is declared to the jury in the form of an instruction in more or less general terms. Since it is impossible to prescribe definite rules of conduct in advance for every combination of circumstances that may arise, and the fact situations are infinitely variable, the law resorts to formulae which state the standard in broad terms without attempt to fill it in in detail. The common formula for the negligence standard is the conduct of a reasonable man under like circumstances. In applying this standard under the instructions of the court, the jury normally is expected to determine what the general standard of conduct would require in the particular case, and so to set a particular standard of its own within the general one. This function is commonly said to be one of the determination of a question of fact, and not of law. It differs from the function of the court, however, only in that it is not reduced to any definite rules, so that the same conclusion will not necessarily be reached in two identical cases, and that it is a secondary function, performed only after the court has reached its initial conclusion that the issue is for the jury.

Comment on Clause (c):

c. Except in a case where there can be no two conclusions, or in which there is some applicable rule of law decisive of the issue, it is the function of the jury to determine whether the defendant's conduct is a legal cause of the harm to the plaintiff. As to this, see § 465.

Comment on Clause (d):

d. In any case where different conclusions may be reached, it is the function of the jury to determine the amount of compensation for legally compensable harm to the plaintiff. Thus where the defendant's negligence results in the plaintiff's broken leg and causes him pain and suffering, it is for the court to rule in the first instance that the jury may award damages for such pain and suffering, and for the jury to determine the amount to be awarded. This too is a question of fact, as to what a proper financial compensation may be; and as in the case of other questions of fact, it is subject to the control of the court when the amount awarded exceeds or falls short of that justified by the facts in evidence.

§ 328D. Res Ipsa Loquitur

(1) **It may be inferred that harm suffered by the plaintiff is caused by negligence of the defendant when**

(a) **the event is of a kind which ordinarily does not occur in the absence of negligence;**

(b) **other responsible causes, including the conduct of the plaintiff and third persons, are sufficiently eliminated by the evidence; and**

(c) **the indicated negligence is within the scope of the defendant's duty to the plaintiff.**

(2) **It is the function of the court to determine whether the inference may reasonably be drawn by the jury, or whether it must necessarily be drawn.**

(3) **It is the function of the jury to determine whether the inference is to be drawn in any case where different conclusions may reasonably be reached.**

Comment:

a. The principle stated in this Section is commonly given the name of res ipsa loquitur. The Latin phrase, which means nothing more than "the thing speaks for itself," originated in a casual word let fall by Baron Pollock in the course of argument with counsel in Byrne v. Boadle, 2 H. & C. 722, 159 Eng.Rep. 299 (1863), where a barrel of flour rolled out of the window of the defendant's warehouse and fell on a passing pedestrian. In itself, the phrase has no more importance or virtue that its English equivalent, and its use has from time to time been criticized as adding unnecessary obscurity to a relatively simple problem.

In its inception the principle of res ipsa loquitur was merely a rule of evidence, permitting the jury to draw from the occurrence of an unusual event the conclusion that it was the defendant's fault. Shortly after its origin, however, it became confused, in cases of injuries to passengers at the hands of carriers, with the older rule which placed the burden of proof upon the carrier to show that its negligence had not caused the injury. (See § 328 A, Comment *b.*) This confusion resulted in a great deal of disagreement among the courts as to the application of the principle and its procedural effect. To some extent this disagreement still continues. The rule stated in this Section is that upon which the great majority of the American courts are now agreed.

b. Circumstantial evidence. Negligence and causation, like other facts, may of course be proved by circumstantial evidence. Without resort to Latin the jury may be permitted to infer, when a runaway horse is found in the street, that its owner has been negligent in looking after it; or when a driver runs down a visible pedestrian, that he has failed to keep a proper lookout. When the Latin phrase is used in such cases, nothing is added. A res ipsa loquitur case is ordinarily merely one kind of case of circumstantial evidence, in which the jury may reasonably infer both negligence and causation from the mere occurrence of the event and the defendant's relation to it.

Some courts occasionally have applied "res ipsa loquitur," against certain defendants, as a rule of policy which goes beyond the probative effect of circumstantial evidence, and requires the defendant to explain the event or be liable. This has been true particularly in actions by passengers against carriers, where it is undoubtedly a survival of the older common law rule placing the burden of proof upon the defendant, still followed by some courts. (See § 328 A, Comment b.) In such cases "res ipsa loquitur" often is given a greater procedural effect, either as requiring the defendant to sustain the burden of proof or as creating a presumption of negligence rather than a mere procedural inference. In general, such decisions have tended to be confined to defendants who have undertaken a special responsibility toward the plaintiff, as in the case of the carrier and the passenger. A few courts consistently define "res ipsa loquitur" as limited to such situations, and as having the greater procedural effect. Such courts usually have been compelled to recognize, under another name, the principle of circumstantial evidence stated in this Section.

Comment on Clause (a) of Subsection (1):

c. *Type of event.* The first requirement for the application of the rule stated in this Section is a basis of past experience which reasonably permits the conclusion that such events do not ordinarily occur unless someone has been negligent. There are many types of accidents which commonly occur without the fault of anyone. The fact that a tire blows out, or that a man falls down stairs is not, in the absence of anything more, enough to permit the conclusion that there was negligence in inspecting the tire, or in the construction of the stairs, because it is common human experience that such events all too frequently occur without such negligence. On the other hand there are many events, such as those of objects falling from the defendant's premises, the fall of an elevator, the escape of gas or water from mains or of electricity from wires or appliances, the derailment of trains or the explosion of boilers, where the conclusion is at least permissible that such things do not usually happen unless someone has been negligent. To such events res ipsa loquitur may apply.

d. *Basis of conclusion.* In the usual case the basis of past experience from which this conclusion may be drawn is common to the community, and is a matter of general knowledge, which the court recognizes on much the same basis as when it takes judicial notice of facts which everyone knows. It may, however, be supplied by the evidence of the parties; and expert testimony that such an event usually does not occur without negligence may afford a sufficient basis for the inference. Such testimony may be essential to the plaintiff's case where, as for example in some actions for medical malpractice, there is no fund of common knowledge which may permit laymen reasonably to draw the conclusion. On the other hand there are other kinds of medical malpractice, as where a sponge is left in the plaintiff's abdomen after an operation, where no expert is needed to tell the jury that such events do not usually occur in the absence of negligence.

e. Permissible conclusion. The plaintiff's burden of proof (see § 328A) requires him to produce evidence which will permit the conclusion that it is more likely than not that his injuries were caused by the defendant's negligence. Where the probabilities are at best evenly divided between negligence and its absence, it becomes the duty of the court to direct the jury that there is no sufficient proof. The plaintiff need not, however, conclusively exclude all other possible explanations, and so prove his case beyond a reasonable doubt. Such proof is not required in civil actions, in contrast to criminal cases. It is enough that the facts proved reasonably permit the conclusion that negligence is the more probable explanation. This conclusion is not for the court to draw, or to refuse to draw, in any case where either conclusion is reasonable; and even though the court would not itself find negligence, it must still leave the question to the jury if reasonable men might do so.

Illustrations:

1. A buys at a grocery store a can of spinach packed by B. While eating the spinach, A is injured by a large piece of glass concealed in it. There is evidence that nothing was done by A or by any third person after the can of spinach was opened which would account for the presence of the glass. Without other evidence, it may be inferred that the presence of the glass was due to the negligence of B.

2. A, a customer in B's restaurant, orders and eats a piece of blueberry pie. He is injured by a small blue tack, of a size and shape which would permit it to become imbedded and concealed in a blueberry, and to escape the most careful scrutiny. It may not be inferred, without other evidence, that the presence of the tack in the pie was due to the negligence of B.

3. A is a passenger in the airplane of B Company, a common carrier. In good flying weather the plane disappears, and no trace

of it is ever found. There is no other evidence. Various explanations are possible, including mechanical failure which could not have been prevented by reasonable care, and bombs planted on the plane. It may, however, be inferred by the jury that the most probable explanation is some negligence on the part of B Company.

4. A goes to bed at night as a guest in B's hotel in a city in California. During the night he is injured by the fall of a large piece of plaster from the ceiling. In the absence of other evidence there are various possible explanations, including activities of persons upstairs or previous guests, jolts from explosions or other sources outside of the hotel, concealed defects not discoverable by reasonable inspection, or an earthquake. It may, however, reasonably be inferred that the most probable explanation is the negligence of B in permitting the plaster to become defective.

Comment on Clause (b) of Subsection (1):

f. Eliminating other responsible causes. It is never enough for the plaintiff to prove that he was injured by the negligence of some person unidentified. It is still necessary to make the negligence point to the defendant. On this too the plaintiff has the burden of proof by a preponderance of the evidence; and in any case where there is no doubt that it is at least equally probable that the negligence was that of a third person, the court must direct the jury that the plaintiff has not proved his case. Again, however, the plaintiff is not required to exclude all other possible conclusions beyond a reasonable doubt, and it is enough that he makes out a case from which the jury may reasonably conclude that the negligence was, more probably than not, that of the defendant.

Illustration:

5. A leaves his automobile parked on the side of a hill. Two minutes later the car runs down the hill and injures B. In the absence of other evidence, the explanation is possible that some meddling stranger has tampered with the car, or that it has been struck by another vehicle. It may, however, reasonably be inferred that, more probably than not, the event occurred because of the negligence of A in parking the car.

g. Defendant's exclusive control. The plaintiff may sustain this burden of proof with the aid of a second inference, based on a showing of some specific cause for the event which was within the defendant's responsibility, or a showing that the defendant is responsible for all reasonably probable causes to which the event can be attributed. Usually this is done by showing that a specific instrumentality which has caused the event, or all reasonably probable causes, were under the exclusive control of the defendant. Thus the responsibility of the defendant is proved by eliminating that of any other person.

It is not, however, necessary to the inference that the defendant have such exclusive control; and exclusive control is merely one way of proving his responsibility. He may be responsible, and the inference may be drawn against him, where he shares the control with another, as in the case of the fall of a party wall which each of two landowners is under a duty to inspect and maintain. He may be responsible where he is under a duty to the plaintiff which he cannot delegate to another, as in the case of a landlord who leases premises dangerous to persons on the public highway, which his tenant undertakes to maintain. He may be responsible where he is under a duty to control the conduct of a third person, as in the case of a host whose guests throw objects from his windows. It may be enough that the defendant was formerly in control, at the time of the probable negligence, as in the case of a beverage bottler whose product poisons the consumer, when there is sufficient evidence to eliminate the responsibility of intermediate dealers. Exclusive control is merely one fact which establishes the responsibility of the defendant; and if it can be established otherwise, exclusive control is not essential to a res ipsa loquitur case. The essential question becomes one of whether the probable cause is one which the defendant was under a duty to the plaintiff to anticipate or guard against.

Illustrations:

6. A's premises are damaged by water escaping from a main under the street. The main was originally installed by B Company, which has at all times had exclusive control of its inspection and maintenance. There is expert evidence that water mains made of proper material and properly installed, inspected and maintained, do not ordinarily break. Without other evidence, it may be inferred that the escape of the water was due to the negligence of B Company.

7. A, a customer in B's store, slips on a banana peel near the door, and falls and is injured. The banana peel is fresh, and there is no evidence as to how long it has been on the floor. Since it is at least equally probable that it was dropped by a third person so short a time before that B had no reasonable opportunity to discover and remove it, it cannot be inferred that its presence was due to the negligence of B.

8. A, a pedestrian on the public sidewalk, is injured by the fall of a sign from the front of a building owned by B and leased to C. Both B and C are under a legal duty to members of the

public using the highway to exercise reasonable care to inspect and maintain the sign. It can be inferred that the event was due to the negligence of both B and C.

9. A undergoes an operation. B, the surgeon performing the operation, leaves it to C, a nurse, to count the sponges used in the course of it. B is under a legal duty to A to exercise reasonable care to supervise the conduct of C in this task. After the operation a sponge is left in B's abdomen. It can be inferred that this is due to the negligence of both B and C.

10. A buys from a retail dealer a bottle of beer, bottled by B. While he is handling the bottle it explodes, and injures him. Without other evidence, it cannot be inferred that the event was, more probably than not, due to the negligence of B. But if there is sufficient evidence that nothing was done by A or the retail dealer or by intermediate handlers of the bottle to cause the explosion, the inference of B's negligence can be drawn.

h. Special responsibility. Against some defendants, such as carriers, who have undertaken a special responsibility to the plaintiff, some courts have made use of the phrase "res ipsa loquitur" to impose upon the defendant a procedural disadvantage, even in the absence of such an inference that the negligence was more probably that of the defendant than of another. Thus where a vehicle operated by a common carrier collides with another vehicle and a passenger is injured, these courts apply res ipsa loquitur in favor of the passenger against the carrier, but not against the driver of the other vehicle. Such an application sometimes is accompanied by an increased procedural effect, creating a presumption against the carrier or imposing upon it the burden of proof. Such cases go beyond the rule stated in this Section, and represent in effect a special rule applicable to such defendants.

i. Eliminating the plaintiff. The inference of negligence does not point to the defendant until the plaintiff's own conduct is eliminated as a responsible cause. Where the evidence fails to show a greater probability that the event was due to the defendant's negligence than that it was caused by the plaintiff's own conduct, the inference of the defendant's responsibility cannot be drawn. This is true not only as to the plaintiff's own contributory negligence, but also as to his innocent conduct, of a kind which would relieve the defendant of responsibility, as where a chattel manufactured by the defendant is put to a use for which it was not intended. Where, however, there is sufficient evidence that the plaintiff's own conduct was not a responsible cause, the fact that he was in "control" of a chattel or other instrumentality will not prevent the inference.

Illustration:

11. A is an engineer operating a locomotive of B Railroad. One of his duties is to keep the water in the boiler, and thus the steam pressure, at a proper level. The boiler explodes and kills A. Without other evidence, it cannot be inferred that the explosion was due to the negligence of B Railroad. But when the fireman testifies that A kept the water and steam at proper levels, and did nothing to cause the explosion, the inference can be drawn.

Comment on Clause (c) of Subsection (1):

j. Defendant's duty. In order to fall within the defendant's responsibility, the indicated negligence must come within the scope of his duty toward the plaintiff. Thus where a landowner owes to a trespasser no duty of care as to the condition of his premises, an injury to a trespasser arising from a defective condition does not permit any inference of negligence. Likewise, where under a statute an automobile driver is liable to a guest in his car only for wilful, wanton, or reckless conduct, an injury to a guest which indicates only ordinary negligence in driving does not permit the inference of a breach of the more limited duty.

Comment:

k. Defendant's superior knowledge. It frequently is said by courts that one basis for the application of the principle of res ipsa loquitur is the defendant's superior knowledge, or his superior opportunity to obtain it, as to how the event occurred. This statement usually is made as an additional reason for permitting the inference of negligence where it can otherwise be drawn, or for refusing to permit the inference where it cannot otherwise be drawn. Undoubtedly the fact that in res ipsa loquitur cases defendants in general have such superior knowledge, or access to it, has been a very persuasive factor in the development of the principle. Cases are, however, very few in which this has ever been the decisive factor. Obviously the inference of the defendant's negligence and responsibility may still be drawn in cases where the event is of a kind which does not usually occur without negligence and all reasonably probable causes were under the control of the defendant, even though it is quite clear from the facts that he does not know and cannot know what has happened. Such superior knowledge, or opportunity to obtain it, is therefore not a requirement for the application of the rule stated in this Section.

Illustration:

12. A's son, with A's consent, takes B for a ride in A's automobile. Under a statute of the particular state, A is liable for

any negligence of his son in driving the car. The car is found in the ditch with both B and the son dead, the son seated behind the steering wheel. There is no evidence as to how or why the car left the road, and it clearly appears that A does not have and cannot possibly obtain such evidence. It may be inferred by the jury that B's death was due to negligence of the son, for which A is subject to liability.

Comment on Subsections (2) and (3):

l. The rules stated in Subsections (2) and (3) are, respectively, special applications of the rules stated in § 328B(a) and 328C(a). They are stated in this Section in order to make it entirely clear that it is the function of the court to determine, in the first instance, whether the jury can reasonably draw the inference, or whether it must necessarily be drawn, and that where different conclusions may reasonably be reached it is the function of the jury to decide whether the inference is to be drawn or not.

Comment:

m. Procedural effect. It is beyond the scope of this Restatement to attempt to state the procedural effect of the res ipsa loquitur principle when it is applied in any particular jurisdiction. In the ordinary case the great majority of the courts now treat res ipsa loquitur as creating nothing more than a permissible inference, which the jury may draw or refuse to draw, unless the facts are so compelling that no reasonable man could reject it. Some courts have tended in the past, and some few still tend, to give res ipsa loquitur the effect of a presumption, which requires a directed verdict for the plaintiff if the defendant offers no evidence to rebut it. An even smaller number treat res ipsa loquitur as imposing the burden of proof upon the defendant. Some courts give the principle the greater procedural effect, whatever it may be, only in actions against defendants such as common carriers, who have undertaken a special responsibility toward the plaintiff.

There has been further disagreement as to the effect, upon the use of res ipsa loquitur, of the plaintiff's allegations of specific negligence in his pleading, or his introduction of evidence of specific negligence. The view which now tends to prevail is that res ipsa loquitur may still be applied, to the extent that the inference to be drawn supports the specific allegation or the specific proof; and that where the specific allegation of negligence is accompanied by a general allegation, res ipsa loquitur may be relied on in support of the general allegation. It is not within the scope of this Restatement to state such procedural rules.

n. Defendant's evidence. When the defendant in turn offers evidence that the event was not due to his negligence, the inference which arises under the conditions stated in this Section is not necessarily overthrown. Although the defendant testifies that he has exercised all reasonable care, the conclusion may still be drawn, on the basis of ordinary human experience, that he has not. Although his evidence is that there was no negligence in operating his train or his bus or his bakeshop, inspecting his elevator or his chandelier or his gas pipes, or parking his car, still the fact remains in evidence that the train went off of the track, the bus into the ditch, the bread was full of glass, the elevator or the chandelier fell, the gas pipe leaked, or the car came down the hill. From this the jury may still be permitted to infer that the defendant's witnesses are not to be believed, that something went wrong with the precautions described, that the full truth has not been told. As the defendant's evidence approaches complete demonstration that the event could not possibly have occurred, it is all the more clearly contradicted by the fact that it has occurred. Normally, therefore, a verdict cannot be directed for the defendant in a res ipsa loquitur case, solely upon the basis of the defendant's evidence of his own due care.

Illustration:

13. A buys from a retail dealer a loaf of bread baked by B. While eating a slice of the bread, A is injured by broken glass embedded in the loaf. In A's action against B for negligence, A proves these facts. B then offers evidence that his bakeshop is conducted with all possible care, and that such precautions have been taken as to make it impossible for any foreign object to be baked into the loaf. Notwithstanding this evidence, the jury may still be permitted to infer that the injury was due to the negligence of B.

o. The inference arising from a res ipsa loquitur case may, however, be destroyed by sufficiently conclusive evidence that it is not in reality a res ipsa loquitur case. If the defendant produces evidence which is so conclusive as to leave no doubt that the event was caused by some outside agency for which he was not responsible, or that it was of a kind which commonly occurs without negligence on the part of anyone and could not be avoided by the exercise of all reasonable care, he may be entitled to a directed verdict.

Chapter 13

LIABILITY FOR CONDITION AND USE OF LAND

TOPIC 1. LIABILITY OF POSSESSORS OF
LAND TO PERSONS ON THE LAND

TITLE A. DEFINITIONS

TOPIC 1. LIABILITY OF POSSESSORS OF
LAND TO PERSONS ON THE LAND

TITLE A. DEFINITIONS

§ 329. Trespasser Defined

A trespasser is a person who enters or remains upon land in the possession of another without a privilege to do so created by the possessor's consent or otherwise.

§ 330. Licensee Defined

A licensee is a person who is privileged to enter or remain on land only by virtue of the possessor's consent.

Comment:

h. Persons included. Included under licensees, among others, are three types of persons:

1. One whose presence upon the land is solely for his own purposes, in which the possessor has no interest, and to whom the privilege of entering is extended as a mere personal favor to the individual, whether by express or tacit consent or as a matter of general or local custom.

2. The members of the possessor's household, except boarders or paying guests and servants, who, as stated in § 332, Comments *i* and *j*, are invitees.

3. Social guests. Some confusion has resulted from the fact that, although a social guest normally is invited, and even urged to come, he is not an "invitee," within the legal meaning of that term, as stated in § 332. He does not come as a member of the public upon premises held open to the public for that purpose, and he does not enter for a purpose directly or indirectly connected with business dealings with the possessor. The use of the premises is extended to him merely as a personal favor to him. The explanation usually given by the courts for the classification of social guests as licensees is that there is a common understanding that the guest is expected to take the premises as the possessor himself uses them, and does not expect and is not entitled to expect that they will be prepared for his reception, or that precautions will be taken for his safety, in any manner in which the possessor does not prepare or take precautions for his own safety, or that of the members of his family. This has not gone without criticism, and an undercurrent of dissent, based upon the contention that it is not in accord with modern social custom and understanding when a guest is invited; but the decisions thus far have been all but unanimous to the effect that the social guest is no more than a licensee.

§ 332. Invitee Defined

(1) An invitee is either a public invitee or a business visitor.

(2) A public invitee is a person who is invited to enter or remain on land as a member of the public for a purpose for which the land is held open to the public.

(3) A business visitor is a person who is invited to enter or remain on land for a purpose directly or indirectly connected with business dealings with the possessor of the land.

Comment:

a. Invitee. "Invitee" is a word of art, with a special meaning in the law. This meaning is more limited than that of "invitation" in the popular sense, and not all of those who are invited to enter upon land are invitees. A social guest may be cordially invited, and strongly urged to come, but he is not an invitee. (See § 330, Comment *h.*) Invitees are limited to those persons who enter or remain on land upon an invitation which carries with it an implied representation, assurance, or understanding that reasonable care has been used to prepare the premises, and make them safe for their reception. Such persons fall generally into two classes: (1) those who enter as members of the public for a purpose for which the land is held open to the public; and (2) those who enter for a purpose connected with the business of the possessor. The second class are sometimes called business visitors; and a business visitor is merely one kind of invitee. There are many visitors, such as customers in shops, who may be placed in either class.

TITLE B. LIABILITY OF POSSESSORS OF LAND TO TRESPASSERS

§ 333. General Rule

Except as stated in §§ 334–339, a possessor of land is not liable to trespassers for physical harm caused by his failure to exercise reasonable care

(a) to put the land in a condition reasonably safe for their reception, or

(b) to carry on his activities so as not to endanger them.

§ 334. Activities Highly Dangerous to Constant Trespassers on Limited Area

A possessor of land who knows, or from facts within his knowledge should know, that trespassers constantly intrude upon a limited area thereof, is subject to liability for bodily harm there caused to them by his failure to carry on an activity involving a risk of death or serious bodily harm with reasonable care for their safety.

Comment:

e. Effect of signs prohibiting trespassers. Knowledge of the persistent trespasses or of facts which should inform the possessor of them, is necessary to subject the possessor to liability under the rule stated in this Section. Therefore, he is not subject to liability if he has taken steps which a reasonable man would believe to be effective in excluding trespassers or in putting an end to their trespasses, unless he discovers that they are ineffective or has some peculiar reason to believe that they will not be effective. Thus it is not enough that the possessor has posted notices to the effect that "trespass is not permitted" or that "trespassers will be prosecuted," if he knows or has reason to know that such notices are disregarded either as a matter of general custom or at the particular place. If the steps taken by the possessor, no matter how reasonable when taken, prove to his knowledge ineffective, he is required to take into account the probable presence of trespassers within such area and to conduct his activities with reasonable regard for their safety.

f. Effect of warnings of dangerous activities. Since a trespasser is not entitled or privileged to enter the land, the possessor, in the absence of reason to know to the contrary, is entitled to expect that a warning of his intention to carry on a dangerous activity will be sufficient to enable even constant trespassers upon a limited area of his land to avoid harm. Therefore, reasonable care to give adequate warning is sufficient to relieve the possessor from liability unless after he has or should have become aware that a trespasser has not heard or does not intend to obey the warning, he has the opportunity by the exercise of reasonable care to avoid injuring the trespasser.

§ 335. Artificial Conditions Highly Dangerous to Constant Trespassers on Limited Area

A possessor of land who knows, or from facts within his knowledge should know, that trespassers constantly intrude upon a limited area of the land, is subject to liability for bodily harm caused to them by an artificial condition on the land, if

(a) the condition

(i) is one which the possessor has created or maintains and

(ii) is, to his knowledge, likely to cause death or seriously bodily harm to such trespassers and

(iii) is of such a nature that he has reason to believe that such trespassers will not discover it, and

(b) the possessor has failed to exercise reasonable care to warn such trespassers of the condition and the risk involved.

Illustration:

1. A, knowing that persons are in the habit of trespassing upon his land at a point close to his unfenced powerhouse, permits a high voltage electric wire, strung at a height of five feet and so concealed by vegetation as to be difficult of observation, to become uninsulated. B, a trespasser, wanders from the adjacent part of the land into the yard of the powerhouse and comes into contact with the wire. The contact causes B's death. A is subject to liability for B's death.

§ 339. Artificial Conditions Highly Dangerous to Trespassing Children

A possessor of land is subject to liability for physical harm to children trespassing thereon caused by an artificial condition upon the land if

(a) the place where the condition exists is one upon which the possessor knows or has reason to know that children are likely to trespass, and

(b) the condition is one of which the possessor knows or has reason to know and which he realizes or should realize will involve an unreasonable risk of death or serious bodily harm to such children, and

(c) the children because of their youth do not discover the condition or realize the risk involved in intermeddling with it or in coming within the area made dangerous by it, and

(d) the utility to the possessor of maintaining the condition and the burden of eliminating the danger are slight as compared with the risk to children involved, and

(e) the possessor fails to exercise reasonable care to eliminate the danger or otherwise to protect the children.

Caveat:

The Institute expresses no opinion as to whether the rule stated in this Section may not apply to natural conditions of the land.

Comment:

a. This Section is concerned only with conditions on the land, and not with activities of the possessor. As to liability to children for such activities, see §§ 333, 334, and 336. A "condition," however, includes controllable forces already in operation, as in the case of machinery in motion. (Cf. § 338.)

b. The rule stated in this Section is now accepted by the great majority of the American courts. It is still rejected in seven or eight jurisdictions, in all of which, however, liability to the trespassing child may be found under various special circumstances. The rule originated in 1873 in Sioux City & Pacific R. Co. v. Stout, 84 U.S. (17 Wall.) 657, 21 L.Ed. 745 (1873), where a child was injured while playing with a railroad turntable. From that case, and others like it, the rule acquired the name of the "turntable doctrine." An early Minnesota decision, Keffe v. Milwaukee & St. Paul R. Co. 21 Minn. 207, 18 Am.Rep 393 (1875), supplied the theory that the child had been allured or enticed onto the premises by the condition created by the defendant, so that the defendant was himself responsible for the trespass, and could not set it up against the child. From this theory the rule also acquired the misnomer of "attractive nuisance," by which it is still known in many courts.

Applying this theory, the United States Supreme Court held, in United Zinc & Chemical Co. v. Britt, 258 U.S. 268, 42 S.Ct. 299, 66 L.Ed. 615, 36 A.L.R. 28, 23 N.C.C.A. 264 (1922), that there was no liability to the child where he had not been attracted onto the premises by the particular condition which injured him. At one time this position had considerable acceptance, but it is now generally rejected. It is now recognized by most of the courts that the basis of the rule is merely the ordinary negligence basis of a duty of reasonable care not to inflict foreseeable harm on another, and that the fact that the child is a trespasser is merely one of the facts to be taken into consideration. The result is a limited obligation to the child, falling short of a duty to prevent all foreseeable harm to him, but requiring reasonable care as to those conditions against which he may be expected to be unable to protect himself.

c. Children. In the great majority of the cases in which the rule here stated has been applied, the plaintiff has been a child of not more than twelve years of age. The earliest decisions as to the turntables all involved children of the age of mischief between six and twelve. The later cases, however, have included a substantial number in which recovery has been permitted, under the rule stated, where the child is of high school age, ranging in a few instances as high as sixteen or seventeen years. The explanation no doubt lies in the fact that in our present hazardous civilization some types of dangers have become common, which an immature adolescent may reasonably not appreciate, although an adult may be expected to do so. The rule stated in this Section is not limited to "young" children, or to those "of tender years," so long as the child is still too young to appreciate the danger, as stated in Clause (c).

A few courts have attempted to state arbitrary age limits, setting a maximum age of fourteen for the possible application of the rule. This usually has been taken over from the rule, in these states, as to the presumed capacity of children over the age of fourteen for contributory negligence, which has in turn been derived from the rule of the criminal law as to their presumed capacity for crime. The great majority of the courts have rejected any such fixed age limit, and have held that there is no definite age beyond which the rule here stated does not apply. As the age of the child increases, conditions become fewer for which there can be recovery under this rule, until at some indeterminate point, probably beyond the age of sixteen, there are no longer any such conditions.

d.   *Conditions upon the land.* The rule stated in this Section is limited to structures or other artificial conditions upon the land. The question of liability for natural conditions is left open in the Caveat, as to which see Comment *p.*

It is not necessary that the particular structure or other artificial condition shall have been created by the possessor, or that he shall have done anything active to maintain it. It is enough that it has been created by some third person, such as his predecessor in title or an independent contractor, or by an adjoining landowner, or even by another trespasser, and that he knows or has reason to know of its existence and realizes or should realize its danger to children, as stated in Clause (b).

Illustration:

1.   A constructs on his land a chute for the removal of goods from his warehouse. The chute is so constructed that it extends onto the adjoining land of B. B, although he does not consent to the encroachment, takes no steps to compel removal of the chute. To B's knowledge the children of the neighborhood habitually come to play on B's premises, and slide down the chute. B also knows that the chute is unsafe for this purpose, and dangerous to the children, because of obstruction formed by supports projecting into it. B does nothing to prevent the risk. C, a boy ten years of age, slides down the chute, strikes his head on one of the supports, and is injured. B is subject to liability to C.

Comment on Clause (a):

e.   *Necessity that children's presence be caused by dangerous condition.* It is not necessary that the defendant shall know that the condition upon his land is likely to attract the trespasses of children, or that the children's trespasses shall be due to the attractiveness of the condition. It is sufficient to satisfy the conditions stated in Clause (a) that the possessor knows or should know that children are likely to trespass upon a part of the land upon which there is a condition which is likely to be dangerous to them, because of their childish propensities to intermeddle or otherwise. Therefore the possessor is subject to liability to children who after entering the land are attracted into dangerous intermeddling by such a condition, although they were ignorant of its existence until after they had entered the land, if he knows or should know that the place is one upon which children are likely to trespass and that the condition is one with which they are likely to meddle.

Illustrations:

2. The A Mining Company knows that the young children in the neighborhood are in the habit of playing around the pit's mouth. One of the employees leaves a cartridge of blasting powder lying in a shed which children, to the knowledge of the Company, have used as a playhouse. Children coming to play find the cartridge and use it as a plaything, causing it to explode and harm B, one of their number. The A Mining Company is subject to liability to B although the children did not know of the presence of the dynamite cartridge until they had entered the shed.

3. The A Manufacturing Company maintains a high-tension electric wire from its powerhouse to its factory. This wire is permitted to become uninsulated and to sag from the poles so that it comes into close proximity to magnolia trees, which are close to the highway at a point where there is no fence. B, a young child, climbs the tree to pick the blossoms and comes into contact with the wire which, in his eagerness to get the flowers, he does not observe. The A Company is liable to B.

f. The rule stated in this Section is not limited to cases in which the trespassing child has intermeddled with anything on the land. It applies although the child has not in any way interfered with anything on the land, and never discovers the particular condition which injures him.

Illustration:

4. A has on his land a ruined wall, which he knows to be in dangerous condition, and likely to fall at any time. He also knows that small children are in the habit of trespassing on the land, playing there, and sitting in the shade at the base of the wall. A does nothing to protect such children. The wall falls on one of them, who has never touched it, and injures him. A is subject to liability to the child.

g. "Has reason to know." In order for the rule stated in this Section to apply, the possessor of the land must know or have reason to know that children are likely to trespass on the land. "Has reason to know" is defined in § 12 to mean that he has information from which a person of reasonable intelligence, or of the superior intelligence of the actor, would infer that the fact in question exists, or would govern his conduct upon the assumption that it does exist. It is not enough that the possessor "should know" of trespasses (see § 12), in the sense that a reasonable man in his position would investigate to discover the fact. The possessor is under no duty to make any investigation or inquiry as to whether children are trespassing, or are likely to trespass, until he is notified, or otherwise receives information, which would lead a reasonable man to that conclusion.

Comment on Clause (b):

h. "Has reason to know." The statement made in Comment g applies equally as to the possessor's knowledge, or reason to know, that the particular condition exists upon his land, and that it is likely to be dangerous to trespassing children. The possessor is under no duty to inspect or police his land to discover whether such conditions exist; and he becomes subject to liability only when he knows or has reason to know that they do exist, and that they are dangerous.

i. When risk such that children can be expected to appreciate it. The duty which the rule stated in this Section imposes upon the possessor of land is based upon the well-known tendency of children to trespass upon the land of others and the necessity of protecting them, even though trespassers, from their childish lack of attention and judgment. The duty of the possessor, therefore, is only to exercise reasonable care to keep the part of the land upon which he should recognize the likelihood of children's trespassing free from those conditions which, though observable by adults, are likely not to be observed by children, or which contain the risks the full extent of which an adult would realize but which are beyond the imperfect realization of children. It does not extend to those conditions the existence of which is obvious even to children and the risk of which should be fully realized by them. This limitation of the possessor's liability to conditions dangerous to children, because of their inability to appreciate their surroundings or to realize the risk involved, frees the possessor of land from the liability to which he would otherwise be subjected by maintaining on the land the normal, necessary and usual implements which are essential to its normal use, but which reckless children can use to their harm in a spirit of bravado or to gratify some other childish desire and with as full a perception of the risks which they are running as though they were adults.

Illustration:

5.   At a point where its factory adjoins an open yard upon its own premises the A Manufacturing Company operates a pulley by which its raw material is raised to the fourth story of the factory. The yard is, to the knowledge of the company, visited by children notwithstanding the efforts of the company's servants to drive them out. The pulley is operated by an engine, and at the end of the cable of the pulley there is a heavy iron ball and hook. The employee of the Company who is in charge of the engine goes to his dinner leaving the engine running, thus causing the ball and hook to descend and ascend. A group of children see this and dare one another to take hold of the ball and chain and be carried up by the pulley. B, one of the children, finally accepts the dare and takes hold of the hook which ascends with him. He loses his nerve when he has been carried up some 20 feet and lets go of the hook and sustains a fall which causes him serious harm. The A Company is not liable to B.

j. There are many dangers, such a those of fire and water, or of falling from a height, which under ordinary conditions may reasonably be expected to be fully understood and appreciated by any child of an age to be allowed at large. To such conditions the rule stated in this Section ordinarily has no application, in the absence of some other factor creating a special risk that the child will not avoid the danger, such as the fact that the condition is so hidden as not to be readily visible, or a distracting influence which makes it likely that the child will not discover or appreciate it.

Where, however, the possessor knows that children too young to appreciate such dangers are likely to trespass on his land, he may still be subject to liability to such children under the rule stated.

Illustrations:

6.   A has on his land a small artificial pond in which, to A's knowledge, children of the neighborhood frequently trespass and swim. A takes no precautions of any kind. B, a boy ten years old who cannot swim, trespasses on A's land, enters the pond, and is drowned. A is not liable to B.

7.   A has on his land a small artificial pond full of goldfish. A's land adjoins a nursery in which children from two to five years of age are left by their parents for the day, and such children are, as A knows, in the habit of trespassing on A's land and going near the pond. A could easily prevent this by closing and locking his gate. A does not do so. B, a child three years of age, trespasses,

enters the pond to catch goldfish, and is drowned. A is subject to liability for the death of B.

k. A condition may be peculiarly dangerous to children because of their tendency to intermeddle with things which are notoriously attractive to them (see Illustration 2), but this is not the only childish characteristic which may make a condition, which involves no serious risk to an adult, highly dangerous to children. Children are notoriously inattentive to their surroundings, and this characteristic may make it unlikely that children will discover a condition which would be obvious to an adult (see Illustration 3). The lack of experience and judgment normal to young children may prevent them from realizing that a condition observed by them is dangerous or, although they realize that it is dangerous, may prevent them from appreciating the full extent of the risk.

l. A condition existing upon the land may be dangerous even to adult trespassers if it is unlikely to be discovered by the attention to be expected of them or is of such a character that, although discovered, the risk involved in it is unlikely to be recognized by an adult of ordinary experience and judgment. The peculiar danger to children involved in such a condition does not lie in the character of the condition, but in the fact that children are known to be far more prone to trespass than are adults. This, together with the fact that young children do not appreciate the wrongfulness and risk involved in trespassing upon the land of another, makes the possessor subject to liability to them, although he would not be subject to adult trespassers harmed by such a condition unless the place upon which the condition was maintained was a limited area known to be subject to constant intrusion, or unless the possessor knew that a trespasser was in dangerous proximity to it, as to which see §§ 335 and 337.

Comment on Clause (c):

m. A possessor of land is, under the statement made in Comment e, under a duty to exercise reasonable care to keep so much of his land as he knows to be subject to the trespasses of young children, free from artificial conditions which involve an unreasonable risk of death or serious bodily harm to them. This does not require him to keep his land free from conditions which even young children are likely to observe and the full extent of the risk involved in which they are likely to realize. The purpose of the duty is to protect children from dangers which they do not appreciate and not to protect them against harm resulting from their own immature recklessness in the case of known and appreciated danger. Therefore, even though the condition is one which the possessor should realize to be such that young children are unlikely to realize the full extent of the danger of meddling with it or encountering it, the possessor is not subject to liability to a child who in fact discovers the condition and appreciates the full risk involved, but none the less chooses to encounter it out of recklessness or bravado.

Illustration:

8. The A Railroad Company maintains upon its land an unlocked turntable, upon which, as it knows, children of the neighborhood frequently trespass, and which involves an unreasonable risk of harm to such children. On two occasions B and C trespass upon the land, play with the turntable, and each is injured when his foot is caught in it. B is a boy sixteen years of age, whose maturity and experience make him fully understand and appreciate the danger. C is a boy nine years of age, who is the son of a railroad engineer, has been repeatedly warned against the turntable, and likewise fully appreciates the danger. A Railroad is not liable to B or to C.

Comment on Clause (d):

n. Balancing risk to children with utility of dangerous condition. In determining whether a particular condition maintained by a possessor upon land which he knows to be subject to the trespasses of children involves an unreasonable risk to them, the comparison of the recognizable risk to the children, with the utility to the possessor of maintaining the condition, is of peculiar importance. The public interest in the possessor's free use of his land for his own purposes is of great significance. A particular condition is, therefore, regarded as not involving unreasonable risk to trespassing children unless it involves a grave risk to them which could be obviated without any serious interference with the possessor's legitimate use of his land. Farming machinery and the like involve inevitable danger to children meddling with them. Nevertheless their essential importance to agriculture permits them to be used and maintained if kept in a proper place and in proper condition. On the other hand, if the installation of devices which would prevent the machine's being set in motion were practicable without burdensome cost or serious interference with the utility of the machine, it might be unreasonable for a farmer to keep a machine without such equipment in a place notoriously open to trespassing children. While wires are necessary to carry high-tension electric current, the burden of properly safeguarding wires maintained at places where trespassing children may be expected to come into contact with them is obviously slight as compared with the gravity of harm which they threaten and the chance that such harm will result.

Illustrations:

9. The A Railway Company maintains a turntable at a point upon its unfenced land close to a highway upon which young children constantly pass on their way to and from school. These children, to the knowledge of the Company, are in the habit of playing about and upon the turntable. A simple locking device would make it very difficult for children to set the turntable in motion, but this device is not installed upon the turntable. While the children are playing about the turntable several of them set it in motion, causing B, one of them, to be caught in the table and seriously hurt. The A Railway Company is subject to liability to B.

10. Under the circumstances stated in Illustration 9, the A Railroad Company would not be liable to B, injured while playing upon its turntable, if a locking device capable of preventing children from setting the turntable in motion would have prevented its effective operation and if to surround it with a reasonably child-proof fence would have seriously interfered with the operation of the railroad.

Comment on Clause (e):

o. The liability covered by this Section is liability for negligence. The possessor of the land is subject to liability to the trespassing child only if he has failed to conform to the standard of conduct of a reasonable man under like circumstances, as stated in § 283. Even though the possessor knows that children are likely to trespass, that the condition on the land involves an unreasonable risk of harm to them, and that they are likely not to discover or appreciate the risk, there is liability only if the possessor fails to take the steps which a reasonable man would take under such circumstances. If the possessor has exercised all reasonable care to make the condition safe, or otherwise to protect the children, and has still not succeeded, there is no liability.

Under some circumstances, a warning to the children is all that can be expected of a reasonable man in the defendant's position. There are some conditions, such as those of moving cars in a railroad yard, as to which no really effective precautions can be taken to make the condition itself safe, and the most that can be done as a practical matter is to warn trespassing children, and so far as is reasonably possible to exclude them. If the children are of sufficient age to understand a warning, it may often reasonably be expected that they will heed it, and will avoid the danger. Where, however, the child is too young to be expected to understand or heed the warning, something more may be required.

Comment on Caveat:

p. The Caveat leaves open the question whether the rule stated in this Section may not apply to natural conditions of the land. The case law thus far indicates that it does not so apply; but in all of the decided cases the condition has been one, such as a body of water, which the child might be expected to understand and appreciate, as stated in Comment *j.* In most instances the burden of improving land in a state of nature in order to make it safe for trespassing children would be disproportionately heavy (see Clause (d)), and for that reason alone there would be no liability. Cases may, however, arise in which there would be no such disproportionate burden, and the natural condition is one which the child could be expected not to understand. The Caveat leaves open the possibility of liability in such a case.

TITLE C. GENERAL LIABILITY OF POSSESSORS OF LAND TO LICENSEES AND INVITEES

§ 341. Activities Dangerous to Licensees

A possessor of land is subject to liability to his licensees for physical harm caused to them by his failure to carry on his activities with reasonable care for their safety if, but only if,

(a) he should expect that they will not discover or realize the danger, and

(b) they do not know or have reason to know of the possessor's activities and of the risk involved.

Comment:

c. When possessor must warn of dangerous act. In determining what is reasonable care account is to be taken of the fact that the licensee is entitled to enter only by the consent of the possessor. Unless the terms of the consent manifest the possessor's intention to subordinate his own activities to the licensee's enjoyment of his license, the licensee should realize that he must give precedence to the possessor's use of his land for his own purpose. Therefore, the possessor need do no more than exercise reasonable care to warn the licensee of his intention to do an act which he should realize is likely to cause harm to the licensee if he comes into or remains within the area endangered by it. He is entitled to expect that such warning will cause the licensee to avoid the danger unless he realizes or should realize that warning would be ineffective, either because the danger is so imminent that a warning will give the licensee no opportunity to avoid it, or because the licensee does not hear the warning or is not able or does not intend to take advantage of it.

§ 341A. Activities Dangerous to Invitees

A possessor of land is subject to liability to his invitees for physical harm caused to them by his failure to carry on his activities with reasonable care for their safety if, but only if, he should expect that they will not discover or realize the danger, or will fail to protect themselves against it.

TITLE E. SPECIAL LIABILITY OF POSSESSORS OF LAND TO INVITEES

§ 344. Business Premises Open to Public: Acts of Third Persons or Animals

A possessor of land who holds it open to the public for entry for his business purposes is subject to liability to members of the public while they are upon the land for such a purpose, for physical harm caused by the accidental, negligent, or intentionally harmful acts of third persons or animals, and by the failure of the possessor to exercise reasonable care to

(a) discover that such acts are being done or are likely to be done, or

(b) give a warning adequate to enable the visitors to avoid the harm, or otherwise to protect them against it.

TOPIC 3. LIABILITY OF LESSORS OF LAND TO PERSONS ON THE LAND

§ 359. Land Leased for Purpose Involving Admission of Public

A lessor who leases land for a purpose which involves the admission of the public is subject to liability for physical harm caused to persons who enter the land for that purpose by a condition of the land existing when the lessee takes possession, if the lessor

(a) knows or by the exercise of reasonable care could discover that the condition involves an unreasonable risk of harm to such persons, and

(b) has reason to expect that the lessee will admit them before the land is put in safe condition for their reception, and

(c) fails to exercise reasonable care to discover or to remedy the condition, or otherwise to protect such persons against it.

Illustrations:

1. A, by a written instrument, leases his rink to B for four nights for B to use as a place in which to give a public exhibition of trained horses. The rink is entered by an outside stairway, the upper landing of which is, as A knows or by a reasonably careful inspection could discover, in a dangerous state of disrepair. A permits B to hold over after the expiration of the four days, and on the sixth day the platform gives way while entering spectators are upon it. C, one of them, is hurt. A is subject to liability to C.

2. A leases his baseball park to the B Baseball Club for the baseball season. The lease contains a covenant by the lessee to make necessary repairs. Two months after B takes possession the grandstand falls because of the bad condition of the woodwork supporting it, which a reasonable inspection would have disclosed to either A or the B Baseball Club when possession was given to the B Club. C, a spectator in the grandstand, is hurt by the collapse of the stand. A is subject to liability to C if, in spite of the covenant, he had reason to believe that the repairs would be neglected.

Chapter 14

LIABILITY OF PERSONS SUPPLYING CHATTELS FOR THE USE OF OTHERS

TOPIC 5. STRICT LIABILITY

TOPIC 5. STRICT LIABILITY

§ 402A. Special Liability of Seller of Product for Physical Harm to User or Consumer

[*Editorial Note:* Section 402A of Restatement Second, Torts, was superseded in 1997 by the promulgation of Restatement Third, Torts: Products Liability, portions of which are included in this volume, infra. Section 402A is reproduced below because of its historical importance in the development of products-liability law and its continuing prominence in the case law.]

(1) One who sells any product in a defective condition unreasonably dangerous to the user or consumer or to his property is subject to liability for physical harm thereby caused to the ultimate user or consumer, or to his property, if

(a) the seller is engaged in the business of selling such a product, and

(b) it is expected to and does reach the user or consumer without substantial change in the condition in which it is sold.

(2) The rule stated in Subsection (1) applies although

(a) the seller has exercised all possible care in the preparation and sale of his product, and

(b) the user or consumer has not bought the product from or entered into any contractual relation with the seller.

Caveat:

The Institute expresses no opinion as to whether the rules stated in this Section may not apply

(1) to harm to persons other than users or consumers;

(2) to the seller of a product expected to be processed or otherwise substantially changed before it reaches the user or consumer; or

(3) to the seller of a component part of a product to be assembled.

Comment:

a. This Section states a special rule applicable to sellers of products. The rule is one of strict liability, making the seller subject to liability to the user or consumer even though he has exercised all possible care in the preparation and sale of the product. The Section is inserted in the Chapter dealing with the negligence liability of suppliers of chattels, for convenience of reference and comparison with other Sections dealing with negligence. The rule stated here is not exclusive, and does not preclude liability based upon the alternative ground of negligence of the seller, where such negligence can be proved.

b. History. Since the early days of the common law those engaged in the business of selling food intended for human consumption have been held to a high degree of responsibility for their products. As long ago as 1266 there were enacted special criminal statutes imposing penalties upon victualers, vintners, brewers, butchers, cooks, and other persons who supplied "corrupt "food and drink.

In the earlier part of this century this ancient attitude was reflected in a series of decisions in which the courts of a number of states sought to find some method of holding the seller of food liable to the ultimate consumer even though there was no showing of negligence on the part of the seller. These decisions represented a departure from, and an exception to, the general rule that a supplier of chattels was not liable to third persons in the absence of negligence or privity of contract. In the beginning, these decisions displayed considerable ingenuity in evolving more or less fictitious theories of liability to fit the case. The various devices included an agency of the intermediate dealer or another to purchase for the consumer, or to sell for the seller; a theoretical assignment of the seller's warranty to the intermediate dealer; a third party beneficiary contract; and an implied representation that the food was fit for consumption because it was placed on the market, as well as numerous others. In later years the courts have become more or less agreed upon the theory of a "warranty" from the seller to the consumer, either "running with the goods" by analogy to a covenant running with the land, or made directly to the consumer. Other decisions have indicated that the basis is merely one of strict liability in tort, which is not dependent upon either contract or negligence.

Recent decisions, since 1950, have extended this special rule of strict liability beyond the seller of food for human consumption. The first extension was into the closely analogous cases of other products intended for intimate bodily use, where, for example, as in the case of cosmetics, the application to the body of the consumer is external rather than internal. Beginning in 1958 with a Michigan case involving cinder building blocks, a number of recent decisions have discarded any limitation to intimate association with the body, and have extended the rule of strict liability to cover the sale of any product which, if it should prove to be defective, may be expected to cause physical harm to the consumer or his property.

c. On whatever theory, the justification for the strict liability has been said to be that the seller, by marketing his product for use and consumption, has undertaken and assumed a special responsibility toward any member of the consuming public who may be injured by it; that the public has the right to and does expect, in the case of products which it needs and for which it is forced to rely upon the seller, that reputable sellers will stand behind their goods; that public policy demands that the burden of accidental injuries caused by products intended for consumption be placed upon those who market them, and be treated as a cost of production against which liability insurance can be obtained; and that the consumer of such products is entitled to the maximum of protection at the hands of someone, and the proper persons to afford it are those who market the products.

d. The rule stated in this Section is not limited to the sale of food for human consumption, or other products for intimate bodily use, although it will obviously include them. It extends to any product sold in the condition, or substantially the same condition, in which it is expected to reach the ultimate user or consumer. Thus the rule stated applies to an automobile, a tire, an airplane, a grinding wheel, a water heater, a gas stove, a power tool, a riveting machine, a chair, and an insecticide. It applies also to products which, if they are defective, may be expected to and do cause only "physical harm" in the form of damage to the user's land or chattels, as in the case of animal food or a herbicide.

e. Normally the rule stated in this Section will be applied to articles which already have undergone some processing before sale, since there is today little in the way of consumer products which will reach the consumer without such processing. The rule is not, however, so limited, and the supplier of poisonous mushrooms which are neither cooked, canned, packaged, nor otherwise treated is subject to the liability here stated.

f. Business of selling. The rule stated in this Section applies to any person engaged in the business of selling products for use or consumption. It therefore applies to any manufacturer of such a product, to any wholesale or retail dealer or distributor, and to the operator of a restaurant. It is not necessary that the seller be engaged solely in the business of selling such products. Thus the rule applies to the owner of a motion picture theatre who sells popcorn or ice cream, either for consumption on the premises or in packages to be taken home.

The rule does not, however, apply to the occasional seller of food or other such products who is not engaged in that activity as a part of his business. Thus it does not apply to the housewife who, on one occasion, sells to her neighbor a jar of jam or a pound of sugar. Nor does it apply to the owner of an automobile who, on one occasion, sells it to his neighbor, or even sells it to a dealer in used cars, and this even though he is fully aware that the dealer plans to resell it. The basis for the rule is the ancient one of the special responsibility for the safety of the public undertaken by one who enters into the business of supplying human beings with products which may endanger the safety of their persons and property, and the forced reliance upon that undertaking on the part of those who purchase such goods. This basis is lacking in the case of the ordinary individual who makes the isolated sale, and he is not liable to a third person, or even to his buyer, in the absence of his negligence. An analogy may be found in the provision of the Uniform Sales Act, § 15, which limits the implied warranty of merchantable quality to sellers who deal in such goods; and in the similar limitation of the Uniform Commercial Code, § 2–314, to a seller who is a merchant. This Section is also not intended to apply to sales of the stock of merchants out of the usual course of business, such as execution sales, bankruptcy sales, bulk sales, and the like.

g. *Defective condition.* The rule stated in this Section applies only where the product is, at the time it leaves the seller's hands, in a condition not contemplated by the ultimate consumer, which will be unreasonably dangerous to him. The seller is not liable when he delivers the product in a safe condition, and subsequent mishandling or other causes make it harmful by the time it is consumed. The burden of proof that the product was in a defective condition at the time that it left the hands of the particular seller is upon the injured plaintiff; and unless evidence can be produced which will support the conclusion that it was then defective, the burden is not sustained.

Safe condition at the time of delivery by the seller will, however, include proper packaging, necessary sterilization, and other precautions required to permit the product to remain safe for a normal length of time when handled in a normal manner.

h. A produce is not in a defective condition when it is safe for normal handling and consumption. If the injury results from abnormal handling, as where a bottled beverage is knocked against a radiator to remove the cap, or from abnormal preparation for use, as where too much salt is added to food, or from abnormal consumption, as where a child eats too much candy and is made ill, the seller is not liable. Where, however, he has reason to anticipate that danger may result from a particular use, as where a drug is sold which is safe only in limited doses, he may be required to give adequate warning of the danger (see Comment *j*), and a product sold without such warning is in a defective condition.

The defective condition may arise not only from harmful ingredients, not characteristic of the product itself either as to presence or quantity, but also from foreign objects contained in the product, from decay or deterioration before sale, or from the way in which the product is prepared or packed. No reason is apparent for distinguishing between the product itself and the container in which it is supplied; and the two are purchased by the user or consumer as an integrated whole. Where the container is itself dangerous, the product is sold in a defective condition. Thus a carbonated beverage in a bottle which is so weak, or cracked, or jagged at the edges, or bottled under such excessive pressure that it may explode or otherwise cause harm to the person who handles it, is in a defective and dangerous condition. The container cannot logically be separated from the contents when the two are sold as a unit, and the liability stated in this Section arises not only when the consumer drinks the beverage and is poisoned by it, but also when he is injured by the bottle while he is handling it preparatory to consumption.

i. Unreasonably dangerous. The rule stated in this Section applies only where the defective condition of the product makes it unreasonably dangerous to the user or consumer. Many products cannot possibly be made entirely safe for all consumption, and any food or drug necessarily involves some risk of harm, if only from over-consumption. Ordinary sugar is a deadly poison to diabetics, and castor oil found use under Mussolini as an instrument of torture. That is not what is meant by "unreasonably dangerous" in this Section. The article sold must be dangerous to an extent beyond that which would be contemplated by the ordinary consumer who purchases it, with the ordinary knowledge common to the community as to its characteristics. Good whiskey is not unreasonably dangerous merely because it will make some people drunk, and is especially dangerous to alcoholics; but bad whiskey, containing a dangerous amount of fuel oil, is unreasonably dangerous. Good tobacco is not unreasonably dangerous merely because the effects of smoking may be harmful; but tobacco containing something like marijuana may be unreasonably dangerous. Good butter is not unreasonably dangerous merely because, if such be the case, it deposits cholesterol in the arteries and leads to heart attacks; but bad butter, contaminated with poisonous fish oil, is unreasonably dangerous.

j. Directions or warning. In order to prevent the product from being unreasonably dangerous, the seller may be required to give directions or warning, on the container, as to its use. The seller may reasonably assume that those with common allergies, as for example to eggs or strawberries, will be aware of them, and he is not required to warn against them. Where, however, the product contains an ingredient to which a substantial number of the population are allergic, and the ingredient is one whose danger is not generally known, or if known is one which the consumer would reasonably not expect to find in the product, the seller is required to give warning against it, if he has knowledge, or by the application of reasonable, developed human skill and foresight should have knowledge, of the presence of the ingredient and the danger. Likewise in the case of poisonous drugs, or those unduly dangerous for other reasons, warning as to use may be required.

But a seller is not required to warn with respect to products, or ingredients in them, which are only dangerous, or potentially so, when consumed in excessive quantity, or over a long period of time, when the danger, or potentiality of danger, is generally known and recognized. Again the dangers of alcoholic beverages are an example, as are also those of foods containing such substances as saturated fats, which may over a period of time have a deleterious effect upon the human heart.

Where warning is given, the seller may reasonably assume that it will be read and heeded; and a product bearing such a warning, which is safe for use if it is followed, is not in defective condition, nor is it unreasonably dangerous.

k. *Unavoidably unsafe products.* There are some products which, in the present state of human knowledge, are quite incapable of being made safe for their intended and ordinary use. These are especially common in the field of drugs. An outstanding example is the vaccine for the Pasteur treatment of rabies, which not uncommonly leads to very serious and damaging consequences when it is injected. Since the disease itself invariably leads to a dreadful death, both the marketing and the use of the vaccine are fully justified, notwithstanding the unavoidable high degree of risk which they involve. Such a product, properly prepared, and accompanied by proper directions and warning, is not defective, nor is it unreasonably dangerous. The same is true of many other drugs, vaccines, and the like, many of which for this very reason cannot legally be sold except to physicians, or under the prescription of a physician. It is also true in particular of many new or experimental drugs as to which, because of lack of time and opportunity for sufficient medical experience, there can be no assurance of safety, or perhaps even of purity of ingredients, but such experience as there is justifies the marketing and use of the drug notwithstanding a medically recognizable risk. The seller of such products, again with the qualification that they are properly prepared and marketed, and proper warning is given, where the situation calls for it, is not to be held to strict liability for unfortunate consequences attending their use, merely because he has undertaken to supply the public with an apparently useful and desirable product, attended with a known but apparently reasonable risk.

l. *User or consumer.* In order for the rule stated in this Section to apply, it is not necessary that the ultimate user or consumer have acquired the product directly from the seller, although the rule applies equally if he does so. He may have acquired it through one or more intermediate dealers. It is not even necessary that the consumer have purchased the product at all. He may be a member of the family of the final purchaser, or his employee, or a guest at his table, or a mere donee from the purchaser. The liability stated is one in tort, and does not require any contractual relation, or privity of contract, between the plaintiff and the defendant.

"Consumers" include not only those who in fact consume the product, but also those who prepare it for consumption; and the housewife who contracts tularemia while cooking rabbits for her husband is included within the rule stated in this Section, as is also the husband who is opening a bottle of beer for his wife to drink. Consumption includes all ultimate uses for which the product is intended, and the customer in a beauty shop to whose hair a permanent wave solution is applied by the shop is a consumer. "User" includes those who are passively enjoying the benefit of the product, as in the case of passengers in automobiles or airplanes, as well as those who are utilizing it for the purpose of doing work upon it, as in the case of an employee of the ultimate buyer who is making repairs upon the automobile which he has purchased.

Illustration:

1. A manufactures and packs a can of beans, which he sells to B, a wholesaler. B sells the beans to C, a jobber, who resells it to D, a retail grocer. E buys the can of beans from D, and gives it to F. F serves the beans at lunch to G, his guest. While eating the beans, G breaks a tooth, on a pebble of the size, shape, and color of a bean, which no reasonable inspection could possibly have discovered. There is satisfactory evidence that the pebble was in the can of beans when it was opened. Although there is no negligence on the part of A, B, C, or D, each of them is subject to liability to G. On the other hand E and F, who have not sold the beans, are not liable to G in the absence of some negligence on their part.

m. "Warranty." The liability stated in this Section does not rest upon negligence. It is strict liability, similar in its nature to that covered by Chapters 20 and 21. The basis of liability is purely one of tort.

A number of courts, seeking a theoretical basis for the liability, have resorted to a "warranty," either running with the goods sold, by analogy to covenants running with the land, or made directly to the consumer without contract. In some instances this theory has proved to be an unfortunate one. Although warranty was in its origin a matter of tort liability, and it is generally agreed that a tort action will still lie for its breach, it has become so identified in practice with a contract of sale between the plaintiff and the defendant that the warranty theory has become something of an obstacle to the recognition of the strict liability where there is no such contract. There is nothing in this Section which would prevent any court from treating the rule stated as a matter of "warranty" to the user or consumer. But if this is done, it should be recognized and understood that the "warranty" is a very different kind of warranty from those usually found in the sale of goods, and that it is not subject to the various contract rules which have grown up to surround such sales.

The rule stated in this Section does not require any reliance on the part of the consumer upon the reputation, skill, or judgment of the seller who is to be held liable, nor any representation or undertaking on the part of that seller. The seller is strictly liable although, as is frequently the case, the consumer does not even know who he is at the time of consumption. The rule stated in this Section is not governed by the provisions of the Uniform Sales Act, or those of the Uniform Commercial Code, as to warranties; and it is not affected by limitations on the scope and content of warranties, or by limitation to "buyer" and "seller" in those statutes. Nor is the consumer required to give notice to the seller of his injury within a reasonable time after it occurs, as is provided by the Uniform Act. The consumer's cause of action does not depend upon the validity of his contract with the person from whom he acquires the product, and it is not affected by any disclaimer or other agreement, whether it be between the seller and his immediate buyer, or attached to and accompanying the product into the consumer's hands. In short, "warranty" must be given a new and different meaning if it is used in connection with this Section. It is much simpler to regard the liability here stated as merely one of strict liability in tort.

n. Contributory negligence. Since the liability with which this Section deals is not based upon negligence of the seller, but is strict liability, the rule applied to strict liability cases (see § 524) applies. Contributory negligence of the plaintiff is not a defense when such negligence consists merely in a failure to discover the defect in the product, or to guard against the possibility of its existence. On the other hand the form of contributory negligence which consists in voluntarily and unreasonably proceeding to encounter a known danger, and commonly passes under the name of assumption of risk, is a defense under this Section as in other cases of strict liability. If the user or consumer discovers the defect and is aware of the danger, and nevertheless proceeds unreasonably to make use of the product and is injured by it, he is barred from recovery.

Comment on Caveat:

o. Injuries to non-users and non-consumers. Thus far the courts, in applying the rule stated in this Section, have not gone beyond allowing recovery to users and consumers, as those terms are defined in Comment *l.* Casual bystanders, and others who may come in contact with the product, as in the case of employees of the retailer, or a passer-by injured by an exploding bottle, or a pedestrian hit by an automobile, have been denied recovery. There may be no essential reason why such plaintiffs should not be brought within the scope of the protection afforded, other than that they do not have the same reasons for expecting such protection as the consumer who buys a marketed product; but the social pressure which has been largely responsible for the development of the rule stated has been a consumers' pressure, and there is not the same demand for the protection of casual strangers. The Institute expresses neither approval nor disapproval of expansion of the rule to permit recovery by such persons.

p. *Further processing or substantial change.* Thus far the decisions applying the rule stated have not gone beyond products which are sold in the condition, or in substantially the same condition, in which they are expected to reach the hands of the ultimate user or consumer. In the absence of decisions providing a clue to the rules which are likely to develop, the Institute has refrained from taking any position as to the possible liability of the seller where the product is expected to, and does, undergo further processing or other substantial change after it leaves his hands and before it reaches those of the ultimate user or consumer.

It seems reasonably clear that the mere fact that the product is to undergo processing, or other substantial change, will not in all cases relieve the seller of liability under the rule stated in this Section. If, for example, raw coffee beans are sold to a buyer who roasts and packs them for sale to the ultimate consumer, it cannot be supposed that the seller will be relieved of all liability when the raw beans are contaminated with arsenic, or some other poison. Likewise the seller of an automobile with a defective steering gear which breaks and injures the driver, can scarcely expect to be relieved of the responsibility by reason of the fact that the car is sold to a dealer who is expected to "service" it, adjust the brakes, mount and inflate the tires, and the like, before it is ready for use. On the other hand, the manufacturer of pig iron, which is capable of a wide variety of uses, is not so likely to be held to strict liability when it turns out to be unsuitable for the child's tricycle into which it is finally made by a remote buyer. The question is essentially one of whether the responsibility for discovery and prevention of the dangerous defect is shifted to the intermediate party who is to make the changes. No doubt there will be some situations, and some defects, as to which the responsibility will be shifted, and others in which it will not. The existing decisions as yet throw no light upon the questions, and the Institute therefore expresses neither approval nor disapproval of the seller's strict liability in such a case.

q. Component parts. The same problem arises in cases of the sale of a component part of a product to be assembled by another, as for example a tire to be placed on a new automobile, a brake cylinder for the same purpose, or an instrument for the panel of an airplane. Again the question arises, whether the responsibility is not shifted to the assembler. It is no doubt to be expected that where there is no change in the component part itself, but it is merely incorporated into something larger, the strict liability will be found to carry through to the ultimate user or consumer. But in the absence of a sufficient number of decisions on the matter to justify a conclusion, the Institute expresses no opinion on the matter.

Chapter 16

THE CAUSAL RELATION NECESSARY TO RESPONSIBILITY FOR NEGLIGENCE

TOPIC 1. CAUSAL RELATION NECESSARY TO THE EXISTENCE OF LIABILITY FOR ANOTHER'S HARM

TITLE A. GENERAL PRINCIPLES

TOPIC 1. CAUSAL RELATION NECESSARY TO THE EXISTENCE OF LIABILITY FOR ANOTHER'S HARM

TITLE A. GENERAL PRINCIPLES

§ 430. Necessity of Adequate Causal Relation

In order that a negligent actor shall be liable for another's harm, it is necessary not only that the actor's conduct be negligent toward the other, but also that the negligence of the actor be a legal cause of the other's harm.

§ 431. What Constitutes Legal Cause

The actor's negligent conduct is a legal cause of harm to another if

(a) his conduct is a substantial factor in bringing about the harm, and

(b) there is no rule of law relieving the actor from liability because of the manner in which his negligence has resulted in the harm.

Comment:

a. *Distinction between substantial cause and cause in the philosophic sense.* In order to be a legal cause of another's harm, it is not enough that the harm would not have occurred had the actor not been negligent. Except as stated in § 432 (2), this is necessary, but it is not of itself sufficient. The negligence must also be a substantial factor in bringing about the plaintiff's harm. The word "substantial" is used to denote the fact that the defendant's conduct has such an effect in producing the harm as to lead reasonable men to regard it as a cause, using that word in the popular sense, in which there always lurks the idea of responsibility, rather than in the so-called "philosophic sense," which includes every one of the great number of events without which any happening would not have occurred. Each of these events is a cause in the so-called "philosophic sense," yet the effect of many of them is so insignificant that no ordinary mind would think of them as causes.

§ 432. Negligent Conduct as Necessary Antecedent of Harm

(1) Except as stated in Subsection (2), the actor's negligent conduct is not a substantial factor in bringing about harm to another if the harm would have been sustained even if the actor had not been negligent.

(2) If two forces are actively operating, one because of the actor's negligence, the other not because of any misconduct on his part, and each of itself is sufficient to bring about harm to another, the actor's negligence may be found to be a substantial factor in bringing it about.

Comment on Subsection (2):

d. The statement in Subsection (2) applies not only when the second force which is operating simultaneously with the force set in motion by the defendant's negligence is generated by the negligent conduct of a third person, but also when it is generated by an innocent act of a third person or when its origin is unknown.

Illustrations:

3. Two fires are negligently set by separate acts of the A and B Railway Companies in forest country during a dry season. The two fires coalesce before setting fire to C's timber land and house. The normal spread of either fire would have been sufficient to burn the house and timber. C barely escapes from his house, suffering burns while so doing. It may be found that the negligence of either the A or the B Company or of both is a substantial factor in bringing about C's harm.

4. The same facts as in Illustration 3, except that the one fire is set by the negligence of the A Company and the other is set by a stroke of lightning or its origin is unknown. It may be found that the negligence of the A Company is a substantial factor in bringing about C's harm.

TITLE B. RULES WHICH DETERMINE THE RESPONSIBILITY OF A NEGLIGENT ACTOR FOR HARM WHICH HIS CONDUCT IS A SUBSTANTIAL FACTOR IN PRODUCING

§ 435. Foreseeability of Harm or Manner of Its Occurrence

(1) If the actor's conduct is a substantial factor in bringing about harm to another, the fact that the actor neither foresaw nor should have foreseen the extent of the harm or the manner in which it occurred does not prevent him from being liable.

(2) The actor's conduct may be held not to be a legal cause of harm to another where after the event and looking back from the harm to the actor's negligent conduct, it appears to the court highly extraordinary that it should have brought about the harm.

§ 436. Physical Harm Resulting From Emotional Disturbance

(1) If the actor's conduct is negligent as violating a duty of care designed to protect another from a fright or other emotional disturbance which the actor should recognize as involving an unreasonable risk of bodily harm, the fact that the harm results solely through the internal operation of the fright or other emotional disturbance does not protect the actor from liability.

(2) If the actor's conduct is negligent as creating an unreasonable risk of causing bodily harm to another otherwise than by subjecting him to fright, shock, or other similar and immediate emotional disturbance, the fact that such harm results solely from the internal operation of fright or other emotional disturbance does not protect the actor from liability.

(3) The rule stated in Subsection (2) applies where the bodily harm to the other results from his shock or fright at harm or peril to a member of his immediate family occurring in his presence.

§ 439. Effect of Contributing Acts of Third Persons When Actor's Negligence Is Actively Operating

If the effects of the actor's negligent conduct actively and continuously operate to bring about harm to another, the fact that the active and substantially simultaneous operation of the effects of a third person's innocent, tortious, or criminal act is also a substantial factor in bringing about the harm does not protect the actor from liability.

TITLE C. SUPERSEDING CAUSE

§ 440. Superseding Cause Defined

A superseding cause is an act of a third person or other force which by its intervention prevents the actor from being liable for harm to another which his antecedent negligence is a substantial factor in bringing about.

§ 442. Considerations Important in Determining Whether an Intervening Force Is a Superseding Cause

The following considerations are of importance in determining whether an intervening force is a superseding cause of harm to another:

(a) the fact that its intervention brings about harm different in kind from that which would otherwise have resulted from the actor's negligence;

(b) the fact that its operation or the consequences thereof appear after the event to be extraordinary rather than normal in view of the circumstances existing at the time of its operation;

(c) the fact that the intervening force is operating independently of any situation created by the actor's negligence, or, on the other hand, is or is not a normal result of such a situation;

(d) the fact that the operation of the intervening force is due to a third person's act or to his failure to act;

(e) the fact that the intervening force is due to an act of a third person which is wrongful toward the other and as such subjects the third person to liability to him;

(f) the degree of culpability of a wrongful act of a third person which sets the intervening force in motion.

§ 442A. Intervening Force Risked by Actor's Conduct

Where the negligent conduct of the actor creates or increases the foreseeable risk of harm through the intervention of another force, and is a substantial factor in causing the harm, such intervention is not a superseding cause.

§ 442B. Intervening Force Causing Same Harm as That Risked by Actor's Conduct

Where the negligent conduct of the actor creates or increases the risk of a particular harm and is a substantial factor in causing that harm, the fact that the harm is brought about through the intervention of another force does not relieve the actor of liability, except where the harm is intentionally caused by a third person and is not within the scope of the risk created by the actor's conduct.

Comment:

b. If the actor's conduct has created or increased the risk that a particular harm to the plaintiff will occur, and has been a substantial factor in causing that harm, it is immaterial to the actor's liability that the harm is brought about in a manner which no one in his position could possibly have been expected to foresee or anticipate. This is true not only where the result is produced by the direct operation of the actor's conduct upon conditions or circumstances existing at the time, but also where it is brought about through the intervention of other forces which the actor could not have expected, whether they be forces of nature, or the actions of animals, or those of third persons which are not intentionally tortious or criminal. This is to say that any harm which is in itself foreseeable, as to which the actor has created or increased the recognizable risk, is always "proximate," no matter how it is brought about, except where there is such intentionally tortious or criminal intervention, and it is not within the scope of the risk created by the original negligent conduct.

Illustrations:

1. A negligently fails to clean petroleum residue out of his oil barge moored at a dock, thus creating the risk of harm to others in the vicinity through fire or explosion of gasoline vapor. The barge is struck by lightning and explodes, injuring B, a workman on the dock. A is subject to liability to B.

§ 443. Normal Intervening Force

The intervention of a force which is a normal consequence of a situation created by the actor's negligent conduct is not a superseding cause of harm which such conduct has been a substantial factor in bringing about.

§ 447. Negligence of Intervening Acts

The fact that an intervening act of a third person is negligent in itself or is done in a negligent manner does not make it a superseding cause of harm to another which the actor's negligent conduct is a substantial factor in bringing about, if

(a) the actor at the time of his negligent conduct should have realized that a third person might so act, or

(b) a reasonable man knowing the situation existing when the act of the third person was done would not regard it as highly extraordinary that the third person had so acted, or

(c) the intervening act is a normal consequence of a situation created by the actor's conduct and the manner in which it is done is not extraordinarily negligent.

Comment on Clause (a):

a. The statement in Clause (a) applies where there is a realizable likelihood of such an act but the likelihood is not enough in itself to make the actor's conduct negligent, the conduct being negligent because of other and greater risks which it entails. If the realizable likelihood that a third person will act in the negligent manner in which a particular third person acts is so great as to be the risk or even one of the risks which make the actor's conduct unreasonably dangerous and therefore negligent, the case is governed by the rule stated in § 449.

Illustration:

1. A loads his truck so carelessly that a slight jolt might cause its heavy contents to fall from it. He parks it in a street where to his knowledge small boys congregate for play. B, one of these boys, tries to climb on the truck. In so doing he so disturbs the load as to cause a heavy article to fall upon and hurt C, a comrade standing close by. B's act is not a superseding cause of C's harm.

§ 449. Tortious or Criminal Acts the Probability of Which Makes Actor's Conduct Negligent

If the likelihood that a third person may act in a particular manner is the hazard or one of the hazards which makes the actor negligent, such an act whether innocent, negligent, intentionally tortious, or criminal does not prevent the actor from being liable for harm caused thereby.

Comment:

a. This Section should be read together with § 302 B, and the Comments to that Section, which deal with the foreseeable likelihood of the intentional or even criminal misconduct of a third person as a hazard which makes the actor's conduct negligent. As is there stated, the mere possibility or even likelihood that there may be such misconduct is not in all cases sufficient to characterize the actor's conduct as negligence. It is only where the actor is under a duty to the other, because of some relation between them, to protect him against such misconduct, or where the actor has undertaken the obligation of doing

97

so, or his conduct has created or increased the risk of harm through the misconduct, that he becomes negligent.

b. The happening of the very event the likelihood of which makes the actor's conduct negligent and so subjects the actor to liability cannot relieve him from liability. The duty to refrain from the act committed or to do the act omitted is imposed to protect the other from this very danger. To deny recovery because the other's exposure to the very risk from which it was the purpose of the duty to protect him resulted in harm to him, would be to deprive the other of all protection and to make the duty a nullity.

Illustrations:

1. A is traveling on the train of the B Railway Company. Her ticket entitles her to ride only to Station X, but she intentionally stays on the train after it has passed that station. When she arrives at Station Y the conductor puts her off the train. This occurs late at night after the station has been closed and the attendants have departed. The station is situated in a lonely district, and the only way in which she can reach the neighboring town is by passing a place where to the knowledge of the conductor there is a construction camp. The construction crew is known to contain many persons of vicious character. While attempting to pass by this camp, A is attacked and ravished by some of the construction crew. The B Railway Company is subject to liability to A.

2. The A Railway Company permits a number of drunken rowdies to ride in its day coach. No effort is made by the conductor or train crew to eject them, although their conduct is insulting and threatening to the other passengers. One of the rowdies attempts to take liberties with B, a female passenger, and in the scuffle harms her. The intentional misconduct of the rowdy is not a superseding cause of B's harm.

3. The train crew of the coal trains of the A Railway Company are in the habit of throwing out coal to their families as the train passes through the streets of a village. The Company knows of this practice but takes no steps to prevent it. B, while walking on the street, is injured by coal so thrown from one of the Company's trains. The trainman's act in throwing out the coal without looking to see whether there was anyone likely to be hit by it is not a superseding cause of B's harm.

TOPIC 2. CAUSAL RELATION AFFECTING THE EXTENT OF LIABILITY BUT NOT ITS EXISTENCE

§ 457. Additional Harm Resulting From Efforts to Mitigate Harm Caused by Negligence

If the negligent actor is liable for another's bodily injury, he is also subject to liability for any additional bodily harm resulting from normal efforts of third persons in rendering aid which the other's injury reasonably requires, irrespective of whether such acts are done in a proper or a negligent manner.

Illustration:

1. A's negligence causes B serious harm. B is taken to a hospital. The surgeon improperly diagnoses his case and performs an unnecessary operation, or, after proper diagnosis, performs a necessary operation carelessly. A's negligence is a legal cause of the additional harm which B sustains.

§ 461. Harm Increased in Extent by Other's Unforeseeable Physical Condition

The negligent actor is subject to liability for harm to another although a physical condition of the other which is neither known nor should be known to the actor makes the injury greater than that which the actor as a reasonable man should have foreseen as a probable result of his conduct.

Comment:

a. The rule stated in this Section applies not only where the peculiar physical condition which makes the other's injuries greater than the actor expected is not known to him, but also where the actor could not have discovered it by the exercise of reasonable care, or, indeed even where it is unknown to the person suffering it or to anyone else until after the harm is sustained. A negligent actor must bear the risk that his liability will be increased by reason of the actual physical condition of the other toward whom his act is negligent.

Illustrations:

1. Through the motorman's negligent management of the A Company's trolley car the control lever strikes the breast of B, a passenger. The injury is apparently slight, but it causes a cancerous tendency to "light up" and localize itself in the injured point,

requiring the amputation of B's breast. A is answerable for the harm caused by the cancer and the amputation.

2. A, a schoolboy, during school hours, inflicts a slight kick upon the shin of B, a fellow student. Ordinarily the kick would have caused only a slight sensation of pain, but because of a latent infection it has serious consequences. A is subject to liability to B for the full extent of his injuries.

b. The rule stated in this Section is an application of a broader rule which applies not only to negligent but also to intentional misconduct. The broad rule applies not only where a physical injury is unexpectedly increased by the unknown physical peculiarities of the other, but also where an injury to another's pecuniary interests is increased by the unexpected and unknown or unknowable value of the article damaged.

Illustration:

3. A sees B, a physician in lucrative practice, doing gardening work on his own country place. B is dressed in shabby, old clothes and A reasonably believes him to be B's gardener. A negligently runs over B, causing harm which prevents him from practicing his profession for a year. A is subject to liability for the damages which B recovers based upon his professional earnings.

DIVISION THREE

STRICT LIABILITY

Chapter 20

LIABILITY OF POSSESSORS AND HARBORERS OF ANIMALS

TOPIC 1. TRESPASS BY LIVESTOCK

TOPIC 1. TRESPASS BY LIVESTOCK

§ **504.** Liability for Trespass by Livestock

(1) Except as stated in Subsections (3) and (4), a possessor of livestock intruding upon the land of another is subject to liability for the intrusion although he has exercised the utmost care to prevent them from intruding.

(2) The liability stated in Subsection (1) extends to any harm to the land or to its possessor or a member of his household, or their chattels, which might reasonably be expected to result from the intrusion of livestock.

(3) The liability stated in Subsection (1) does not extend to harm

(a) not reasonably to be expected from the intrusion;

(b) done by animals straying onto abutting land while driven on the highway; or

(c) brought about by the unexpectable operation of a force of nature, action of another animal or intentional, reckless or negligent conduct of a third person.

(4) A possessor of land who fails to erect and maintain a fence required by the applicable common law or by statute to prevent the intrusion of livestock, can not recover under the rule stated in Subsection (1).

TOPIC 2. HARM CAUSED BY ANIMALS OTHERWISE THAN BY TRESPASS BY LIVESTOCK

§ **506.** Wild Animal and Domestic Animal Defined

(1) A wild animal as that term is used in this Restatement is an animal that is not by custom devoted to the service of mankind at the time and in the place in which it is kept.

(2) A domestic animal as that term is used in this Restatement is an animal that is by custom devoted to the service of mankind at the time and in the place in which it is kept.

§ **507.** Liability of Possessor of Wild Animal

(1) A possessor of a wild animal is subject to liability to another for harm done by the animal to the other, his person, land or chattels, although the possessor has exer-

cised the utmost care to confine the animal, or otherwise prevent it from doing harm.

(2) This liability is limited to harm that results from a dangerous propensity that is characteristic of wild animals of the particular class, or of which the possessor knows or has reason to know.

Illustration:

1. A keeps a pet chimpanzee that is thoroughly tamed and accustomed to playing with its owner's children. The chimpanzee escapes, notwithstanding every precaution to keep it upon its owner's premises. It approaches a group of children. B, the mother of one of the children, erroneously thinking the chimpanzee is about to attack the children, rushes to her child's assistance and in her hurry and excitement stumbles and falls, breaking her leg. A is subject to liability to B.

§ 509. Harm Done by Abnormally Dangerous Domestic Animals

(1) A possessor of a domestic animal that he knows or has reason to know has dangerous propensities abnormal to its class, is subject to liability for harm done by the animal to another, although he has exercised the utmost care to prevent it from doing the harm.

(2) This liability is limited to harm that results from the abnormally dangerous propensity of which the possessor knows or has reason to know.

Illustrations:

1. A keeps a dog, which he knows to be in the habit of running after automobiles and yapping at their wheels. A chains the dog in his yard. The dog escapes, without any negligence on the part of A, runs into the street, and barks at the wheels of B's passing automobile. The dog is caught under one of the wheels, B's car is thrown into the ditch, and B is injured. A is subject to liability to B under this Section.

2. A keeps a dog in his apartment on the second floor. A knows that the dog is in the habit of rushing at the window and leaning out of it in order to bark at pedestrians passing below. The dog rushes to the window to bark at B, loses its footing, and falls on B and injures him. A is subject to liability to B under this Section.

§ **518.** **Liability for Harm Done by Domestic Animals That Are Not Abnormally Dangerous**

Except for animal trespass, one who possesses or harbors a domestic animal that he does not know or have reason to know to be abnormally dangerous, is subject to liability for harm done by the animal if, but only if,

(a) he intentionally causes the animal to do the harm, or

(b) he is negligent in failing to prevent the harm.

Chapter 21

ABNORMALLY DANGEROUS ACTIVITIES

Section

§ **519.** **General Principle**

(1) One who carries on an abnormally dangerous activity is subject to liability for harm to the person, land or chattels of another resulting from the activity, although he has exercised the utmost care to prevent the harm.

(2) This strict liability is limited to the kind of harm, the possibility of which makes the activity abnormally dangerous.

Comment:

a. The general rule stated in this Section is subject to exceptions and qualifications, too numerous to be included within a single Section. It should therefore be read together with §§ 520 to 524A, by which it is limited.

b. As to the factors to be considered in determining whether an activity is abnormally dangerous, see § 520.

c. The word "care" includes care in preparation, care in operation and skill both in operation and preparation.

d. The liability stated in this Section is not based upon any intent of the defendant to do harm to the plaintiff or to affect his interests, nor is it based upon any negligence, either in attempting to carry on the activity itself in the first instance, or in the manner in which it is carried on. The defendant is held liable although he has exercised the utmost care to prevent the harm to the plaintiff that has ensued. The liability arises out of the abnormal danger of the activity itself, and the risk that it creates, of harm to those in the vicinity. It is founded upon a policy of the law that imposes upon anyone who for his own purposes creates an abnormal risk of harm to his neighbors, the responsibility of relieving against that harm when it does in fact occur. The defendant's enterprise, in other words, is required to pay its way by compensating for the harm it causes, because of its special, abnormal and dangerous character.

Comment on Subsection (2):

e. Extent of protection. The rule of strict liability stated in Subsection (1) applies only to harm that is within the scope of the abnormal risk that is the basis of the liability. One who carries on an abnormally dangerous activity is not under strict liability for every possible harm that may result from carrying it on. For example, the thing that makes the storage of dynamite in a city abnormally dangerous is the risk of harm to those in the vicinity if it should explode. If an explosion occurs and does harm to persons, land or chattels in the vicinity, the rule stated in Subsection (1) applies. If, however, there is no explosion and for some unexpected reason a part of the wall of the magazine in which the dynamite is stored falls upon a pedestrian on the highway upon which the magazine abuts, the rule stated in Subsection (1) has no application. In this case the liability, if any, will be dependent upon proof of negligence in the construction or maintenance of the wall. So also, the transportation of dynamite or other high explosives by truck through the streets of a city is abnormally dangerous for the same reason as that which makes the storage of the explosives abnormally dangerous. If the dynamite explodes in the course of the transportation, a private person transporting it is subject to liability under the rule stated in Subsection (1), although he has exercised the utmost care. On the other hand, if the vehicle containing the explosives runs over a pedestrian, he cannot recover unless the vehicle was driven negligently.

Illustration:

1. A, with reasonable care, carries on blasting operations in a closely settled rural district. A has no reason to know of the presence of B's mink ranch nearby. The noise of the blasting

frightens the mink and the fright causes them to kill their young. A is not subject to strict liability to B for the loss of the mink.

§ 520. Abnormally Dangerous Activities

In determining whether an activity is abnormally dangerous, the following factors are to be considered:

(a) existence of a high degree of risk of some harm to the person, land or chattels of others;

(b) likelihood that the harm that results from it will be great;

(c) inability to eliminate the risk by the exercise of reasonable care;

(d) extent to which the activity is not a matter of common usage;

(e) inappropriateness of the activity to the place where it is carried on; and

(f) extent to which its value to the community is outweighed by its dangerous attributes.

Comment:

a. This Section deals only with the factors which determine whether an activity is abnormally dangerous. The general principle of strict liability for abnormally dangerous activities is stated in § 519. The limitations upon strict liability for abnormally dangerous activities are stated in §§ 521–524A.

b. Distinguished from negligence. The rule stated in § 519 is applicable to an activity that is carried on with all reasonable care, and that is of such utility that the risk which is involved in it cannot be regarded as so great or so unreasonable as to make it negligence merely to carry on the activity at all. (See § 282). If the utility of the activity does not justify the risk it creates, it may be negligence merely to carry it on, and the rule stated in this Section is not then necessary to subject the defendant to liability for harm resulting from it.

c. Relation to nuisance. If the abnormally dangerous activity involves a risk of harm to others that substantially impairs the use and enjoyment of neighboring lands or interferes with rights common to all members of the public the impairment or interference may be actionable on the basis of a public or a private nuisance. (See § 822, and Comment a under that Section). The rule of strict liability stated in § 519 frequently is applied by many courts in these cases under the name of "absolute nuisance," even when the harm that results is physical harm to person, land or chattels.

  d. *Purpose of activity.* In the great majority of the cases that involve abnormally dangerous activities the activity is carried on by the actor for purposes in which he has a financial interest, such as a business conducted for profit. This, however, is not necessary for the existence of such an activity. The rule here stated is equally applicable when there is no pecuniary benefit to the actor. Thus a private owner of an abnormally dangerous body of water who keeps it only for his own use and pleasure as a swimming pool is subject to the same liability as one who operates a reservoir of water for profit.

  e. *Not limited to the defendant's land.* In most of the cases to which the rule of strict liability is applicable the abnormally dangerous activity is conducted on land in the possession of the defendant. This, again, is not necessary to the existence of such an activity. It may be carried on in a public highway or other public place or upon the land of another.

  f. *"Abnormally dangerous."* For an activity to be abnormally dangerous, not only must it create a danger of physical harm to others but the danger must be an abnormal one. In general, abnormal dangers arise from activities that are in themselves unusual, or from unusual risks created by more usual activities under particular circumstances. In determining whether the danger is abnormal, the factors listed in Clauses (a) to (f) of this Section are all to be considered, and are all of importance. Any one of them is not necessarily sufficient of itself in a particular case, and ordinarily several of them will be required for strict liability. On the other hand, it is not necessary that each of them be present, especially if others weigh heavily. Because of the interplay of these various factors, it is not possible to reduce abnormally dangerous activities to any definition. The essential question is whether the risk created is so unusual, either because of its magnitude or because of the circumstances surrounding it, as to justify the imposition of strict liability for the harm that results from it, even though it is carried on with all reasonable care. In other words, are its dangers and inappropriateness for the locality so great that, despite any usefulness it may have for the community, it should be required as a matter of law to pay for any harm it causes, without the need of a finding of negligence.

Comment on Clauses (a) and (b):

  g. *Risk of harm.* An activity that is abnormally dangerous ordinarily involves a high degree of risk of serious harm to the person, land or chattels of others. The harm threatened must be major in degree, and sufficiently serious in its possible consequences to justify holding the defendant strictly responsible for subjecting others to an unusual risk. It is not enough that there is a recognizable risk of some relatively slight harm, even though that risk might be sufficient to make the actor's conduct negligent if the utility of his conduct did not outweigh it, or if he did not exercise reasonable care in conducting it. If the potential harm is sufficiently great, however, as in the case of a nuclear explosion, the likelihood that it will take place may be comparatively slight and yet the activity be regarded as abnormally dangerous.

Some activities, such as the use of atomic energy, necessarily and inevitably involve major risks of harm to others, no matter how or where they are carried on. Others, such as the storage of explosives, necessarily involve major risks unless they are conducted in a remote place or to a very limited extent. Still others, such as the operation of a ten-ton traction engine on the public highway, which crushes conduits beneath it, involve such a risk only because of the place where they are carried on. In determining whether there is such a major risk, it may therefore be necessary to take into account the place where the activity is conducted, as to which see Comment *j.*

Comment on Clause (c):

h. Risk not eliminated by reasonable care. Another important factor to be taken into account in determining whether the activity is abnormally dangerous is the impossibility of eliminating the risk by the exercise of reasonable care. Most ordinary activities can be made entirely safe by the taking of all reasonable precautions; and when safety cannot be attained by the exercise of due care there is reason to regard the danger as an abnormal one.

There is probably no activity, unless it is perhaps the use of atomic energy, from which all risks of harm could not be eliminated by the taking of all conceivable precautions, and the exercise of the utmost care, particularly as to the place where it is carried on. Thus almost any other activity, no matter how dangerous, in the center of the Antarctic continent, might be expected to involve no possible risk to any one except those who engage in it. It is not necessary, for the factor stated in Clause (c) to apply, that the risk be one that no conceivable precautions or care could eliminate. What is referred to here is the unavoidable risk remaining in the activity, even though the actor has taken all reasonable precautions in advance and has exercised all reasonable care in his operation, so that he is not negligent. The utility of his conduct may be such that he is socially justified in proceeding with his activity, but the unavoidable risk of harm that is inherent in it requires that it be carried on at his peril, rather than at the expense of the innocent person who suffers harm as a result of it. Thus the manufacture in a city of certain explosives may involve a risk of detonation in spite of everything that the manufacturer may reasonably be expected to do; and although he may not be negligent in manufacturing them at all, he is subject to strict liability for an abnormally dangerous activity.

A combination of the factors stated in Clauses (a), (b) and (c), or sometimes any one of them alone, is commonly expressed by saying that the activity is "ultrahazardous," or "extra-hazardous." Liability for abnormally dangerous activities is not, however, a matter of these three factors alone, and those stated in Clauses (d), (e), and (f) must still be taken into account.

As to strict liability for ground damage resulting from aviation, see § 520A.

Comment on Clause (d):

i. Common usage. An activity is a matter of common usage if it is customarily carried on by the great mass of mankind or by many people in the community. It does not cease to be so because it is carried on for a purpose peculiar to the individual who engages in it. Certain activities, notwithstanding their recognizable danger, are so generally carried on as to be regarded as customary. Thus automobiles have come into such general use that their operation is a matter of common usage. This, notwithstanding the residue of unavoidable risk of serious harm that may result even from their careful operation, is sufficient to prevent their use from being regarded as an abnormally dangerous activity. On the other hand, the operation of a tank or any other motor vehicle of such size and weight as to be unusually difficult to control safely, or to be likely to damage the ground over which it is driven, is not yet a usual activity for many people, and therefore the operation of such a vehicle may be abnormally dangerous.

Although blasting is recognized as a proper means of excavation for building purposes or of clearing woodland for cultivation, it is not carried on by any large percentage of the population, and therefore it is not a matter of common usage. Likewise the manufacture, storage, transportation and use of high explosives, although necessary to the construction of many public and private works, are carried on by only a comparatively small number of persons and therefore are not matters of common usage. So likewise, the very nature of oil lands and the essential interest of the public in the production of oil require that oil wells be drilled, but the dangers incident to the operation are characteristic of oil lands and not of lands in general, and relatively few persons are engaged in the activity.

The usual dangers resulting from an activity that is one of common usage are not regarded as abnormal, even though a serious risk of harm cannot be eliminated by all reasonable care. The difference is sometimes not so much one of the activity itself as of the manner in which it is carried on. Water collected in large quantity in a hillside reservoir in the midst of a city or in coal mining country is not the activity of any considerable portion of the population, and may therefore be regarded as abnormally dangerous; while water in a cistern or in household pipes or in a barnyard tank supplying cattle, although it may involve much the same danger of escape, differing only in degree if at all, still is a matter of common usage and therefore not abnormal. The same is true of gas and electricity in household pipes and wires, as contrasted with large gas storage tanks or high tension power lines. Fire in a fireplace or in an ordinary railway engine is a matter of common usage, while a traction engine shooting out sparks in its passage along the public highway is an abnormal danger.

Comment on Clause (e):

j. Locality. Another factor to be taken into account in determining whether an activity is abnormally dangerous is the place where it is carried on. If the place is one inappropriate to the particular activity, and other factors are present, the danger created may be regarded as an abnormal one.

Even a magazine of high explosives, capable of destroying everything within a distance of half a mile, does not necessarily create an abnormal danger if it is located in the midst of a desert area, far from human habitation and all property of any considerable value. The same is true of a large storage tank filled with some highly inflammable liquid such as gasoline. Blasting, even with powerful high explosives, is not abnormally dangerous if it is done on an uninhabited mountainside, so far from anything of considerable value likely to be harmed that the risk if it does exist is not a serious one. On the other hand, the same magazine of explosives, the hugh storage tank full of gasoline or the blasting operations all become abnormally dangerous if they are carried on in the midst of a city.

So likewise, the collection of large quantities of water in irrigation ditches or in a reservoir in open country usually is not a matter of any abnormal danger. On the other hand, if the reservoir is constructed in a coal mining area that is honeycombed with mine passages, or on a bluff overhanging a large city or if water is collected in an enormous standing tank above the same city, there is abnormal danger and strict liability when, without any negligence, the water escapes and does harm.

In other words, the fact that the activity is inappropriate to the place where it is carried on is a factor of importance in determining whether the danger is an abnormal one. This is sometimes expressed, particularly in the English cases, by saying there is strict liability for a "non-natural" use of the defendant's land.

There are some highly dangerous activities, that necessarily involve a risk of serious harm in spite of all possible care, that can be carried on only in a particular place. Coal mining must be done where there is coal; oil wells can be located only where there is oil; and a dam impounding water in a stream can be situated only in the bed of the stream. If these activities are of sufficient value to the community (see Comment k), they may not be regarded as abnormally dangerous when they are so located, since the only place where the activity can be carried on must necessarily be regarded as an appropriate one.

Comment on Clause (f):

k. *Value to the community.* Even though the activity involves a serious risk of harm that cannot be eliminated with reasonable care and it is not a matter of common usage, its value to the community may be such that the danger will not be regarded as an abnormal one. This is true particularly when the community is largely devoted to the dangerous enterprise and its prosperity largely depends upon it. Thus the interests of a particular town whose livelihood depends upon such an activity as manufacturing cement may be such that cement plants will be regarded as a normal activity for that community notwithstanding the risk of serious harm from the emission of cement dust. There is an analogy here to the consideration of the same elements in determining the existence of a nuisance, under the rule stated in § 831; and the Comments under that Section are applicable here, so far as they are pertinent.

Thus in Texas and Oklahoma, a properly conducted oil or gas well, at least in a rural area, is not regarded as abnormally dangerous, while a different conclusion has been reached in Kansas and Indiana. California, whose oil industry is far from insignificant, has concluded that an oil well drilled in a thickly settled residential area in the city of Los Angeles is a matter of strict liability.

In England, "a pluvial country, where constant streams and abundant rains make the storage of water unnecessary for ordinary or general purposes," a large reservoir in an inappropriate place has been found to be abnormally dangerous. In west Texas, a dry land whose livestock must have water, such a reservoir is regarded as "a natural and common use of the land." The same conclusion has been reached by many of the western states as to irrigation ditches.

Comment:

l. Function of court. Whether the activity is an abnormally dangerous one is to be determined by the court, upon consideration of all the factors listed in this Section, and the weight given to each that it merits upon the facts in evidence. In this it differs from questions of negligence. Whether the conduct of the defendant has been that of a reasonable man of ordinary prudence or in the alternative has been negligent is ordinarily an issue to be left to the jury. The standard of the hypothetical reasonable man is essentially a jury standard, in which the court interferes only in the clearest cases. A jury is fully competent to decide whether the defendant has properly driven his horse or operated his train or guarded his machinery or repaired his premises, or dug a hole. The imposition of strict liability, on the other hand, involves a characterization of the defendant's activity or enterprise itself, and a decision as to whether he is free to conduct it at all without becoming subject to liability for the harm that ensues even though he has used all reasonable care. This calls for a decision of the court; and it is no part of the province of the jury to decide whether an industrial enterprise upon which the community's prosperity might depend is located in the wrong place or whether such an activity as blasting is to be permitted without liability in the center of a large city.

§ 520A. Ground Damage From Aircraft

If physical harm to land or to persons or chattels on the ground is caused by the ascent, descent or flight of aircraft, or by the dropping or falling of an object from the aircraft,

(a) the operator of the aircraft is subject to liability for the harm, even though he has exercised the utmost care to prevent it, and

(b) the owner of the aircraft is subject to similar liability if he has authorized or permitted the operation.

§ 522. Contributing Actions of Third Persons, Animals and Forces of Nature

One carrying on an abnormally dangerous activity is subject to strict liability for the resulting harm although it is caused by the unexpectable

(a) innocent, negligent or reckless conduct of a third person, or

111

(b) action of an animal, or

(c) operation of a force of nature.

Caveat:

The Institute expresses no opinion as to whether the fact that the harm is done by an act of a third person that is not only deliberate but also intended to bring about the harm, relieves from liability one who carries on an abnormally dangerous activity.

Comment:

a. Rationale. The reason for imposing strict liability upon those who carry on abnormally dangerous activities is that they have for their own purposes created a risk that is not a usual incident of the ordinary life of the community. If the risk ripens into injury, it is immaterial that the harm occurs through the unexpectable action of a human being, an animal or a force of nature. This is true irrespective of whether the action of the human being which makes the abnormally dangerous activity harmful is innocent, negligent or even reckless. (Compare § 510 and contrast § 504(3)).

§ 523. Assumption of Risk

The plaintiff's assumption of the risk of harm from an abnormally dangerous activity bars his recovery for the harm.

Comment:

a. As to the defense of assumption of risk in general, see §§ 496A–496G.

b. Although, as stated in § 524, the ordinary contributory negligence of the plaintiff in failing to discover an abnormally dangerous activity or to take precautions against it is not a defense to the strict liability of the actor who carries it on, the plaintiff's voluntary acceptance of the abnormal risk is a defense. Thus, for example, a possessor of land who expressly agrees that the defendant may conduct blasting operations in close proximity to his land, with knowledge of the abnormal risk of harm to his person or property from the operations, can not recover when the activity miscarries and the harm results.

c. As in other situations involving assumption of risk, the plaintiff does not assume the risk unless he knows of its existence. The risk

112

inseparable from the great majority of abnormally dangerous activities is, however, a matter of such common knowledge and general notoriety that in the absence of special circumstances, as when he has been misled by the defendant or when he is too young to appreciate the risk, a plaintiff may often be found to have the knowledge notwithstanding his own denial. It is not necessary that he know or understand all of the causes or elements of the risk inseparable from the activity. It is enough that he knows that there is an abnormal risk of serious harm, to which those who take part in the activity or come within its range will be subjected. (See § 496D).

d. The risk is commonly assumed by one who takes part in the activity himself, as a servant, an independent contractor, a member of a group carrying on a joint enterprise or as the employer of an independent contractor hired to carry on the activity or to do work that must necessarily involve it. Thus a plaintiff who accepts employment driving a tank truck full of nitroglycerin, with knowledge of the danger must be taken to assume the risk when he is injured by an explosion.

e. Likewise the risk is commonly assumed when the plaintiff, knowing that the activity is being carried on and aware of the risk that it involves, voluntarily proceeds to encounter the risk by coming within range of it. Thus one who voluntarily enters land on which he knows that blasting is going on and so brings himself within range of the abnormal risk that he knows to exist, must be taken to assume the risk of harm resulting from any unpreventable miscarriage of the activity, although he does not assume the risk of any negligence in the operation unless he knows of it.

f. As in other situations involving assumption of risk the plaintiff's acceptance of the risk must be voluntary, and he does not assume the risk when the defendant's conduct has forced upon him the choice of two unreasonable alternatives. (See § 496E). In particular, he is not required to forego the exercise of a valuable right or privilege merely because the defendant's activity has made it dangerous unless the danger is so extreme that the continued exercise of the right or privilege is clearly unreasonable. A possessor of land is not required to abandon the land and move away from it, merely because the defendant has set up a powder mill in such proximity to it that there is danger in the continued use of the land. In these cases, however, the plaintiff may be entitled to assume, until he knows the contrary, that the danger has been reduced to a minimum by all reasonable precautions.

Illustrations:

> 1. A maintains a magazine of explosives in dangerous proximity to a public highway. Knowing of the presence of the magazine, B drives along the highway past it. While he is doing so he is injured by the explosion of the magazine. B is not barred from recovery from A by assumption of the risk.

> 2. A carries on blasting operations in dangerous proximity to the public highway. He posts a large warning sign, and stations a flagman to stop automobile drivers and inform them that there will be a delay of five minutes. B, driving on the highway, is stopped by the flagman, told of the blasting and is asked to wait. B refuses to wait, insists on proceeding on the highway and is injured by the blasting. B is barred from recovery from A by his assumption of the risk.

g. A plaintiff who makes use of the services of a common carrier or other public utility may ordinarily assume that they involve no abnormal danger. His right as a member of the public to make use of the services is a factor to be considered in determining whether he voluntarily assumes the risk of anything abnormal. When, however, the services rendered are of a kind that will necessarily involve an abnormally dangerous activity, and the plaintiff, knowing this, voluntarily elects to avail himself of them, with free alternatives open to him, he may still assume the risk. Thus a passenger who chooses to travel by air in an abnormally dangerous jet plane, still of an experimental character, at supersonic speed, will assume the risk inseparable from that type of transportation, even though the plane is provided by a common carrier.

Illustration:

> 3. A operates a factory in which it is necessary to use electric current of very high voltage. He contracts with B Electric Company, a public utility, for the necessary current. B constructs high tension poles and wires that carry a current of 20,000 volts into A's plant. Without any negligence on the part of B, the current escapes and damages A's factory. A is barred from recovery from B Company by his assumption of the risk.

§ 524. Contributory Negligence

(1) Except as stated in Subsection (2), the contributory negligence of the plaintiff is not a defense to the strict liability of one who carries on an abnormally dangerous activity.

(2) The plaintiff's contributory negligence in knowingly and unreasonably subjecting himself to the risk of harm from the activity is a defense to the strict liability.

Comment:

a. Since the strict liability of one who carries on an abnormally dangerous activity is not founded on his negligence, the ordinary contributory negligence of the plaintiff is not a defense to an action based on strict liability. The reason is the policy of the law that places the full responsibility for preventing the harm resulting from abnormally dangerous activities upon the person who has subjected others to the abnormal risk.

Thus in the ordinary case the contributory negligence will not bar recovery on the basis of strict liability. This is true when the plaintiff merely fails to exercise reasonable care to discover the existence or presence of the activity or to take precautions against the harm that may result from it. Thus one who is inattentive while driving along the highway, and therefore fails to discover a sign that would warn him of blasting operations ahead endangering his passage is not barred from recovery by his contributory negligence.

b. On the other hand, the plaintiff is barred by his voluntary assumption of the risk, as stated in § 523; and on the same basis, he is barred by his contributory negligence when he intentionally and unreasonably subjects himself to a risk of harm from the abnormally dangerous activity, of which he knows. This kind of contributory negligence, which consists of voluntarily and unreasonably encountering a known risk, frequently is called either contributory negligence or assumption of risk, or both. As to the relation between the two defenses, see § 496A.

Thus one who, without any necessity for doing so that is commensurate with the risk involved, knowingly brings himself within range of an abnormally dangerous activity, cannot recover against the person who carries on the activity. One who, driving along the highway, sees a sign and a flagman warning him that blasting operations are under way ahead that will endanger his passage, and nevertheless insists upon proceeding, cannot recover when he is injured by the blast.

Illustrations:

1. A, driving on the highway, attempts to pass a truck of the B Company on a narrow road. The truck is plainly marked "Danger, Dynamite," but A, being intent on the road and upon passing B, negligently fails to observe the sign. In passing, A negligently tries to drive through so narrow a space that he collides with the truck and causes the dynamite to explode. A's

115

personal representative is not barred from recovery against B Company under a death statute.

2. The same facts as Illustration 1, except that A reads the sign. A's representative is barred from recovery.

§ 524A. Plaintiff's Abnormally Sensitive Activity

There is no strict liability for harm caused by an abnormally dangerous activity if the harm would not have resulted but for the abnormally sensitive character of the plaintiff's activity.

Comment:

a. Since the basis for the strict liability for abnormally dangerous activities is the unusual risk inflicted upon those in the vicinity, it is limited to such harm as may reasonably be expected to result from such an activity, or from its miscarriage, to normal conditions around it and the normal activities of others. The plaintiff cannot, by himself resorting to an abnormally sensitive activity, impose upon the defendant an additional burden of liability, even though the defendant is aware of the fact. When the harm would not have resulted but for the abnormal and unduly sensitive character of the plaintiff's own activity or conditions arising in the course of it, the defendant's strict liability does not extend to the result, although he may still be liable for any negligence.

Illustrations:

1. A Company maintains and operates an electric transmission line carrying a current of 20,000 volts. Without any negligence on the part of A Company the line causes electrical induction currents in B Company's telegraph wires in the vicinity, which interfere with the transmission of messages. A Company is not liable to B Company.

2. A, constructing a building, operates pile-driving machinery that causes excessive vibration, abnormally dangerous to buildings in the vicinity. B, in an adjoining building, is conducting scientific experiments with extremely delicate instruments. Although the vibration causes no other harm to B or to the building, it ruins the instruments and prevents the experiments. A is not liable to B unless he is found to be negligent in his operation.

116

DIVISION FOUR

MISREPRESENTATION

Chapter 22

MISREPRESENTATION AND NONDISCLOSURE CAUSING PECUNIARY LOSS

117

TOPIC 1. FRAUDULENT MISREPRESENTATION (DECEIT)

§ 525. Liability for Fraudulent Misrepresentation

One who fraudulently makes a misrepresentation of fact, opinion, intention or law for the purpose of inducing another to act or to refrain from action in reliance upon it, is subject to liability to the other in deceit for pecuniary loss caused to him by his justifiable reliance upon the misrepresentation.

Comment:

d. *Representations of fact, opinion and law.* Strictly speaking, "fact "includes not only the existence of a tangible thing or the happening of a particular event or the relationship between particular persons or things, but also the state of mind, such as the entertaining of an intention or the holding of an opinion, of any person, whether the maker of a representation or a third person. Indeed, every assertion of the existence of a thing is a representation of the speaker's state of mind, namely, his belief in its existence. There is sometimes, however, a marked difference between what constitutes justifiable reliance upon statements of the maker's opinion and what constitutes justifiable reliance upon other representations. Therefore, it is convenient to distinguish between misrepresentations of opinion and misrepresentations of all other facts, including intention.

A statement of law may have the effect of a statement of fact or a statement of opinion. It has the effect of a statement of fact if it asserts that a particular statute has been enacted or repealed or that a particular decision has been rendered upon particular facts. It has the effect of a statement of opinion if it expresses only the actor's judgment as to the legal consequence that would be attached to the particular state of facts if the question were litigated. It is therefore convenient to deal separately with misrepresentations of law.

e. *Representation implied from statement of fact.* A misrepresentation of fact may concern either an existing or past fact. A statement about the future may imply a representation concerning an existing or past fact. (See Comment *f*). To be actionable, a misrepresentation of fact must be one of a fact that is of importance in determining the recipient's course of action at the time the representation is made. Thus a statement that a horse has recently and consistently trotted a mile in less than two minutes may justifiably be taken as an implied assertion of the capacity of the horse to repeat the performance at the time the statement is made. So, too, a past fact may be one that makes it obligatory or advisable for the recipient to take a particular course of action, as when A falsely tells B that he has caused the arrest of a criminal for whose arrest B has offered a reward, or when in an insurance policy the insured has falsely stated that his father did not die of tuberculosis. A fraudulent misrepresentation of such a fact may be the basis of liability.

f. Representation implied from statement promissory in form. Similarly a statement that is in form a prediction or promise as to the future course of events may justifiably be interpreted as a statement that the maker knows of nothing which will make the fulfillment of his prediction or promise impossible or improbable. Thus a statement that a second-hand car will run fifteen miles on a gallon of gasoline is an implied assertion that the condition of the car makes it capable of so doing, and is an actionable misrepresentation if the speaker knows that it has never run more than seven miles per gallon of gasoline.

Illustrations:

2. A, in order to induce B to buy a heating device, states that it will give a stated amount of heat while consuming only a stated amount of fuel. B is justified in accepting A's statement as an assurance that the heating device is capable of giving the services that A promises.

TITLE A. FRAUDULENT CHARACTER OF MISREPRESENTATION

§ 526. Conditions Under Which Misrepresentation Is Fraudulent (Scienter)

A misrepresentation is fraudulent if the maker

(a) knows or believes that the matter is not as he represents it to be,

(b) does not have the confidence in the accuracy of his representation that he states or implies, or

(c) knows that he does not have the basis for his representation that he states or implies.

§ 530. Misrepresentation of Intention

(1) A representation of the maker's own intention to do or not to do a particular thing is fraudulent if he does not have that intention.

(2) A representation of the intention of a third person is fraudulent under the conditions stated in § 526.

Comment on Subsection (1):

a. The state of a man's mind is as much a fact as the state of his digestion. A false representation of the actor's own intention to do or

119

not to do a particular thing is actionable if the statement is reasonably to be interpreted as expressing a firm intention and not merely as one of those "puffing "statements which are so frequent and so little regarded in negotiations for a business transaction as to make it unjustifiable for the recipient to rely upon them. As to the rules that determine whether the recipient may justifiably rely upon the statement of intention as an inducement to enter into the transaction, see s 544.

b. To be actionable the statement of the maker's own intention must be fraudulent, which is to say that he must in fact not have the intention stated. If he does not have it, he must of course be taken to know that he does not have it. If the statement is honestly made and the intention in fact exists, one who acts in justifiable reliance upon it cannot maintain an action of deceit if the maker for any reason changes his mind and fails or refuses to carry his expressed intention into effect. If the recipient wishes to have legal assurance that the intention honestly entertained will be carried out, he must see that it is expressed in the form of an enforceable contract, and his action must be on the contract.

TITLE B. EXPECTATION OF INFLUENCING CONDUCT

§ 531. General Rule

One who makes a fraudulent misrepresentation is subject to liability to the persons or class of persons whom he intends or has reason to expect to act or to refrain from action in reliance upon the misrepresentation, for pecuniary loss suffered by them through their justifiable reliance in the type of transaction in which he intends or has reason to expect their conduct to be influenced.

Caveat:

The Institute expresses no opinion on whether the liability of the maker of a fraudulent representation may extend beyond the rule stated in this Section to other persons or other types of transactions, if reliance upon the representation in acting or in refraining from action may reasonably be foreseen.

Comment:

d. "Reason to expect." One has reason to expect a result if he has information from which a reasonable man would conclude that the result will follow or would govern his conduct upon the assumption that it will do so. (Compare, in § 12(1), the meaning of "reason to know.")

In order for the maker of a fraudulent misrepresentation to have reason to expect that it will reach third persons and influence their conduct it is not enough that he recognizes, or as a reasonable man should recognize, the risk that it may be communicated to them and they may act upon it. When physical harm results from the misrepresentation, the maker may be liable under the rules stated in §§ 310 and 552A. When only pecuniary loss results, the magnitude of the extent to which misrepresentations may be circulated and the losses that may result from reliance upon them has induced the courts to limit the liability to the narrower rule stated in this Section.

Virtually any misrepresentation is capable of being transmitted or repeated to third persons, and if sufficiently convincing may create an obvious risk that they may act in reliance upon it. This risk is not enough for the liability covered in this Section. The maker of the misrepresentation must have information that would lead a reasonable man to conclude that there is an especial likelihood that it will reach those persons and will influence their conduct. There must be something in the situation known to the maker that would lead a reasonable man to govern his conduct on the assumption that this will occur. If he has the information, the maker is subject to liability under the rule stated here. For example, one who gives fraudulent information concerning his finances to a commercial credit agency cannot be heard to say that he does not expect that it will be communicated to its subscribers.

Illustrations:

4. A, a certified public accountant, fraudulently certifies an erroneous balance sheet for B Company. A is informed that B Company intends to exhibit the balance sheet to one or more of a group of banks or other lenders or investors for the purpose of obtaining a loan. A does not know the identity of any of the persons whom B Company may decide to approach. B Company exhibits the balance sheet to C Company, which, in reliance upon it, makes a loan to B Company, and as a result suffers pecuniary loss. A is subject to liability to C Company.

5. A, an architect, fraudulently furnishes erroneous specifications for a building to B, who is under contract to construct it. A is informed that B intends to obtain bids from subcontractors for work on the building as called for by the specifications, but A does not know the identity of any of the persons who may bid. B publishes an invitation for bids. In response to it C, in reliance upon the specifications, bids for the plumbing work on the build-

ing, is awarded the contract and as a result suffers pecuniary loss. A is subject to liability to C.

§ 533. Representation Made to a Third Person

The maker of a fraudulent misrepresentation is subject to liability for pecuniary loss to another who acts in justifiable reliance upon it if the misrepresentation, although not made directly to the other, is made to a third person and the maker intends or has reason to expect that its terms will be repeated or its substance communicated to the other, and that it will influence his conduct in the transaction or type of transaction involved.

TITLE C. JUSTIFIABLE RELIANCE

§ 537. General Rule

The recipient of a fraudulent misrepresentation can recover against its maker for pecuniary loss resulting from it if, but only if,

(a) he relies on the misrepresentation in acting or refraining from action, and

(b) his reliance is justifiable.

§ 538. Materiality of Misrepresentation

(1) Reliance upon a fraudulent misrepresentation is not justifiable unless the matter misrepresented is material.

(2) The matter is material if

(a) a reasonable man would attach importance to its existence or nonexistence in determining his choice of action in the transaction in question; or

(b) the maker of the representation knows or has reason to know that its recipient regards or is likely to regard the matter as important in determining his choice of action, although a reasonable man would not so regard it.

§ 545A. Contributory Negligence

One who justifiably relies upon a fraudulent misrepresentation is not barred from recovery by his contributory negligence in doing so.

TITLE D. CAUSATION

§ 546. Causation in Fact

The maker of a fraudulent misrepresentation is subject to liability for pecuniary loss suffered by one who justifiably relies upon the truth of the matter misrepresented, if his reliance is a substantial factor in determining the course of conduct that results in his loss.

§ 548A. Legal Causation of Pecuniary Loss

A fraudulent misrepresentation is a legal cause of a pecuniary loss resulting from action or inaction in reliance upon it if, but only if, the loss might reasonably be expected to result from the reliance.

TITLE E. DAMAGES FOR FRAUDULENT MISREPRESENTATION

§ 549. Measure of Damages for Fraudulent Misrepresentation

(1) The recipient of a fraudulent misrepresentation is entitled to recover as damages in an action of deceit against the maker the pecuniary loss to him of which the misrepresentation is a legal cause, including

(a) the difference between the value of what he has received in the transaction and its purchase price or other value given for it; and

(b) pecuniary loss suffered otherwise as a consequence of the recipient's reliance upon the misrepresentation.

(2) The recipient of a fraudulent misrepresentation in a business transaction is also entitled to recover additional damages sufficient to give him the benefit of his contract with the maker, if these damages are proved with reasonable certainty.

Comment on Clause (1)(a):

b. Under the rule stated in Clause (1)(a), the recipient of a fraudulent misrepresentation is entitled to recover from its maker in all cases the actual out-of-pocket loss which, because of its falsity, he sustains through his action or inaction in reliance on it. If, notwithstanding the falsity of the representation, the thing that the plaintiff acquires through the fraudulent transaction is of equal or greater value than the price paid and he has suffered no harm through using it

123

in reliance upon its being as represented, he has suffered no loss and can recover nothing under the rule stated in this Clause. His recovery, if any, must be upon the basis of the rule stated in Subsection (2).

Comment on Subsection (2):

g. Subsection (1) states the rules normally applicable to determine the measure of damages recoverable for a fraudulent misrepresentation in a tort action of deceit. If the plaintiff is content with these damages, he can always recover them. The rules stated in Subsection (1) are the logical rules for a tort action, since the purpose of a tort action is to compensate for loss sustained and to restore the plaintiff to his former position, and not to give him the benefit of any contract he has made with the defendant. When the plaintiff has not entered into any transaction with the defendant but has suffered his pecuniary loss through reliance upon the misrepresentation in dealing with a third person, these are the rules that must of necessity be applied.

When the plaintiff has made a bargain with the defendant, however, situations arise in which the rules stated in Subsection (1), and particularly that stated in Clause (a) of that Subsection, do not afford compensation that is just and satisfactory. If the value of what the plaintiff has received from the defendant is fully equal to the price he has paid for it or other value he has parted with and he has suffered no consequential damages, he may be unable to recover at all under the rules stated in Subsection (1). He may nevertheless be left with something acquired under the transaction which, because of the matter misrepresented, he does not want and cannot use. He may have lost the opportunity of acquiring a substitute at the same price and because of his commitments made or expenses incurred or for a variety of other reasons he may find rescission of the transaction and recovery of the price paid an unsatisfactory and insufficient remedy. In this case, under the rules stated in Subsection (1), the defrauding party would escape all liability.

The frequency of these situations has led the great majority of the American courts to adopt a broad general rule giving the plaintiff, in an action of deceit, the benefit of his bargain with the defendant in all cases, and making that the normal measure of recovery in actions of deceit.

The rule adopted in Subsection (2) does not take this position. One reason is that in occasional cases the out-of-pocket measure of damages will actually be more profitable and satisfactory from the point of view of the plaintiff than the benefit-of-the-bargain rule. This would be the case, for example, if the owner of valuable property were induced to sell it for less than its value by a representation that it had defects that made it practically worthless. On the basis of the representations, taken to be true, the seller would have sold worthless property for a substantial price and suffered no loss at all. Another and a more important, reason is that there are many cases in which the value that the plaintiff would have received if the bargain made with him had been performed cannot be proved with any satisfactory degree of certainty, because it must necessarily turn upon the estimated value of something non-existent and never in fact received. In this case the benefit-of-the-bargain harm to the plaintiff becomes mere speculation, and ordinary rules of the law of damages preclude the award.

h. This Section therefore follows a compromise position adopted by some jurisdictions, giving the plaintiff the option of either the out-of-pocket or the benefit-of-the-bargain rule in any case in which the latter measure can be established by proof in accordance with the usual rules of certainty in damages. The comments and illustrations that follow deal with the more common situations in which the plaintiff may wish to elect to receive the benefit of his bargain.

i. Value received equal to value paid. When the value of what the plaintiff has received under the transaction with the defendant is fully equal to the value of what he has parted with, he has suffered no out-of-pocket loss, and under the rule stated in Subsection (1), Clause (a), he could recover no damages. This would mean that the defrauding defendant has successfully accomplished his fraud and is still immune from an action in deceit. Even though the plaintiff may rescind the transaction and recover the price paid, the defendant is enabled to speculate on his fraud and still be assured that he can suffer no pecuniary loss. This is not justice between the parties. The admonitory function of the law requires that the defendant not escape liability and justifies allowing the plaintiff the benefit of his bargain.

Illustration:

   4. A, seeking to sell land to B, fraudulently tells B that half of the land is covered with good pine timber. B buys the land from A for $5,000. There is no timber on the land but it is still worth $5,000. Competent evidence establishes that if the representation had been true the land, with the timber, would have been worth $9,000. B may recover $4,000 from A.

Comment:

l. Benefit of the bargain. The damages necessary to give the plaintiff the benefit of the bargain that he has made with the defendant will depend, first of all, upon the nature of the bargain. If the defendant has undertaken to convey property of a certain description to the plaintiff, the plaintiff is entitled to an amount sufficient to give him the value of property of that description. If the defendant has undertaken merely to give the plaintiff accurate information about the property, he is entitled to a sufficient amount to place him in the position he would have occupied if he had had the information. If the defendant has undertaken merely to use care to give accurate information, the plaintiff is entitled only to an amount sufficient to compensate him by placing him in the position he would have occupied if that care had been used.

In order to give the plaintiff the benefit of the bargain, it is not necessary in all cases to give him the value of the thing as represented. He may be fully and fairly compensated if he is given the cost of making it as represented.

Illustrations:

> 7. A, seeking to sell a farm to B, fraudulently tells B that there is a well on the farm, with an ample supply of water. B buys the farm for $3,000. There is no well but there is water under the land, and a well can easily and quickly be dug for $250. With the well the land would be worth $5,000. B is entitled to recover $250 from A.

> 8. A, seeking to acquire students for his dental college, fraudulently tells B that the college gives a good dental education and awards a degree. B takes the dental course, paying A $1,000. The dental education is a good one and worth $1,000, but at the end of the course B finds that the college is not licensed to award a degree, without which B cannot obtain a license to practice dentistry. B is entitled to recover from A the cost of attendance at a licensed dental college for the additional time necessary to obtain a degree.

TOPIC 2. CONCEALMENT AND NONDISCLOSURE

§ 550. Liability for Fraudulent Concealment

One party to a transaction who by concealment or other action intentionally prevents the other from acquiring material information is subject to the same liability to the other, for pecuniary loss as though he had stated the nonexistence of the matter that the other was thus prevented from discovering.

§ 551. Liability for Nondisclosure

(1) One who fails to disclose to another a fact that he knows may justifiably induce the other to act or refrain

from acting in a business transaction is subject to the same liability to the other as though he had represented the nonexistence of the matter that he has failed to disclose, if, but only if, he is under a duty to the other to exercise reasonable care to disclose the matter in question.

(2) One party to a business transaction is under a duty to exercise reasonable care to disclose to the other before the transaction is consummated,

(a) matters known to him that the other is entitled to know because of a fiduciary or other similar relation of trust and confidence between them; and

(b) matters known to him that he knows to be necessary to prevent his partial or ambiguous statement of the facts from being misleading; and

(c) subsequently acquired information that he knows will make untrue or misleading a previous representation that when made was true or believed to be so; and

(d) the falsity of a representation not made with the expectation that it would be acted upon, if he subsequently learns that the other is about to act in reliance upon it in a transaction with him; and

(e) facts basic to the transaction, if he knows that the other is about to enter into it under a mistake as to them, and that the other, because of the relationship between them, the customs of the trade or other objective circumstances, would reasonably expect a disclosure of those facts.

Comment on Subsection (1):

a. Unless he is under some one of the duties of disclosure stated in Subsection (2), one party to a business transaction is not liable to the other for harm caused by his failure to disclose to the other facts of which he knows the other is ignorant and which he further knows the other, if he knew of them, would regard as material in determining his course of action in the transaction in question. The interest in knowing those facts that are important in determining the advisability of a course of action in a financial or commercial matter is given less protection by the rule stated in this Subsection than is given to the interest in knowing facts that are important in determining the recipient's course of action in regard to matters that involve the security of the person, land or chattels of himself or a third person.

b. The conditions under which liability is imposed for nondisclosure in an action for deceit differ in one particular from those under which a similar nondisclosure may confer a right to rescind the transaction or to recover back money paid or the value of other benefits conferred. In the absence of a duty of disclosure, under the rule stated in Subsection (2) of this Section, one who is negotiating a business transaction is not liable in deceit because of his failure to disclose a fact that he knows his adversary would regard as material. On the other hand, as is stated in Restatement, Second, Contracts § 303(b) the other is entitled to rescind the transaction if the undisclosed fact is basic; and under Restatement of Restitution, § 8, Comment e, and § 28, he would be entitled to recover back any money paid or benefit conferred in consummation of the transaction.

Comment on Clause (e):

j. *"Facts basic to the transaction."* The word "basic" is used in this Clause in the same sense in which it is used in Comment c under § 16 of the Restatement of Restitution. A basic fact is a fact that is assumed by the parties as a basis for the transaction itself. It is a fact that goes to the basis, or essence, of the transaction, and is an important part of the substance of what is bargained for or dealt with. Other facts may serve as important and persuasive inducements to enter into the transaction, but not go to its essence. These facts may be material, but they are not basic. If the parties expressly or impliedly place the risk as to the existence of a fact on one party or if the law places it there by custom or otherwise the other party has no duty of disclosure. (Compare Restatement, Second, Contracts § 296).

Illustrations:

3. A sells to B a dwelling house, without disclosing to B the fact that the house is riddled with termites. This is a fact basic to the transaction.

4. A sells to B a dwelling house, knowing that B is acting in the mistaken belief that a highway is planned that will pass near the land and enhance its value. A does not disclose to B the fact that no highway is actually planned. This is not a fact basic to the transaction.

5. Having purchased a certain tract of land for $25,000, A hears that B may have a claim to it. He goes to B and offers to purchase B's interest. B does not believe he has a valid legal claim but agrees to give A a quit-claim deed for $250. B's lack of a valid legal claim is not a fact that he is under a duty to disclose.

Comment:

k. Nondisclosure of basic facts. The rule stated in Subsection (1) reflects the traditional ethics of bargaining between adversaries, in the absence of any special reason for the application of a different rule. When the facts are patent, or when the plaintiff has equal opportunity for obtaining information that he may be expected to utilize if he cares to do so, or when the defendant has no reason to think that the plaintiff is acting under a misapprehension, there is no obligation to give aid to a bargaining antagonist by disclosing what the defendant has himself discovered. To a considerable extent, sanctioned by the customs and mores of the community, superior information and better business acumen are legitimate advantages, which lead to no liability. The defendant may reasonably expect the plaintiff to make his own investigation, draw his own conclusions and protect himself; and if the plaintiff is indolent, inexperienced or ignorant, or his judgment is bad, or he does not have access to adequate information, the defendant is under no obligation to make good his deficiencies. This is true, in general, when it is the buyer of land or chattels who has the better information and fails to disclose it. Somewhat less frequently, it may be true of the seller.

Illustrations:

6. A is a violin expert. He pays a casual visit to B's shop, where second-hand musical instruments are sold. He finds a violin which, by reason of his expert knowledge and experience, he immediately recognizes as a genuine Stradivarius, in good condition and worth at least $50,000. The violin is priced for sale at $100. Without disclosing his information or his identity, A buys the violin from B for $100. A is not liable to B.

7. The same facts as in Illustration 6, except that the violin is sold at auction and A bids it in for $100. The same conclusion.

8. B has a shop in which he sells second-hand musical instruments. In it he offers for sale for $100 a violin, which he knows to be an imitation Stradivarius and worth at most $50. A enters the shop, looks at the violin and is overheard by B to say to his companion that he is sure that the instrument is a genuine Stradivarius. B says nothing, and A buys the violin for $100. B is not liable to A.

l. The continuing development of modern business ethics has, however, limited to some extent this privilege to take advantage of ignorance. There are situations in which the defendant not only knows that his bargaining adversary is acting under a mistake basic to the transaction, but also knows that the adversary, by reason of the relation between them, the customs of the trade or other objective circumstances, is reasonably relying upon a disclosure of the unrevealed fact if it exists. In this type of case good faith and fair dealing may require a disclosure.

It is extremely difficult to be specific as to the factors that give rise to this known, and reasonable, expectation of disclosure. In general, the cases in which the rule stated in Clause (e) has been applied have been those in which the advantage taken of the plaintiff's ignorance is so shocking to the ethical sense of the community, and is so extreme and unfair, as to amount to a form of swindling, in which the plaintiff is led by appearances into a bargain that is a trap, of whose essence and substance he is unaware. In such a case, even in a tort action for deceit, the plaintiff is entitled to be compensated for the loss that he has sustained. Thus a seller who knows that his cattle are infected with tick fever or contagious abortion is not free to unload them on the buyer and take his money, when he knows that the buyer is unaware of the fact, could not easily discover it, would not dream of entering into the bargain if he knew and is relying upon the seller's good faith and common honesty to disclose any such fact if it is true.

There are indications, also, that with changing ethical attitudes in many fields of modern business, the concept of facts basic to the transaction may be expanding and the duty to use reasonable care to disclose the facts may be increasing somewhat. This Subsection is not intended to impede that development.

Illustrations:

9. A sells B a dwelling house, without disclosing the fact that drain tile under the house is so constructed that at periodic intervals water accumulates under the house. A knows that B is not aware of this fact, that he could not discover it by an ordinary inspection, and that he would not make the purchase if he knew it. A knows also that B regards him as an honest and fair man and one who would disclose any such fact if he knew it. A is subject to liability to B for his pecuniary loss in an action of deceit.

10. A is engaged in the business of removing gravel from the bed of a navigable stream. He is notified by the United States government that the removal is affecting the channel of the stream, and ordered to stop it under threat of legal proceedings to compel him to do so. Knowing that B is unaware of this notice, could not reasonably be expected to discover it and would not buy if he knew, A sells the business to B without disclosing the fact. A is subject to liability to B for his pecuniary loss in an action of deceit.

11.   A, who owns an amusement center, sells it to B without disclosing the fact that it has just been raided by the police, and that A is being prosecuted for maintaining prostitution and the sale of marijuana on the premises. These facts have seriously affected the reputation and patronage of the center, and greatly reduced its monthly income. A knows that B is unaware of these facts, could not be expected to discover them by ordinary investigation and would not buy if he knew them. He also knows that B believes A to be a man of high character, who would disclose any serious defects in the business. A is subject to liability to B for his pecuniary loss in an action of deceit.

12.   A sells a summer resort to B, without disclosing the fact that a substantial part of it encroaches on the public highway. A knows that B is unaware of the fact and could not be expected to discover it by ordinary inquiry, and that B trusts him to disclose any such facts. A is subject to liability to B for his pecuniary loss in an action of deceit.

m.   Court and jury. Whether there is a duty to the other to disclose the fact in question is always a matter for the determination of the court. If there are disputed facts bearing upon the existence of the duty, as for example the defendant's knowledge of the fact, the other's ignorance of it or his opportunity to ascertain it, the customs of the particular trade, or the defendant's knowledge that the plaintiff reasonably expects him to make the disclosure, they are to be determined by the jury under appropriate instructions as to the existence of the duty.

TOPIC 3. NEGLIGENT MISREPRESENTATION

§ 552.   Information Negligently Supplied for the Guidance of Others

(1) One who, in the course of his business, profession or employment, or in any other transaction in which he has a pecuniary interest, supplies false information for the guidance of others in their business transactions, is subject to liability for pecuniary loss caused to them by their justifiable reliance upon the information, if he fails to exercise reasonable care or competence in obtaining or communicating the information.

(2) Except as stated in Subsection (3), the liability stated in Subsection (1) is limited to loss suffered

(a) by the person or one of a limited group of persons for whose benefit and guidance he intends to supply the information or knows that the recipient intends to supply it; and

(b) through reliance upon it in a transaction that he intends the information to influence or knows that the recipient so intends or in a substantially similar transaction.

(3) The liability of one who is under a public duty to give the information extends to loss suffered by any of the class of persons for whose benefit the duty is created, in any of the transactions in which it is intended to protect them.

Comment:

a. Although liability under the rule stated in this Section is based upon negligence of the actor in failing to exercise reasonable care or competence in supplying correct information, the scope of his liability is not determined by the rules that govern liability for the negligent supplying of chattels that imperil the security of the person, land or chattels of those to whom they are supplied (see §§ 388–402), or other negligent misrepresentation that results in physical harm. (See § 311). When the harm that is caused is only pecuniary loss, the courts have found it necessary to adopt a more restricted rule of liability, because of the extent to which misinformation may be, and may be expected to be, circulated, and the magnitude of the losses which may follow from reliance upon it.

The liability stated in this Section is likewise more restricted than that for fraudulent misrepresentation stated in § 531. When there is no intent to deceive but only good faith coupled with negligence, the fault of the maker of the misrepresentation is sufficiently less to justify a narrower responsibility for its consequences.

The reason a narrower scope of liability is fixed for negligent misrepresentation than for deceit is to be found in the difference between the obligations of honesty and of care, and in the significance of this difference to the reasonable expectations of the users of information that is supplied in connection with commercial transactions. Honesty requires only that the maker of a representation speak in good faith and without consciousness of a lack of any basis for belief in the truth or accuracy of what he says. The standard of honesty is unequivocal and ascertainable without regard to the character of the transaction in which the information will ultimately be relied upon or the situation of the party relying upon it. Any user of commercial information may reasonably expect the observance of this standard by a supplier of information to whom his use is reasonably foreseeable.

On the other hand, it does not follow that every user of commercial information may hold every maker to a duty of care. Unlike the duty of honesty, the duty of care to be observed in supplying information for use in commercial transactions implies an undertaking to observe a relative standard, which may be defined only in terms of the use to which the information will be put, weighed against the magnitude and probability of loss that might attend that use if the information proves to be incorrect. A user of commercial information cannot reasonably expect its maker to have undertaken to satisfy this obligation unless the terms of the obligation were known to him. Rather, one who relies upon information in connection with a commercial transaction may reasonably expect to hold the maker to a duty of care only in circumstances in which the maker was manifestly aware of the use to which the information was to be put and intended to supply it for that purpose.

By limiting the liability for negligence of a supplier of information to be used in commercial transactions to cases in which he manifests an intent to supply the information for the sort of use in which the plaintiff's loss occurs, the law promotes the important social policy of encouraging the flow of commercial information upon which the operation of the economy rests. The limitation applies, however, only in the case of information supplied in good faith, for no interest of society is served by promoting the flow of information not genuinely believed by its maker to be true.

Comment on Subsection (2):

h. Persons for whose guidance the information is supplied. The rule stated in this Section subjects the negligent supplier of misinformation to liability only to those persons for whose benefit and guidance it is supplied. In this particular his liability is somewhat more narrowly restricted than that of the maker of a fraudulent representation (see § 531), which extends to any person whom the maker of the representation has reason to expect to act in reliance upon it.

Under this Section, as in the case of the fraudulent misrepresentation (see § 531), it is not necessary that the maker should have any particular person in mind as the intended, or even the probable, recipient of the information. In other words, it is not required that the person who is to become the plaintiff be identified or known to the defendant as an individual when the information is supplied. It is enough that the maker of the representation intends it to reach and influence either a particular person or persons, known to him, or a group or class of persons, distinct from the much larger class who might reasonably be expected sooner or later to have access to the information and foreseeably to take some action in reliance upon it. It

133

is enough, likewise, that the maker of the representation knows that his recipient intends to transmit the information to a similar person, persons or group. It is sufficient, in other words, insofar as the plaintiff's identity is concerned, that the maker supplies the information for repetition to a certain group or class of persons and that the plaintiff proves to be one of them, even though the maker never had heard of him by name when the information was given. It is not enough that the maker merely knows of the ever-present possibility of repetition to anyone, and the possibility of action in reliance upon it, on the part of anyone to whom it may be repeated.

Even when the maker is informed of the identity of a definite person to whom the recipient intends to transmit the information, the circumstances may justify a finding that the name and identity of that person was regarded by the maker, and by the recipient, as important only because the person in question was one of a group whom the information was intended to reach and for whose guidance it was being supplied. In many situations the identity of the person for whose guidance the information is supplied is of no moment to the person who supplies it, although the number and character of the persons to be reached and influenced, and the nature and extent of the transaction for which guidance is furnished may be vitally important. This is true because the risk of liability to which the supplier subjects himself by undertaking to give the information, while it may not be affected by the identity of the person for whose guidance the information is given, is vitally affected by the number and character of the persons, and particularly the nature and extent of the proposed transaction. On the other hand, the circumstances may frequently show that the identity of the person for whose guidance the information is given is regarded by the person supplying it, and by the recipient, as important and material; and therefore the person giving the information understands that his liability is to be restricted to the named person and to him only. Thus when the information is procured for transmission to a named or otherwise described person, whether the maker is liable to another, to whom in substitution the information is transmitted in order to influence his conduct in an otherwise identical transaction, depends upon whether it is understood between the one giving the information and the one bringing about its transmission, that it is to be given to the named individual and to him only.

Illustrations:

4. A, having lots for sale, negligently supplies misinformation concerning the lots to a real estate board, for the purpose of having the information incorporated in the board's multiple listing of available lots, which is distributed by the board to approximate-

ly 1,000 prospective purchasers of land each month. The listing is sent by the board to B, and in reliance upon the misinformation B purchases one of A's lots and in consequence suffers pecuniary loss. A is subject to liability to B.

5. A is negotiating with X Bank for a credit of $50,000. The Bank requires an audit by independent public accountants. A employs B & Company, a firm of accountants, to make the audit, telling them that the purpose of the audit is to meet the requirements of X Bank in connection with a credit of $50,000. B & Company agrees to make the audit, with the express understanding that it is for transmission to X Bank only. X Bank fails, and A, without any further communication with B & Company, submits its financial statements accompanied by B & Company's opinion to Y Bank, which in reliance upon it extends a credit of $50,000 to A. The audit is so carelessly made as to result in an unqualified favorable opinion on financial statements that materially misstates the financial position of A, and in consequence Y Bank suffers pecuniary loss through its extension of credit. B & Company is not liable to Y Bank.

6. The same facts as in Illustration 5, except that nothing is said about supplying the information for the guidance of X Bank only, and A merely informs B & Company that he expects to negotiate a bank loan, for $50,000, requires the audit for the purpose of the loan, and has X Bank in mind. B & Company is subject to liability to Y Bank.

§ 552A. Contributory Negligence

The recipient of a negligent misrepresentation is barred from recovery for pecuniary loss suffered in reliance upon it if he is negligent in so relying.

§ 552B. Damages for Negligent Misrepresentation

(1) The damages recoverable for a negligent misrepresentation are those necessary to compensate the plaintiff for the pecuniary loss to him of which the misrepresentation is a legal cause, including

(a) the difference between the value of what he has received in the transaction and its purchase price or other value given for it; and

(b) pecuniary loss suffered otherwise as a consequence of the plaintiff's reliance upon the misrepresentation.

135

(2) the damages recoverable for a negligent misrepresentation do not include the benefit of the plaintiff's contract with the defendant.

TOPIC 4. INNOCENT MISREPRESENTATION

§ 552C. Misrepresentation in Sale, Rental or Exchange Transaction

(1) One who, in a sale, rental or exchange transaction with another, makes a misrepresentation of a material fact for the purpose of inducing the other to act or to refrain from acting in reliance upon it, is subject to liability to the other for pecuniary loss caused to him by his justifiable reliance upon the misrepresentation, even though it is not made fraudulently or negligently.

(2) Damages recoverable under the rule stated in this section are limited to the difference between the value of what the other has parted with and the value of what he has received in the transaction.

Caveat:

The Institute expresses no opinion as to whether there may be other types of business transactions, in addition to those of sale, rental and exchange, in which strict liability may be imposed for innocent misrepresentation under the conditions stated in this Section.

Comment on Subsection (1):

a. History. The rule developed by the English courts, following the leading case of Derry v. Peek (1889) 14 A.C. 337, was that there was no liability for a misrepresentation causing only pecuniary loss unless the misrepresentation was fraudulent, as that term is defined in § 526. This rule received wide application in the United States. As to the extent to which it has been modified to permit recovery for misrepresentation that is not fraudulent but merely negligent, see § 552 and Comments. The rule stated in this Section represents a further modification reflected in the decisions of a number of American jurisdictions, some of which, in the case of bargaining transactions, rejected the rule of Derry v. Peek or never really accepted the holding of that case despite some judicial language seemingly to the contrary. It is a rule of strict liability for innocent misrepresentation of a material fact, made to another in a sale, rental or exchange transaction.

The courts that apply this rule have expressed it in differing ways. Some have imposed upon a party to a bargaining transaction a "duty" to know. Others have held that an unqualified statement of fact, which is susceptible of personal knowledge and which turns out to be false, is fraudulent insofar as there was no disclaimer of personal knowledge; and this view seems to have been taken without regard to whether the other party was actually deceived by the absence of the disclaimer. Although these courts use the language of scienter, their decisions actually constitute the imposition of liability for innocent misrepresentation.

More significantly, other courts have utilized the rule originating in equity that when a party seeks rescission of a transaction on the ground of a misrepresentation of a material fact by the other party relief will be granted even though the misrepresentation was innocent (just as rescission is also granted for mutual mistake). (See, generally, Restatement of Restitution, §§ 6, 8; Restatement, Second, Contracts §§ 304, 306). This rule of the law of restitution has also been regularly applied in actions at law, at least in situations in which the plaintiff is seeking to recover money paid and has already effected a rescission, so that a decree establishing the rescission is not required. (See Restatement of Restitution, § 28). Under similar circumstances a number of courts have permitted a tort action for damages without regard to the requirement that the transaction be completely rescinded, either by the plaintiff or by the court, and without limiting the action to the restitutionary concept of recovery of money paid.

DIVISION FIVE

DEFAMATION

Chapter 24

INVASION OF INTEREST IN REPUTATION

TOPIC 1. ELEMENTS OF A CAUSE OF ACTION FOR DEFAMATION

Section

TOPIC 2. DEFAMATORY COMMUNICATIONS

TOPIC 3. TYPES OF DEFAMATORY COMMUNICATION

TOPIC 1. ELEMENTS OF A CAUSE OF ACTION FOR DEFAMATION

§ 558. Elements Stated

To create liability for defamation there must be:

(a) a false and defamatory statement concerning another;

(b) an unprivileged publication to a third party;

(c) fault amounting at least to negligence on the part of the publisher; and

(d) either actionability of the statement irrespective of special harm or the existence of special harm caused by the publication.

TOPIC 2. DEFAMATORY COMMUNICATIONS

§ 559. Defamatory Communication Defined

A communication is defamatory if it tends so to harm the reputation of another as to lower him in the estimation of the community or to deter third persons from associating or dealing with him.

§ 564A. Defamation of a Group or Class

One who publishes defamatory matter concerning a group or class of persons is subject to liability to an individual member of it if, but only if,

(a) the group or class is so small that the matter can reasonably be understood to refer to the member, or

(b) the circumstances of publication reasonably give rise to the conclusion that there is particular reference to the member.

TOPIC 3. TYPES OF DEFAMATORY COMMUNICATION

§ 566. Expressions of Opinion

A defamatory communication may consist of a statement in the form of an opinion, but a statement of this nature is actionable only if it implies the allegation of undisclosed defamatory facts as the basis for the opinion.

TOPIC 4. FORMS OF DEFAMATORY COMMUNICATIONS

§ 568. Libel and Slander Distinguished

(1) Libel consists of the publication of defamatory matter by written or printed words, by its embodiment in physical form or by any other form of communication that has the potentially harmful qualities characteristic of written or printed words.

(2) Slander consists of the publication of defamatory matter by spoken words, transitory gestures or by any form of communication other than those stated in Subsection (1).

(3) The area of dissemination, the deliberate and premeditated character of its publication and the persistence of the defamation are factors to be considered in determining whether a publication is a libel rather than a slander.

§ **568A.** Radio and Television

Broadcasting of defamatory matter by means of radio or television is libel, whether or not it is read from a manuscript.

TOPIC 5. DEFAMATION ACTIONABLE IRRESPECTIVE OF SPECIAL HARM (DEFAMATION ACTIONABLE PER SE)

§ **569.** Liability Without Proof of Special Harm—Libel

One who falsely publishes matter defamatory of another in such a manner as to make the publication a libel is subject to liability to the other although no special harm results from the publication.

§ **570.** Liability Without Proof of Special Harm—Slander

One who publishes matter defamatory to another in such a manner as to make the publication a slander is subject to liability to the other although no special harm results if the publication imputes to the other

(a) a criminal offense, as stated in § 571, or

(b) a loathsome disease, as stated in § 572, or

(c) matter incompatible with his business, trade, profession, or office, as stated in § 573, or

(d) serious sexual misconduct, as stated in § 574.

§ **571.** Slanderous Imputations of Criminal Conduct

One who publishes a slander that imputes to another conduct constituting a criminal offense is subject to liability to the other without proof of special harm if the offense imputed is of a type which, if committed in the place of publication, would be

(a) punishable by imprisonment in a state or federal institution, or

(b) regarded by public opinion as involving moral turpitude.

§ **572.** Slanderous Imputations of Loathsome Disease

One who publishes a slander that imputes to another an existing venereal disease or other loathsome and communicable disease is subject to liability without proof of special harm.

§ 573. Slanderous Imputations Affecting Business, Trade, Profession or Office

One who publishes a slander that ascribes to another conduct, characteristics or a condition that would adversely affect his fitness for the proper conduct of his lawful business, trade or profession, or of his public or private office, whether honorary or for profit, is subject to liability without proof of special harm.

§ 574. Slanderous Imputations of Sexual Misconduct

One who publishes a slander that imputes serious sexual misconduct to another is subject to liability to the other without proof of special harm.

TOPIC 6. DEFAMATORY COMMUNICATIONS CAUSING SPECIAL HARM

§ 575. Slander Creating Liability Because of Special Harm

One who publishes a slander that, although not actionable per se, is the legal cause of special harm to the person defamed, is subject to liability to him.

§ 576. Harm Caused by Repetition

The publication of a libel or slander is a legal cause of any special harm resulting from its repetition by a third person if, but only if,

(a) the third person was privileged to repeat it, or

(b) the repetition was authorized or intended by the original defamer, or

(c) the repetition was reasonably to be expected.

TOPIC 7. PUBLICATION OF DEFAMATORY MATTER

§ 577. What Constitutes Publication

(1) Publication of defamatory matter is its communication intentionally or by a negligent act to one other than the person defamed.

(2) One who intentionally and unreasonably fails to remove defamatory matter that he knows to be exhibited on

141

land or chattels in his possession or under his control is subject to liability for its continued publication.

Comment:

a. *Manner of making publication.* A publication of the defamatory matter is essential to liability. (See § 558). Any act by which the defamatory matter is intentionally or negligently communicated to a third person is a publication. In the case of slander, the act is usually the speaking of the words, although under some circumstances there may be an act of publication by transitory gestures. (See § 568, Comment *d*). In the case of libel, there is usually some act by which written or printed words are brought to the attention of a third person although here again there are other methods of making a publication in libelous form. (See § 568, Comment *d*).

b. *Communication to third person.* To constitute a publication it is necessary that the defamatory matter be communicated to some one other than the person defamed. The law of defamation primarily protects only the interest in reputation. Therefore, unless the defamatory matter is communicated to a third person there has been no loss of reputation, since reputation is the estimation in which one's character is held by his neighbors or associates. The communication of disparaging matter only to the person to whom it refers is not actionable defamation, irrespective of the vile or scandalous character of the communication and its effects upon the feelings of that person. If the conduct is intended or likely to result in severe emotional distress, or in illness or other bodily harm on the part of the person thus vilified and if it does so result, the actor may be liable under the rules stated in §§ 46 and 48, and in §§ 312 and 313. He is not liable, however, for defamation under any of the rules stated in this Chapter. It is not necessary that the defamatory matter be communicated to a large or even a substantial group of persons. It is enough that it is communicated to a single individual other than the one defamed.

§ 578. Liability of Republisher

Except as to those who only deliver or transmit defamation published by a third person, one who repeats or otherwise republishes defamatory matter is subject to liability as if he had originally published it.

TOPIC 8. REQUIREMENT OF FAULT

§ 580A. Defamation of Public Official or Public Figure

One who publishes a false and defamatory communication concerning a public official or public figure in regard to his conduct, fitness or role in that capacity is subject to liability, if, but only if, he

(a) knows that the statement is false and that it defames the other person, or

(b) acts in reckless disregard of these matters.

Comment:

e. "Constitutional privilege"; burden of alleging and proving. The effect of the Constitution upon a cause of action for defamation may be described in two different ways. One method is to state that the Constitution imposes a limitation on the action so that the plaintiff cannot maintain it unless he shows that his cause of action does not come within the limitation. The other method is to say that the Constitution affords a privilege to the defendant so that he is not liable if he comes within the scope of the privilege and does not exceed or abuse the privilege. Either description is meaningful, but the use of the term, privilege, in this connection can give rise to a misleading impression. For a privilege created by the law to apply, the person who seeks to dispel the seemingly tortious character of his conduct normally has the burden of raising the issue of the privilege and proving the existence of its elements. (See § 10, Comment *c*; also § 891). This is true, for example, of the common law privileges to an action for defamation, whether they are absolute or conditional. (See § 613. Comment *i*). It is not true of the "constitutional privilege" of publishing false and defamatory statements regarding a public official or public figure when there is no knowledge of falsity or recklessness regarding truth or falsity. Here it is held that the plaintiff has the burden of alleging and proving that the defendant had knowledge or acted in reckless disregard.

TOPIC 9. TRUTH

§ 581A. True Statements

One who publishes a defamatory statement of fact is not subject to liability for defamation if the statement is true.

Chapter 25

DEFENSES TO ACTIONS FOR DEFAMATION

TOPIC 2. ABSOLUTE PRIVILEGES

TITLE A. CONSENT

TOPIC 2. ABSOLUTE PRIVILEGES

TITLE A. CONSENT

§ 583. General Principle

Except as stated in § 584, the consent of another to the publication of defamatory matter concerning him is a complete defense to his action for defamation.

144

TITLE B. ABSOLUTE PRIVILEGE IRRESPECTIVE OF CONSENT

§ 585. Judicial Officers

A judge or other officer performing a judicial function is absolutely privileged to publish defamatory matter in the performance of the function if the publication has some relation to the matter before him.

§ 586. Attorneys at Law

An attorney at law is absolutely privileged to publish defamatory matter concerning another in communications preliminary to a proposed judicial proceeding, or in the institution of, or during the course and as a part of, a judicial proceeding in which he participates as counsel, if it has some relation to the proceeding.

§ 587. Parties to Judicial Proceedings

A party to a private litigation or a private prosecutor or defendant in a criminal prosecution is absolutely privileged to publish defamatory matter concerning another in communications preliminary to a proposed judicial proceeding, or in the institution of or during the course and as a part of, a judicial proceeding in which he participates, if the matter has some relation to the proceeding.

§ 588. Witnesses in Judicial Proceedings

A witness is absolutely privileged to publish defamatory matter concerning another in communications preliminary to a proposed judicial proceeding or as a part of a judicial proceeding in which he is testifying, if it has some relation to the proceeding.

§ 589. Jurors

A member of a grand or petit jury is absolutely privileged to publish defamatory matter concerning another in the performance of his function as a juror, if the defamatory matter has some relation to the proceedings in which he is acting as juror.

§ 590. Legislators

A member of the Congress of the United States or of a State or local legislative body is absolutely privileged to publish defamatory matter concerning another in the performance of his legislative functions.

§ 590A. Witnesses in Legislative Proceedings

A witness is absolutely privileged to publish defamatory matter as part of a legislative proceeding in which he is testifying or in communications preliminary to the proceeding, if the matter has some relation to the proceeding.

§ 591. Executive and Administrative Officers

An absolute privilege to publish defamatory matter concerning another in communications made in the performance of his official duties exists for

(a) any executive or administrative officer of the United States; or

(b) a governor or other superior executive officer of a state.

§ 592. Husband and Wife

A husband or a wife is absolutely privileged to publish to the other spouse defamatory matter concerning a third person.

TOPIC 3. CONDITIONAL PRIVILEGES

TITLE A. OCCASIONS MAKING A PUBLICATION CONDITIONALLY PRIVILEGED

SUBTITLE II. FACTORS DETERMINING THE EXISTENCE OF A CONDITIONAL PRIVILEGE ARISING FROM AN OCCASION

§ 594. Protection of the Publisher's Interest

An occasion makes a publication conditionally privileged if the circumstances induce a correct or reasonable belief that

(a) there is information that affects a sufficiently important interest of the publisher, and

(b) the recipient's knowledge of the defamatory matter will be of service in the lawful protection of the interest.

146

§ 595. Protection of Interest of Recipient or a Third Person

(1) An occasion makes a publication conditionally privileged if the circumstances induce a correct or reasonable belief that

(a) there is information that affects a sufficiently important interest of the recipient or a third person, and

(b) the recipient is one to whom the publisher is under a legal duty to publish the defamatory matter or is a person to whom its publication is otherwise within the generally accepted standards of decent conduct.

(2) In determining whether a publication is within generally accepted standards of decent conduct it is an important factor that

(a) the publication is made in response to a request rather than volunteered by the publisher or

(b) a family or other relationship exists between the parties.

§ 597. Family Relationships

(1) An occasion makes a publication conditionally privileged if the circumstances induce a correct or reasonable belief that

(a) there is information that affects the well-being of a member of the immediate family of the publisher, and

(b) the recipient's knowledge of the defamatory matter will be of service in the lawful protection of the well-being of the member of the family.

(2) An occasion makes a publication conditionally privileged when the circumstances induce a correct or reasonable belief that

(a) there is information that affects the well-being of a member of the immediate family of the recipient or of a third person, and

(b) the recipient's knowledge of the defamatory matter will be of service in the lawful protection of the well-being of the member of the family, and

(c) the recipient has requested the publication of the defamatory matter or is a person to whom its publication is otherwise within generally accepted standards of decent conduct.

147

Comment on Subsection (1):

    c. Everyone has a sufficient interest in the physical, moral and social well-being of the members of his immediate family to make it proper for him to protect their well-being by the publication of defamatory matter concerning another when, if the matter were true, the recipient's knowledge would be of service in protecting their well-being.

    d. The statement in this Subsection gives a conditional privilege to communications between members of a family, other than those between husband and wife, which were absolutely privileged under the rule stated in § 592, and to communications between one member of a family and a third person. In either case, the person to whom the defamatory publication is made must be one whose knowledge of it is reasonably believed to be of value for the protection of the publisher's interest in the well-being of other members of his immediate family. Thus a person is conditionally privileged to communicate to his brother, sister, child or parent defamatory matter concerning another family member's companions or associates.

Illustration:

    1. A tells his sister B that he has seen C, B's husband, in the company of prostitutes. The communication is conditionally privileged.

Comment on Subsection (2):

    e. The statement in this Subsection gives a conditional privilege to publish defamatory matter concerning another for the purpose of protecting the well-being of some member of the immediate family of the recipient or other third person. Here, as in the case of the privilege to publish defamatory matter that is believed to be necessary for the protection of the recipient's interest, the fact that the information is volunteered rather than given in answer to an inquiry is of importance. Here, as in the case of the privilege covered in § 595, the existence of the privilege will turn primarily upon a comparison between the harm likely to result to the interest of a member of the recipient's family through the recipient's ignorance of the matter communicated, with the harm likely to be caused to the plaintiff through the injury to his reputation.

    On the other hand, here, as under the rule stated in § 595, the fact that a request is made for information may be sufficient to justify the publication of defamatory matter in response to it, although the publisher would not regard the information as essential to the well-being of a member of the recipient's family. Here again, as in § 595, the particular social relationship between the publisher and the recipient may be such as to give him a privilege to communicate information even without a request for it which otherwise he would not be privileged to volunteer.

Illustrations:

2. A, a minister, writes an unsolicited letter to B, a parishioner, telling him that he understands that the fiance of B's daughter is a felon. The occasion is conditionally privileged.

3. A tells B, a close friend, that C, B's infant son, has been guilty of petty thievery. The occasion is conditionally privileged.

§ 598. Communication to One Who May Act in the Public Interest

An occasion makes a publication conditionally privileged if the circumstances induce a correct or reasonable belief that

(a) there is information that affects a sufficiently important public interest, and

(b) the public interest requires the communication of the defamatory matter to a public officer or a private citizen who is authorized or privileged to take action if the defamatory matter is true.

§ 598A. Inferior State Officers

An occasion makes a publication conditionally privileged if an inferior administrative officer of a state or any of its subdivisions who is not entitled to an absolute privilege makes a defamatory communication required or permitted in the performance of his official duties.

SUBTITLE III. ABUSE OF PRIVILEGE

§ 599. General Principle

One who publishes defamatory matter concerning another upon an occasion giving rise to a conditional privilege is subject to liability to the other if he abuses the privilege.

§ 600. Knowledge of Falsity or Reckless Disregard as to Truth

Except as stated in § 602, one who upon an occasion giving rise to a conditional privilege publishes false and defamatory matter concerning another abuses the privilege if he

(a) knows the matter to be false, or

(b) acts in reckless disregard as to its truth or falsity.

§ 603. Purpose of the Privilege

One who upon an occasion giving rise to a conditional privilege publishes defamatory matter concerning another abuses the privilege if he does not act for the purpose of protecting the interest for the protection of which the privilege is given.

Chapter 26

BURDEN OF PROOF AND FUNCTION OF JUDGE AND JURY IN ACTIONS FOR DEFAMATION

TOPIC 1. BURDEN OF PROOF

TOPIC 2. FUNCTION OF COURT AND JURY

TOPIC 1. BURDEN OF PROOF

§ 613. Burden of Proof

(1) In an action for defamation the plaintiff has the burden of proving, when the issue is properly raised,

(a) the defamatory character of the communication,

(b) its publication by the defendant,

(c) its application to the plaintiff,

(d) the recipient's understanding of its defamatory meaning,

(e) the recipient's understanding of it as intended to be applied to the plaintiff,

(f) special harm resulting to the plaintiff from its publication,

(g) the defendant's negligence, reckless disregard or knowledge regarding the truth or falsity and the defamatory character of the communication, and

(h) the abuse of a conditional privilege.

(2) In an action for defamation the defendant has the burden of proving, when the issue is properly raised, the presence of the circumstances necessary for the existence of a privilege to publish the defamatory communication.

Caveat:

The Institute expresses no opinion on the extent to which the common law rule placing on the defendant the burden of proof to show the truth of the defamatory communication has been changed by the constitutional requirement that the plaintiff must prove defendant's negligence or greater fault regarding the falsity of the communication.

TOPIC 2. FUNCTION OF COURT AND JURY

§ 614. Determination of Meaning and Defamatory Character of Communication

(1) The court determines

(a) whether a communication is capable of bearing a particular meaning, and

(b) whether that meaning is defamatory.

(2) The jury determines whether a communication, capable of a defamatory meaning, was so understood by its recipient.

Chapter 27

MEASURE OF DAMAGES IN ACTIONS FOR DEFAMATION

Section

§ 620. Nominal Damages

One who is liable for a slander actionable per se or for a libel is liable for at least nominal damages.

§ 621. General Damages

One who is liable for a defamatory communication is liable for the proved, actual harm caused to the reputation of the person defamed.

Caveat:

The Institute takes no position on whether the traditional common law rule allowing recovery in the absence of proof of actual harm, for the harm that normally results from such a defamation, may constitutionally be applied if the defendant knew of the falsity of the communication or acted in reckless disregard of its truth or falsity.

Comment:

a. Meaning of general damages. General damages are a form of compensatory damages. On their character in general, see § 904. In defamation actions general damages are imposed for the purpose of compensating the plaintiff for the harm that the publication has caused to his reputation.

This Section applies to slander actions if the slander is actionable without proof of special harm (§ 570), or if the requisite special harm is proved to exist. (See § 575). It applies to all libel actions, since proof of special harm is not required. (See § 569).

General damages differ from damages for special harm of the type that is required to be shown in the case of slander that is not actionable per se. Special harm is the loss of something having economic or pecuniary value. (See § 575, Comment *b*). If special harm is shown, damages for it may also be recovered. (See § 622). Recovery may also be had for emotional distress and resulting bodily harm. (See § 623).

At common law general damages have traditionally been awarded not only for harm to reputation that is proved to have occurred, but also, in the absence of this proof, for harm to reputation that would normally be assumed to flow from a defamatory publication of the nature involved. This presumption of general damage to reputation from a defamatory publication that is actionable per se affords little control by the court over the jury in assessing the amount of damages.

b. Constitutional limitations on recovery of general damages. In Gertz v. Robert Welch, Inc., (1974) 418 U.S. 323, the Supreme Court held that the common law rule of presumed damages is incompatible with the First Amendment freedoms and therefore unconstitutional. So long, at least, as the action is based on negligence of the defendant, as described in s 580B, a plaintiff's recovery is confined to compensation for "actual injury." The court has not specifically defined actual injury, but it has explained that the term is not confined to out-of-pocket loss. It includes "impairment of reputation and standing in the community," but this must be supported by competent evidence and cannot be presumed in the absence of proof. Unless the harm is pecuniary in nature, the evidence need not "assign an actual dollar

value" to it. "Actual injury" is also held to include "personal humiliation, and mental anguish and suffering," provided they are proved to
have been sustained. The Constitution does not require proof of
impairment of reputation before damages for emotional distress can be
recovered. Damages for emotional distress are treated in § 623.

§ 622. Special Harm as Affecting the Measure of Recovery

**One who is liable for either a slander actionable per se or
a libel is also liable for any special harm legally caused by
the defamatory publication.**

§ 623. Emotional Distress and Resulting Bodily Harm

**One who is liable to another for a libel or slander is liable
also for emotional distress and bodily harm that is proved
to have been caused by the defamatory publication.**

Special Note on Remedies for Defamation Other Than Damages

The tort law of libel and slander has been conceived as of serving
three separate functions: (1) to compensate the plaintiff for the injury
to his reputation, for his pecuniary losses and for his emotional
distress, (2) to vindicate him and aid in restoring his reputation and (3)
to punish the defendant and dissuade him and others from publishing
defamatory statements. The traditional remedy has been an award of
damages, whether compensatory, nominal or punitive. The award of
damages has served all three purposes, to a greater or lesser degree.

But the damage remedy has proved to have many inadequacies,
and it has become less useful as a remedy for the injured party as a
result of recent developments in the law of defamation. In the first
place, there has always been a serious anomaly in trying to convert
damage to reputation in the absence of proof of specific pecuniary loss
and injury to feelings into exact monetary figures.

Second, and more important, the damage remedy is frequently
not available even though the communication is both false and defamatory and causes actual provable harm. The defendant is often found to
be privileged. If he is absolutely privileged, there is certainly no point
in bringing suit for damages. The common law of conditional privilege
has been built up over the years as a careful balancing of the
conflicting interests of the plaintiff and of the defendant, together with
those of other people. But no matter how desirable it is to protect
significant interests of other parties the fact remains that it is the
plaintiff who has innocently suffered the damage. Now that strict
liability for defamation is no longer constitutional, the plaintiff may
lose because he was unable to prove that the defendant published the
statement with knowledge of its falsity or in reckless disregard of its

truth or falsity, or even negligently in this regard. If the plaintiff fails to win on any one of these bases, he not only fails to obtain damages, but the impression created among those who were aware of the suit is that the defamatory charge must have been true. As a result, the plaintiff's reputation is damaged all the more, and he would have been better off never to have brought the suit.

Third, the damage remedy has sometimes proved to be unfair to the defendant. Defamation actions have not infrequently been brought—or jury verdicts have been rendered, irrespective of the plaintiff's motivation in bringing the action—not to compensate for actual pecuniary loss or to vindicate the plaintiff, but instead to cudgel the defendant and to mulct him for substantial damages that may be like a windfall to the plaintiff. It is cases of this sort that have helped to persuade the Supreme Court to intervene and set restrictions and standards that will protect the country's commitment to free speech and free press.

These inadequacies make it very doubtful whether the damage remedy fully serves the purposes for which the law of defamation was established, especially the vindication of plaintiff's reputation. Consideration should therefore be given to alternative legal remedies that may more adequately serve one or more of the purposes enumerated. Several of these alternatives may be considered.

(1) Declaratory relief. In a jurisdiction where declaratory relief is available as a general remedy and statutory provisions do not preclude it, resort may be had to a suit for a declaratory judgment that the defamatory statement is untrue. This action would provide no compensation for injury but it could vindicate the plaintiff and aid in restoring his reputation. Libel or slander suits similar to this are those in which the plaintiff seeks only nominal damages or announces that he will donate to charity any award that he receives.

There is presently no established practice for bringing suit to obtain a declaratory judgment that a defamatory statement about the plaintiff is false. A number of questions will arise if the practice develops. Thus, since there is no request for award of damages, can an action for slander be maintained for a communication that was not slanderous per se, even in the absence of any proof of special damages? Again, now that the common law strict liability for defamation is no longer constitutional (see §§ 580A, 580B), would it still be necessary to prove fault on the part of the defendant in order to maintain an action solely for declaratory relief? Could the declaratory action be sustained even though the defendant was able to claim a privilege, on the basis that the purpose of the privilege is to protect the defendant from the burden of a monetary obligation? Should the affirmative defense of truth in a regular defamation action be converted into a specific element of the plaintiff's cause of action in a suit for declaratory relief, so that the burden of proof as to falsity is on the plaintiff? How should costs of suit be allocated? Would it be desirable to develop a technique for eliminating suits based on trivial defamation? Substantial policy issues abound in each of these problems.

If the remedy of a formal action for a declaratory judgment is not available in a particular jurisdiction there remain two possible methods of using the ordinary action for defamation to obtain declaratory relief. The first is to bring the action expressly requesting only nominal damages and stating that the suit is for the purpose of vindicating the plaintiff's reputation and not for the purpose of recovering compensatory damages. It has been tacitly assumed that a suit of this nature would be subject to all of the defenses and restrictions of a suit for regular damages. But the issues involved are different and the competing interests may produce a different balance. Decisions consciously treating these issues have not been rendered. A suit brought solely for nominal damages may well come to be treated as one for declaratory relief, with different restrictions and defenses. (See § 620).

The second possible method of obtaining declaratory relief in a regular defamation suit involves the utilization of a special verdict. Thus, if a fact issue is presented as to whether the defendant published a defamatory communication negligently (or recklessly or with knowledge of the falsity) and the case goes to the jury, the trial judge may call for a special verdict indicating (1) whether the communication was true or false and (2) whether the defendant acted negligently. In this way, even if the jury finds that the defendant was not negligent, so that he wins the suit, the plaintiff will have had an opportunity to obtain a formal declaration that the defamatory statement about him was false.

(2) *Retraction.* There are numerous retraction statutes in the United States. They usually provide that if a newspaper receives a notification as to the falsity of a defamatory news item and complies with a request for retraction its liability for damages will be reduced. At an earlier time the English manorial courts sometimes required an apology and the ecclesiastical courts required the defendant to acknowledge his false witness and beg the pardon of the injured party. The core of the idea might be utilized today as a supplement to the action for declaratory relief. A news medium might be directed to publish a news item covering the judgment against it and thus aid in vindicating the plaintiff's reputation. On the constitutionality of a statute to this effect, see Miami Herald Pub. Co. v. Tornillo (1974) 418 U.S. 241, 258 (Brennan, J., concurring).

(3) Injunctive relief. Equity courts have never been inclined to grant freely injunctive remedies against personal defamation, and ever since Near v. Minnesota (1931) 283 U.S. 697, it has been recognized that prior restraint of a publication runs afoul of the First Amendment. Nevertheless, it remains possible that injunctive relief might on some occasions become a suitable supplement to declaratory relief. When it has been formally determined by a court that a statement is both defamatory and untrue and the defendant persists in continuing to publish it, a carefully worded injunction might meet the need and be available against further publication of the statement that has already been determined by the court to be false and defamatory.

(4) Self-help. The Supreme Court has said: "The first remedy of any victim of defamation is self-help—using available opportunities to contradict the lie or correct the error and thereby to minimize its adverse impact on reputation." This remedy, of course, does not require suit or court action. The law can nevertheless help. It gives a conditional privilege to a person who is seeking to protect his reputation by answering a defamatory charge. (See § 594). But a statute requiring a news medium to publish a reply offered to a statement made by it would apparently be unconstitutional. The party seeking to vindicate his reputation by self-help must find his own means of publication. If he finds the means, he may in some situations succeed in fully vindicating himself.

Self-help may be restored to, not only to reveal the falsity of the defamatory statement and to vindicate the reputation, but also to punish the defamer and retaliate against him. In earlier times the principal method of this type of self-help was the clan or blood feud. It was supplanted for a time by the challenge to a duel or the horsewhip. One of the primary reasons for developing the tort law of defamation was to induce the defamed person to resort to the courts for relief instead of wreaking his own vengeance. With the increasing unavailability of the damage remedy for defamation and the consequent heightened temptation to resort to extralegal methods like these which are presently regarded as uncivilized, the need grows for making available legal and civilized methods of protecting the defamed person's reputation. Development of a declaratory remedy seems best calculated to do this.

Further Reform of the Damage Remedy. The Supreme Court has on numerous occasions expressed concern regarding the rendering of verdicts for large sums of damages and the effect of this in unconstitutionally impairing freedom of speech and freedom of the press by producing a form of self-censorship to avoid the possibility of these verdicts. The Court has now held in Gertz v. Robert Welch, Inc., (1974) 418 U.S. 323, that the Constitution limits recoverable damages to "compensation for actual injury ... at least when liability is not based on a showing of knowledge of falsity or reckless disregard for the truth." But actual injury is "not limited to out-of-pocket loss" and may include "impairment of reputation and standing in the community, personal humiliation, and mental anguish and suffering." Although this places more restraint on discretion to determine the size of the damage award and gives more control over jury conduct to the courts, it still leaves a considerable amount of uncertainty regarding the ultimate figure. At the same time it leaves out one important element of pecuniary or out-of-pocket damages, for which the amount can be determined on an objective basis—the cost of reasonable attorney's fees.

The normal common law rule in America is not to award damages for attorney's fees in a tort action. At the same time it has been the traditional, though unexpressed, practice to treat the award for emotional distress as providing the funds for paying the plaintiff's counsel fees. The common law rule can be changed by a statute providing for recovery of the counsel fees. Since this might, however, create constitutional problems because of the potential overall size of verdicts, a provision in the statute would be advisable, indicating that if counsel fees are sought, other damages will be limited to pecuniary loss. The statute might leave the election as to whether to seek attorney's fees and forego recovery for mental suffering to the plaintiff, or it might make the choice for him.

DIVISION SIX–A

PRIVACY

Chapter 28A

INVASION OF PRIVACY

§ 652A. General Principle

(1) One who invades the right of privacy of another is subject to liability for the resulting harm to the interests of the other.

(2) The right of privacy is invaded by

(a) unreasonable intrusion upon the seclusion of another, as stated in § 652B; or

(b) appropriation of the other's name or likeness, as stated in § 652C; or

(c) unreasonable publicity given to the other's private life, as stated in § 652D; or

(d) publicity that unreasonably places the other in a false light before the public, as stated in § 652E.

Comment:

a. History. The right of privacy has been defined as the right to be let alone. Prior to 1890 no English or American court had ever expressly recognized the existence of the right, although there were decisions that in retrospect appear to have protected it in one manner or another. In 1890 a noted article, by Warren and Brandeis, The Right to Privacy, in 4 Harv.L.Rev. 193, reviewed these cases, and concluded that they were in reality based upon a broader principle that was entitled to separate recognition. Although this conclusion was first rejected in Michigan and New York, it was accepted by the Georgia court in Pavesich v. New England Life Insurance Co. (1905) 122 Ga. 190, 50 S.E. 68. Following that decision, the existence of a right of privacy is now recognized in the great majority of the American jurisdictions that have considered the question.

b. Forms of invasion. As it has developed in the courts, the invasion of the right of privacy has been a complex of four distinct wrongs, whose only relation to one another is that each involves interference with the interest of the individual in leading, to some reasonable extent, a secluded and private life, free from the prying eyes, ears and publications of others. Even this nexus becomes tenuous in the case of the appropriation of name or likeness covered by § 652C, which appears rather to confer something analogous to a property right upon the individual. This Section states the four forms of invasion thus far recognized as tortious, and refers to following Sections in which each is dealt with.

c. Thus far, as indicated in the decisions of the courts, the four forms of invasion of the right of privacy stated in this Section are the ones that have clearly become crystallized and generally been held to be actionable as a matter of tort liability. Other forms may still appear, particularly since some courts, and in particular the Supreme Court of the United States, have spoken in very broad general terms of a somewhat undefined "right of privacy" as a ground for various constitutional decisions involving indeterminate civil and personal rights. These and other references to the right of privacy, particularly as a protection against various types of governmental interference and the compilation of elaborate written or computerized dossiers, may give rise to the expansion of the four forms of tort liability for invasion of privacy listed in this Section or the establishment of new forms. Nothing in this Chapter is intended to exclude the possibility of future developments in the tort law of privacy.

   d. *Overlapping of sections.* It is possible and not infrequent for privacy to be invaded by the same act or by a series of acts in two or more of the ways stated in §§ 652B to 652E. When this occurs, the plaintiff may maintain his action for invasion of privacy upon any or all of the grounds available to him. He may, however, have only one recovery of his damages upon one or all of the different grounds.

Illustration:

   1.   A breaks and enters B's home, steals a photograph of B, and publishes it to advertise his whiskey, together with false statements about B that would be highly objectionable to a reasonable man. A is subject to liability to B for invasion of privacy by intrusion upon B's seclusion, as stated in § 652B; by the appropriation of his likeness, as stated in § 652C; by giving publicity to B's private photograph, as stated in § 652D; and by giving publicity to B that places him in a false light before the public, as stated in § 652E. B may proceed upon any or all of these grounds, but he may have only one recovery of damages for invasion of privacy.

§ 652B. Intrusion Upon Seclusion

One who intentionally intrudes, physically or otherwise, upon the solitude or seclusion of another or his private affairs or concerns, is subject to liability to the other for invasion of his privacy, if the intrusion would be highly offensive to a reasonable person.

Comment:

   a. The form of invasion of privacy covered by this Section does not depend upon any publicity given to the person whose interest is invaded or to his affairs. It consists solely of an intentional interference with his interest in solitude or seclusion, either as to his person or as to his private affairs or concerns, of a kind that would be highly offensive to a reasonable man.

b. The invasion may be by physical intrusion into a place in which the plaintiff has secluded himself, as when the defendant forces his way into the plaintiff's room in a hotel or insists over the plaintiff's objection in entering his home. It may also be by the use of the defendant's senses, with or without mechanical aids, to oversee or overhear the plaintiff's private affairs, as by looking into his upstairs windows with binoculars or tapping his telephone wires. It may be by some other form of investigation or examination into his private concerns, as by opening his private and personal mail, searching his safe or his wallet, examining his private bank account, or compelling him by a forged court order to permit an inspection of his personal documents. The intrusion itself makes the defendant subject to liability, even though there is no publication or other use of any kind of the photograph or information outlined.

§ 652C. Appropriation of Name or Likeness

One who appropriates to his own use or benefit the name or likeness of another is subject to liability to the other for invasion of his privacy.

§ 652D. Publicity Given to Private Life

One who gives publicity to a matter concerning the private life of another is subject to liability to the other for invasion of his privacy, if the matter publicized is of a kind that

(a) would be highly offensive to a reasonable person, and

(b) is not of legitimate concern to the public.

Special Note on Relation of § 652D to the First Amendment to the Constitution. This Section provides for tort liability involving a judgment for damages for publicity given to true statements of fact. It has not been established with certainty that liability of this nature is consistent with the free-speech and free-press provisions of the First Amendment to the Constitution, as applied to state law through the Fourteenth Amendment. Since 1964, with the decision of New York Times Co. v. Sullivan, 376 U.S. 254, the Supreme Court has held that the First Amendment has placed a number of substantial restrictions on tort actions involving false and defamatory publications. These restrictions are treated in Division Five of this Restatement. See especially §§ 580A, 580B and 621.

The Supreme Court has rendered several decisions on invasion of the right of privacy involving this Section and § 652E. The case of Cox Broadcasting Co. v. Cohn (1975) 420 U.S. 469, holds that under the First Amendment there can be no recovery for disclosure of and publicity to facts that are a matter of public record. The case leaves open the question of whether liability can constitutionally be imposed for other private facts that would be highly offensive to a reasonable person and that are not of legitimate concern.

Comment on Clause (a):

c. *Highly offensive publicity.* The rule stated in this Section gives protection only against unreasonable publicity, of a kind highly offensive to the ordinary reasonable man. The protection afforded to the plaintiff's interest in his privacy must be relative to the customs of the time and place, to the occupation of the plaintiff and to the habits of his neighbors and fellow citizens. Complete privacy does not exist in this world except in a desert, and anyone who is not a hermit must expect and endure the ordinary incidents of the community life of which he is a part. Thus he must expect the more or less casual observation of his neighbors as to what he does, and that his comings and goings and his ordinary daily activities, will be described in the press as a matter of casual interest to others. The ordinary reasonable man does not take offense at a report in a newspaper that he has returned from a visit, gone camping in the woods or given a party at his house for his friends. Even minor and moderate annoyance, as for example through public disclosure of the fact that the plaintiff has clumsily fallen downstairs and broken his ankle, is not sufficient to give him a cause of action under the rule stated in this Section. It is only when the publicity given to him is such that a reasonable person would feel justified in feeling seriously aggrieved by it, that the cause of action arises.

Comment on Clause (b):

d. *Matter of legitimate public concern.* When the matter to which publicity is given is true, it is not enough that the publicity would be highly offensive to a reasonable person. The common law has long recognized that the public has a proper interest in learning about many matters. When the subject-matter of the publicity is of legitimate public concern, there is no invasion of privacy.

This has now become a rule not just of the common law of torts, but of the Federal Constitution as well. In the case of Cox Broadcasting Co. v. Cohn (1975) 420 U.S. 469, the Supreme Court indicated that an action for invasion of privacy cannot be maintained when the subject-matter of the publicity is a matter of "legitimate concern to the public." The Court held specifically that the "States may not impose sanctions for the publication of truthful information contained in official court records open to public inspection." Other language indicates that this position applies to public records in general.

It seems clear that the common law restrictions on recovery for publicity given to a matter of proper public interest will now become a part of the constitutional law of freedom of the press and freedom of speech. To the extent that the constitutional definition of a matter that is of legitimate concern to the public is broader than the definition given in any State, the constitutional definition will of course control. In the absence of additional holdings of the Supreme Court, the succeeding Comments are based on decisions at common law.

Illustration:

> 12. A state statute prohibits the public disclosure of the name of a victim of rape. In a news broadcast covering a prosecution for rape, a broadcasting company discloses the name of the victim, who had been identified in the indictment. A State decision awarding damages for invasion of privacy is unconstitutional.

§ 652E. Publicity Placing Person in False Light

One who gives publicity to a matter concerning another that places the other before the public in a false light is subject to liability to the other for invasion of his privacy, if

> **(a) the false light in which the other was placed would be highly offensive to a reasonable person, and**

> **(b) the actor had knowledge of or acted in reckless disregard as to the falsity of the publicized matter and the false light in which the other would be placed.**

Caveat:

The Institute takes no position on whether there are any circumstances under which recovery can be obtained under this Section if the actor did not know of or act with reckless disregard as to the falsity of the matter publicized and the false light in which the other would be placed but was negligent in regard to these matters.

Comment:

a. Nature of Section. The form of invasion of privacy covered by the rule stated in this Section does not depend upon making public any facts concerning the private life of the individual. On the contrary, it is essential to the rule stated in this Section that the matter published concerning the plaintiff is not true. The rule stated here is, however, limited to the situation in which the plaintiff is given publicity. On what constitutes publicity and the publicity of application to a simple disclosure, see § 652D, Comment a, which is applicable to the rule stated here.

   b. *Relation to defamation.* The interest protected by this Section is the interest of the individual in not being made to appear before the public in an objectionable false light or false position, or in other words, otherwise than as he is. In many cases to which the rule stated here applies, the publicity given to the plaintiff is defamatory, so that he would have an action for libel or slander under the rules stated in Chapter 24. In such a case the action for invasion of privacy will afford an alternative or additional remedy, and the plaintiff can proceed upon either theory, or both, although he can have but one recovery for a single instance of publicity.

   It is not, however, necessary to the action for invasion of privacy that the plaintiff be defamed. It is enough that he is given unreasonable and highly objectionable publicity that attributes to him characteristics, conduct or beliefs that are false, and so is placed before the public in a false position. When this is the case and the matter attributed to the plaintiff is not defamatory, the rule here stated affords a different remedy, not available in an action for defamation.

§ 652F.   Absolute Privileges

The rules on absolute privileges to publish defamatory matter stated in §§ 583 to 592A apply to the publication of any matter that is an invasion of privacy.

§ 652G.   Conditional Privileges

The rules on conditional privileges to publish defamatory matter stated in §§ 594 to 598A, and on the special privileges stated in §§ 611 and 612, apply to the publication of any matter that is an invasion of privacy.

§ 652I.   Personal Character of Right of Privacy

Except for the appropriation of one's name or likeness, an action for invasion of privacy can be maintained only by a living individual whose privacy is invaded.

DIVISION NINE

INTERFERENCE WITH ADVANTAGEOUS ECONOMIC RELATIONS

Chapter 37

INTERFERENCE WITH CONTRACT OR PROSPECTIVE CONTRACTUAL RELATION

§ 766. Intentional Interference with Performance of Contract by Third Person

One who intentionally and improperly interferes with the performance of a contract (except a contract to marry) between another and a third person by inducing or otherwise causing the third person not to perform the contract, is subject to liability to the other for the pecuniary loss resulting to the other from the failure of the third person to perform the contract.

Comment:

h. Inducing or otherwise causing. The word "inducing" refers to the situations in which A causes B to choose one course of conduct rather than another. Whether A causes the choice by persuasion or by intimidation, B is free to choose the other course if he is willing to suffer the consequences. Inducement operates on the mind of the person induced. The phrase "otherwise causing "refers to the situations in which A leaves B no choice, as, for example, when A imprisons or commits such a battery upon B that he cannot perform his contract with C, or when A destroys the goods that B is about to deliver to C. This is also the case when performance by B of his contract with C necessarily depends upon the prior performance by A of his contract with B and A fails to perform in order to disable B from performing for C. The rule stated in this Section applies to any intentional causation whether by inducement or otherwise. The essential thing is the intent to cause the result. If the actor does not have this intent, his conduct does not subject him to liability under this rule even if it has the unintended effect of deterring the third person from dealing with the other. (On purpose and intent, see Comment *j*).

i. Actor's knowledge of other's contract. To be subject to liability under the rule stated in this Section, the actor must have knowledge of the contract with which he is interfering and of the fact that he is interfering with the performance of the contract. Although the actor's conduct is in fact the cause of another's failure to perform a contract, the actor does not induce or otherwise intentionally cause that failure if he has no knowledge of the contract. But it is not necessary that the actor appreciate the legal significance of the facts giving rise to the contractual duty, at least in the case of an express contract. If he knows those facts, he is subject to liability even though he is mistaken as to their legal significance and believes that the agreement is not legally binding or has a different legal effect from what it is judicially held to have.

j. Intent and purpose. The rule stated in this Section is applicable if the actor acts for the primary purpose of interfering with the performance of the contract, and also if he desires to interfere, even though he acts for some other purpose in addition. The rule is broader, however, in its application than to cases in which the defendant has acted with this purpose or desire. It applies also to intentional interference, as that term is defined in § 8A, in which the actor does not act for the purpose of interfering with the contract or desire it but knows that the interference is certain or substantially certain to occur as a result of his action. The rule applies, in other words, to an interference that is incidental to the actor's independent purpose and desire but known to him to be a necessary consequence of his action.

The fact that this interference with the other's contract was not desired and was purely incidental in character is, however, a factor to be considered in determining whether the interference is improper. If the actor is not acting criminally nor with fraud or violence or other means wrongful in themselves but is endeavoring to advance some interest of his own, the fact that he is aware that he will cause interference with the plaintiff's contract may be regarded as such a minor and incidental consequence and so far removed from the defendant's objective that as against the plaintiff the interference may be found to be not improper. (See § 767, especially Comment *d*).

k. Means of interference. There is no technical requirement as to the kind of conduct that may result in interference with the third party's performance of the contract. The interference is often by inducement. The inducement may be any conduct conveying to the third person the actor's desire to influence him not to deal with the other. Thus it may be a simple request or persuasion exerting only moral pressure. Or it may be a statement unaccompanied by any specific request but having the same effect as if the request were specifically made. Or it may be a threat by the actor of physical or economic harm to the third person or to persons in whose welfare he is interested. Or it may be the promise of a benefit to the third person if he will refrain from dealing with the other.

On the other hand, it is not necessary to show that the third party was induced to break the contract. Interference with the third party's performance may be by prevention of the performance, as by physical force, by depriving him of the means of performance or by misdirecting the performance, as by giving him the wrong orders or information.

l.   Inducement by refusal to deal. A refusal to deal is one means by which a person may induce another to commit a breach of his contract with a third person. Thus A may induce B to break his contract with C by threatening not to enter into, or to sever, business relations with B unless B does break the contract. This situation frequently presents a nice question of fact. While, under the rule stated in this Section, A may not, without some justification induce B to break his contract with C, A is ordinarily free to refuse to deal with B for any reason or no reason. The difficult question of fact presented in this situation is whether A is merely exercising his freedom to select the persons with whom he will do business or is inducing B not to perform his contract with C. That freedom is not restricted by the relationship between B and C; and A's aversion to C is as legitimate a reason for his refusal to deal with B as his aversion to B. If he is merely exercising that freedom, he is not liable to C for the harm caused by B's choice not to lose A's business for the sake of getting C's.

On the other hand, if A, instead of merely refusing to deal with B and leaving B to make his own decision on what to do about it, goes further and uses his own refusal to deal or the threat of it as a means of affirmative inducement, compulsion or pressure to make B break his contract with C, he may be acting improperly and subject to liability under the rule stated in this Section.

Illustrations:

1.   Upon hearing of B's contract with C, A ceases to buy from B. When asked by B to explain his conduct, A replies that his reason is B's contract with C. Thereupon B breaks his contract

with C in order to regain A's business. A has not induced the breach and is not subject to liability to C under the rule stated in this Section.

2. Upon hearing of B's contract with C, A writes to B as follows: "I cannot tolerate your contract with C. You must call it off. I am sure that our continued relations will more than compensate you for any payment you may have to make to C. If you do not advise me within ten days that your contract with C is at an end, you may never expect further business from me." Thereupon B breaks his contract with C. A has induced the breach and is subject to liability under the rule stated in this Section.

m. Inducement by offer of better terms. Another method of inducing B to sever his business relations with C is to offer B a better bargain than that which he has with C. Here, as in the situation dealt with in Comment *l*, a nice question of fact is presented. A's freedom to conduct his business in the usual manner, to advertise his goods, to extol their qualities, to fix their prices and to sell them is not restricted by the fact that B has agreed to buy similar goods from C. Even though A knows of B's contract with C, he may nevertheless send his regular advertising to B and may solicit business in normal course. This conduct does not constitute inducement of breach of the contract. The illustration below is a case of solicitation that does constitute inducement.

Illustration:

3. A writes to B: "I know you are under contract to buy these goods from C. Therefore I offer you a special price way below my cost. If you accept this offer, you can break your contract with C, pay him something in settlement and still make money. I am confident that you will find it more satisfactory to deal with me than with C." As a result of this letter, B breaks his contract with C. A has induced the breach.

n. Making agreement with knowledge of the breach. One does not induce another to commit a breach of contract with a third person under the rule stated in this Section when he merely enters into an agreement with the other with knowledge that the other cannot perform both it and his contract with the third person. (Compare Comment *m*). For instance, B is under contract to sell certain goods to C. He offers to sell them to A, who knows of the contract. A accepts the offer and receives the goods. A has not induced the breach and is not subject to liability under the rule stated in this Section. In some cases, however, B may be enjoined at the suit of C from performing for A, or B may be compelled specifically to perform the contract with C. (On the normal availability of injunctive relief, see Comment *u*). In some cases, too, as in the case of a contract for the sale of land, the purchaser acquires an equitable interest good against subsequent transferees of the vendor who are not bona fide purchasers. The rules relating to the protection of this interest against subsequent transferees are not within the scope of this Restatement.

o.   Causation. The question whether the actor's conduct caused the third person to break his contract with the other raises an issue of fact. The reasonableness of the claimed reaction of the third person to the actor's conduct is material evidence on this issue, but it is not conclusive. Thus the fact that only a coward or a fool would have been influenced by the defendant's conduct is evidence that may warrant a finding that the third person was not in fact influenced by it. On the other hand, if other evidence establishes that the actor did in fact induce the third person's conduct, the actor is liable even though the third person was cowardly or foolish or otherwise unreasonable in permitting himself to be so influenced and is himself liable for his own misconduct. (See §§ 546–548).

p.   The person protected. The person protected by the rule stated in this Section is the specified person with whom the third person had a contract that the actor caused him not to perform. To subject the actor to liability under this rule, his conduct must be intended to affect the contract of a specific person. It is not enough that one has been prevented from obtaining performance of a contract as a result of the actor's conduct. (Cf. § 766A). Thus, if A induces B to break a contract with C, persons other than C who may be harmed by the action as, for example, his employees or suppliers, are not within the scope of the protection afforded by this rule, unless A intends to affect them. Even then they may not be able to recover unless A acted for the purpose of interfering with their contracts. (See § 767, Comment *h*). The rule does not require, however, that the person who loses the performance of the contract as a result of the conduct of the actor should be specifically mentioned by name. It is sufficient that he is identified in some manner,—that he is the person intended by the actor and understood by those whom the actor seeks to induce. Thus inducement to break a contract to purchase an identified brand of cigarettes, "Saspan," may subject the inducer to liability to the commercial source identified by that trade symbol, the "Russo–Germanic Alliance Co.," but not to other distributors who sell the product.

In some cases the expression of one's general opinions or advice may cause persons not to perform their contracts with another. Thus a prominent person's opinion that economic opportunities are greater in the West than in the East and his advice to young men in general that they "go West" may cause some young man to leave an existing employment in breach of his contract and seek new fortune in the

West. Again a person's lecture on the perils of eating meat may cause another to break his contract and cease buying meat from his butcher; or in a public lecture or private conversation, one may persuade others not to buy foreign or union made goods. The rule stated in this Section does not afford protection against harm thus caused. Only when the actor's conduct is intended to affect a specific person is the actor subject to liability under this rule.

q. Persons intended to be induced. When inducement of a breach of contract is involved, the situation is ordinarily one in which a single person is induced to commit a breach of a single contract. However, the situation may be one in which many persons are induced to act. Thus a boycott campaign may be intended to induce numerous persons to break their contracts with the plaintiff.

r. Ill will. Ill will on the part of the actor toward the person harmed is not an essential condition of liability under the rule stated in this Section. He may be liable even when he acts with no desire to harm the other. But the freedom to act in the manner stated in this Section may depend in large measure on the purposes of his conduct. Although the actor is acting for the purpose of advancing an interest of his own, that interest may not be of sufficient importance to make his interference one that is not improper and avoid liability. Satisfying one's spite or ill will is not an adequate basis to justify an interference and keep it from being improper. The presence or absence of ill will toward the person harmed may clarify the purposes of the actor's conduct and may be, accordingly, an important factor in determining whether the interference was improper.

s. "Malice." There are frequent expressions in judicial opinions that "malice "is requisite for liability in the cases treated in this Section. But the context and the course of the decisions make it clear that what is meant is not malice in the sense of ill will but merely "intentional interference without justification." Malicious conduct may be an obvious type of this interference, but it is only one of several types. Compare Introductory Note to Chapter 29 (Wrongful Prosecution of Criminal Proceedings). If the plaintiff is required to show malicious interference in this latter sense, however, it is sometimes held to impose upon him the burden of alleging and proving "lack of justification. "(See § 767, Comment *k*).

t. Damages. On the elements of damages, see § 774A. The cause of action is for pecuniary loss resulting from the interference. Recovery may be had also for consequential harms for which the interference was a legal cause. (See § 774A).

u. Equitable relief. In appropriate circumstances under the general rules relating to equitable relief (see §§ 933–951), one may be enjoined from conduct that would subject him to liability under the rule stated in this section.

v. Relation to action for breach of contract. The fact that the plaintiff has an available action for breach of contract against the third person does not prevent him from maintaining an action under the rule stated in this Section against the person who has induced or otherwise caused the breach. The two are both wrongdoers, and each is liable to the plaintiff for the harm caused to him by the loss of the benefits of the contract. (Compare § 875). Even a judgment obtained against the third person for the breach of contract will not bar the action under this Section so long as the judgment is not satisfied. Payments made by the third person in settlement of the claim against him must, however, be credited against the liability for causing the breach and so go to reduce the damages for the tort. (See § 774A(2)).

§ 766A. Intentional Interference With Another's Performance of His Own Contract

One who intentionally and improperly interferes with the performance of a contract (except a contract to marry) between another and a third person, by preventing the other from performing the contract or causing his performance to be more expensive or burdensome, is subject to liability to the other for the pecuniary loss resulting to him.

§ 766B. Intentional Interference With Prospective Contractual Relation

One who intentionally and improperly interferes with another's prospective contractual relation (except a contract to marry) is subject to liability to the other for the pecuniary harm resulting from loss of the benefits of the relation, whether the interference consists of

(a) inducing or otherwise causing a third person not to enter into or continue the prospective relation or

(b) preventing the other from acquiring or continuing the prospective relation.

Comment:

a. Cross-references. In order for the actor to be held liable, this Section requires that his interference be improper. The factors of importance in determining this issue are stated and explained in § 767, which must be read closely with this Section.

This Section uses the expression, "subject to liability," as defined in § 5, meaning that the actor is liable if his conduct was a legal cause of the interference and he has no defense to the action.

This Section is concerned only with intentional interference with prospective contractual relations, not yet reduced to contract. The rule for the actor's intentional interference with a third person's performance of his existing contract with the plaintiff is stated in § 766. The rule for the actor's intentional interference with the plaintiff's performance of his own contract with a third person is stated in § 766A. The rule for negligent interference with either a contract or prospective contractual relations is stated in § 766C.

b. Historical development and rationale. As early as 1621 the court of King's Bench held one liable to another in an action on the case for interfering with his prospective contracts by threatening to "mayhem and vex with suits" those who worked for or bought from him, "whereby they durst not work or buy. "Garrett v. Taylor, Cro.Jac. 567, 79 Eng.Rep. 485. In 1793, the same court held one similarly liable who shot at some African natives in order to prevent them from trading with the plaintiff until the debts claimed by the defendant were paid. Tarleton v. McGawley, Peake N.P. 205, 170 Eng.Rep. 153. Precedent for these decisions is found as early as the fifteenth century, and even earlier. Thus in 1410 it was said that "if the comers to my market are disturbed or beaten, by which I lose my toll, I shall have a good action of trespass on the case." 11 Hen. IV 47; see also (1356) 29 Edw. III 18. An action for threatening plaintiff's tenants in life and limb "so that they departed from their tenures to the plaintiff's damage" was not uncommon, and there was a special writ adapted to this complaint. See (1494) 9 Hen. VII 7, and Reg.Brev. III—quare tenentibus de vita et mutilatione membrorum suorum comminatus. In Keeble v. Hickeringill, (1706) 11 East 574, 103 Eng. Rep. 127, Holt, C.J., explains the "reason" and "principle" upon which liability in these cases was based and illustrates the application of the rule to a variety of situations.

In another line of cases liability was imposed upon one who diverted another's business by fraudulently palming off his own goods as those of the other, or by infringing another's trade mark or trade name. Liability was later extended to cases in which the diversion of business was accomplished by fraudulent misrepresentations of different types. Again, in an independent development, liability was imposed for loss of business caused by defamation of another in his business or profession or by disparagement of his goods. (See §§ 623A–629).

In all of these cases liability was imposed for interference with business expectancies and was not limited to interference with existing contracts; but in all of them the actor's conduct was characterized by violence, fraud or defamation, and was tortious in character.

In 1853 the decision in Lumley v. Gye, 2 El. & Bl. 216, 118 Eng.Rep. 749, which involved inducement of the breach of an existing contract, imposed liability when the means of inducement were not tortious in themselves, and it was the intentional interference with the relation that was the basis of liability. (See § 766, Comment *b*). Later English decisions, and notably Temperton v. Russell, [1893] 1 Q.B. 715, extended the same principle to interference with business relations that are merely prospective and potential.

c. *Type of relation.* The relations protected against intentional interference by the rule stated in this Section include any prospective contractual relations, except those leading to contracts to marry (see § 698), if the potential contract would be of pecuniary value to the plaintiff. Included are interferences with the prospect of obtaining employment or employees, the opportunity of selling or buying land or chattels or services, and any other relations leading to potentially profitable contracts. Interference with the exercise by a third party of an option to renew or extend a contract with the plaintiff is also included. Also included is interference with a continuing business or other customary relationship not amounting to a formal contract. In many respects, a contract terminable at will is closely analogous to the relationship covered by this Section. (See § 766, Comment *g* and § 768, Comment *i*).

The expression, prospective contractual relation, is not used in this Section in a strict, technical sense. It is not necessary that the prospective relation be expected to be reduced to a formal, binding contract. It may include prospective quasi-contractual or other restitutionary rights or even the voluntary conferring of commercial benefits in recognition of a moral obligation.

On interference with noncommercial expectancies involving pecuniary loss, see § 774B and the Special Note following it. Of course, interference with personal, social and political relations is not covered in either Section.

d. *Intent and purpose.* The intent required for this Section is that defined in § 8A. The interference with the other's prospective contractual relation is intentional if the actor desires to bring it about or if he knows that the interference is certain or substantially certain to occur as a result of his action. (See § 766, Comment *j*).

The interference, however, must also be improper. The factors to be considered in determining whether an interference is improper are stated in § 767. One of them is the actor's motive and another is the interest sought to be advanced by him. Together these factors mean that the actor's purpose is of substantial significance. If he had no desire to effectuate the interference by his action but knew that it would be a mere incidental result of conduct he was engaging in for another purpose, the interference may be found to be not improper. Other factors come into play here, however, particularly the nature of the actor's conduct. If the means used is innately wrongful, predatory in character, a purpose to produce the interference may not be necessary. On the other hand, if the sole purpose of the actor is to vent his ill will, the interference may be improper although the means are less blameworthy. For a more complete treatment see § 767, especially Comment *d*.

e. Inducing or otherwise causing. The cause of action arising under the rule stated in this Section closely parallels that covered by § 766, and Comments *h, k, l* and m under that Section are applicable here so far as they are pertinent. The fact that the interference is not with a subsisting contract but only with a prospective relation not yet reduced to contract form is, however, important in determining whether the actor was acting properly in pursuing his own purposes. (See §§ 767 and 768). If the means of interference is itself tortious, as in the case of defamation, injurious falsehood, fraud, violence or threats, there is no greater justification to interfere with prospective relations than with existing contracts; but when the means adopted is not innately wrongful and it is only the resulting interference that is in question as a basis of liability, the interference is more likely to be found to be not improper.

f. Malice and ill will. On this, see § 766, Comments *r* and *s*.

g. Damages and equitable relief. On these, see § 766, Comments *t* and *u*.

§ 766C. Negligence Interference With Contract or Prospective Contractual Relation

One is not liable to another for pecuniary harm not deriving from physical harm to the other, if that harm results from the actor's negligently

(a) causing a third person not to perform a contract with the other, or

(b) interfering with the other's performance of his contract or making the performance more expensive or burdensome, or

(c) interfering with the other's acquiring a contractual relation with a third person.

§ 767. Factors in Determining Whether Interference Is Improper

In determining whether an actor's conduct in intentionally interfering with a contract or a prospective contractual relation of another is improper or not, consideration is given to the following factors:

(a) the nature of the actor's conduct,

(b) the actor's motive,

(c) the interests of the other with which the actor's conduct interferes,

(d) the interests sought to be advanced by the actor,

(e) the social interests in protecting the freedom of action of the actor and the contractual interests of the other,

(f) the proximity or remoteness of the actor's conduct to the interference and

(g) the relations between the parties.

Comment on Clause (b):

d. The actor's motive. Since interference with contractual relations is an intentional tort, it is required that in any action based upon §§ 766, 766A or 766B the injured party must show that the interference with his contractual relations was either desired by the actor or known by him to be a substantially certain result of his conduct. (See § 8A). Intent alone, however, may not be sufficient to make the interference improper, especially when it is supplied by the actor's knowledge that the interference was a necessary consequence of his conduct rather than by his desire to bring it about. In determining whether the interference is improper, it may become very important to ascertain whether the actor was motivated, in whole or in part, by a desire to interfere with the other's contractual relations. If this was the sole motive the interference is almost certain to be held improper. A motive to injure another or to vent one's ill will on him serves no socially useful purpose.

The desire to interfere with the other's contractual relations need not, however, be the sole motive. If it is the primary motive it may carry substantial weight in the balancing process and even if it is only a casual motive it may still be significant in some circumstances. On the other hand, if there is no desire at all to accomplish the interference and it is brought about only as a necessary consequence of the conduct of the actor engaged in for an entirely different purpose, his knowledge of this makes the interference intentional, but the factor of motive carries little weight toward producing a determination that the interference was improper.

Motive as a factor is often closely interwoven with the other factors listed in this Section, so that they cannot be easily separated. There is obviously a very intimate relation between the factors of motive and of the interests that the actor is trying to promote by his conduct. So close is the relationship that the two factors might well be merged into a single one. The basis for the separation in this Section is that the factor of motive is concerned with the issue of whether the actor desired to bring about the interference as the sole or a partial reason for his conduct, while the factor of the actor's interests is concerned with the individual and social value or significance of any interests that he is seeking to promote.

The relation of the factor of motive to that of the nature of the actor's conduct is an illustration of the interplay between factors in reaching a determination of whether the actor's conduct was improper. If the conduct is independently wrongful—as, for example, if it is illegal because it is in restraint of trade or if it is tortious toward the third person whose conduct is influenced—the desire to interfere with the other's contractual relations may be less essential to a holding that the interference is improper. On the other hand, if the means used by the actor are innocent or less blameworthy, the desire to accomplish the interference may be more essential to a holding that the interference is improper.

A similar interplay exists between the factor of motive and that of the proximity of the actor's conduct to the actual interference. If the relationship is direct and immediate, as when A induces B to sell a particular article to him, knowing that B is under contract to sell it to C, it makes no difference that A did not desire to have the contract broken between B and C or that he is quite sorry that this was a necessary consequence of his action. On the other hand, if in the same situation A also knows that C has contracted to sell the chattel to D and that his conduct will also prevent that contract from being carried out, this result is so consequential and indirect that a motive or purpose to accomplish that interference may be necessary to a finding that the interference was improper.

Comment on Clause (c):

e.   The interests of the other with which the actor's conduct interferes. Some contractual interests receive greater protection than others. Thus, depending upon the relative significance of the other factors, the actor's conduct in interfering with the other's prospective

175

contractual relations with a third party may be held to be not improper, although his interference would be improper if it involved persuading the third party to commit a breach of an existing contract with the other. (See, for example, § 768). The result in the latter case is due in part to the greater definiteness of the other's expectancy and his stronger claim to security for it and in part to the lesser social utility of the actor's conduct. Again, the fact that a contract violates public policy, as, for example, a contract in unreasonable restraint of trade, or that its performance will enable the party complaining of the interference to maintain a condition that shocks the public conscience (see § 774), may justify an inducement of breach that, in the absence of this fact, would be improper. Even with reference to contracts not subject to these objections, however, it may be found to be not improper to induce breach when the inducement is justified by the other factors stated in this Section. (See, for example, § 770).

Comment on Clause (d):

  f.   The actor's interest. The correlative of the interest with which the actor interferes (see Comment *e*) is the interest that his conduct is intended to promote. Both are important in determining whether the interference is improper. And both are to be appraised in the light of the social interests that would be advanced by their protection.

  Usually the actor's interest will be economic, seeking to acquire business for himself. An interest of this type is important and will normally prevail over a similar interest of the other if the actor does not use wrongful means. (See § 768). If the interest of the other has been already consolidated into the binding legal obligation of a contract, however, that interest will normally outweigh the actor's own interest in taking that established right from him. Of course, the interest in gratifying one's feeling of ill will toward another carries no weight. Some interests of the actor that do carry weight are depicted in §§ 770–773.

  In some cases the actor may be seeking to promote not solely an interest of his own but a public interest. The actor may believe that certain practices used in another's business are prejudicial to the public interest, as, for example, his maintenance of a gambling den in the rear room of his cigar store and in plain sight of his patrons, or his despoiling the environment by polluting a stream or strip-mining an area without restoring the natural conditions, or his racial or sexual discrimination in his employment policy. If the actor causes a third person not to perform a contract or not to enter into or continue a contractual relation with the other in order to protect the public interest affected by these practices, relevant questions in determining whether his interference is improper are: whether the practices are actually being used by the other, whether the actor actually believes that the practices are prejudicial to the public interest, whether his belief is reasonable, whether he is acting in good faith for the protection of the public interest, whether the contractual relation involved is incident or foreign to the continuance of the practices and whether the actor employs wrongful means to accomplish the result.

Comment on Clause (e):

g. *The social interests*. Appraisal of the private interests of the persons involved may lead to a stalemate unless the appraisal is enlightened by a consideration of the social utility of these interests. Moreover, the rules stated in §§ 766–766B deal with situations affecting both the existence and the plan of competitive enterprise. The social interest in this enterprise may frequently require the sacrifice of the claims of the individuals to freedom from interference with their pursuit of gain. Thus it is thought that the social interest in competition would be unduly prejudiced if one were to be prohibited from in any manner persuading a competitor's prospective customers not to deal with him. On the other hand, both social and private interests concur in the determination that persuasion only by suitable means is permissible, that predatory means like violence and fraud are neither necessary nor desirable incidents of competition. (See further § 768).

Comment on Clause (f):

h. *Proximity or remoteness of actor's conduct to interference.* One who induces a third person not to perform his contract with another interferes directly with the other's contractual relation. The interference is an immediate consequence of the conduct, and the other factors need not play as important a role in the determination that the actor's interference was improper. The actor's conduct need not be predatory or independently tortious, for example, and mere knowledge that this consequence is substantially certain to result may be sufficient.

If, however, A induces B to sell certain goods to him and thereby causes him not to perform his contract to supply the goods to C, this may also have the effect of preventing C from performing his contractual obligations to supply them to D and E. C's failure to perform his contracts is a much more indirect and remote consequence of A's conduct than B's breach of his contract with C, even assuming that A was aware of all of the contractual obligations and the interference can be called intentional. This remoteness conduces toward a finding that the interference was not improper. The weight of this factor, however, may be controverted by the factor of motive if it was the actor's primary purpose to interfere with C's obligation to D and E, or perhaps by the factor of the actor's conduct if that conduct was inherently unlawful or independently tortious. Similar results follow in cases in which the person whose contract was the subject of the initial interference has contracts of his own with his employees, his subcontractors or his suppliers, which he is now unable to perform.

Recovery for A's interference with B's obtaining performance of a contract by C by preventing B from performing himself and thus becoming entitled to C's performance may also be affected by this factor. The injury to B is his failure to obtain the benefit of C's performance. That consequence is an indirect one and if it was not a part of A's motivation but a mere incidental result of his conduct and if that conduct was not independently tortious or unlawful, the interference will ordinarily be held not to be improper.

Comment on Clause (g):

i. Relations between the parties. The relation between the parties is often an important factor in determining whether an interference is proper or improper. In a case where A is the actor, B is the injured party and C is the third party influenced by A's conduct, the significant relationship may be between any two of the three parties. Thus A and B may be competitors, and A's conduct in inducing C not to deal with B may be proper, though it would have been improper if he had not been a competitor. (See § 768). Or, if A is C's business advisor, it is proper for him to advise C, in good faith and within the scope of C's request for advice, that it would be to his financial advantage to break his contract with B, while it would be improper if he were a volunteer. (See § 772). Again, it is important whether the relationship between B and C is that of a prospective contract, an existing contract or a contract terminable at will. (See § 768).

j. Determination of whether the actor's conduct is improper or not. The weighing process described in this Section does not necessarily reach the same result in regard to each of the three forms of interference with business relations stated in §§ 766, 766A and 766B. As indicated in Comment *e*, for example, greater protection is given to the interest in an existing contract than to the interest in acquiring prospective contractual relations, and as a result permissible interference is given a broader scope in the latter instance. (See § 768). In some situations the process of weighing the conflicting factors set forth in this Section has already been performed by the courts, and incipient privileges and rules defining conduct as not improper are developing. When this has been accomplished and the scope of the more or less crystallized rule or privilege has been indicated by the decisions, the responsibility in the particular case is simply to apply it to the facts involved; and there is no need to go through the balancing process afresh. Some of the situations in which this development has occurred are stated in §§ 769–773.

When no crystallized pattern is applicable, however, the balancing process must be followed for the individual case. Though consideration must be given to the factors stated in this Section, generalizations utilizing a standard are sometimes offered. Thus, it has been suggested that the real question is whether the actor's conduct was fair and reasonable under the circumstances. Recognized standards of business ethics and business customs and practices are pertinent, and consideration is given to concepts of fair play and whether the defendant's interference is not "sanctioned by the 'rules of the game.'" The determination is whether the actor's interference is "improper" or not. But an attempt to apply these broad, general standards is materially helped by breaking the conflicting elements into the factors stated in this Section.

k. Burden of proof. The intentional tort of interference with contractual relations differs from most other intentional torts, which have rather clearly defined requirements for establishing a prima facie case and for setting up an affirmative defense based upon a privilege. This tort has not fully developed to this stage and some of the factors stated in this Section may be significant in ascertaining whether the actor's conduct is to be regarded as initially wrongful or culpable in nature. This tort is sometimes treated like the tort of negligence, with the result that it is a part of the plaintiff's case to show all of the factors making the defendant's interference improper. This is especially true in jurisdictions where the courts speak of malicious interference and define it as meaning intentional interference without justification. (See Comment *b*).

DIVISION TEN

INVASIONS OF INTERESTS IN LAND OTHER THAN BY TRESPASS

Chapter 40

NUISANCE

TOPIC 1. TYPES OF NUISANCE

179

TOPIC 1. TYPES OF NUISANCE

§ 821A. Types of Nuisance

In this Restatement "nuisance" is used to denote either

> **(a) a public nuisance as defined in s 821B, or**

> **(b) a private nuisance as defined in s 821D.**

Comment:

a. This Section is intended to be exclusive. Any harm to person or property that does not fall within either of the two stated categories is not a nuisance and is not included within any of the Sections of this Chapter. It may possibly result in liability based on other grounds such as ordinary negligence, but the particular rules stated as applicable to nuisances do not apply to it.

b. Meaning of "nuisance." The term frequently is used in several different senses. In popular speech it often has a very loose connotation of anything harmful, annoying, offensive or inconvenient, as when it is said that a man makes a nuisance of himself by bothering others. Occasionally this careless usage has crept into a court opinion. If the term is to have any definite legal significance, these cases must be completely disregarded.

In its legal significance, "nuisance" has been employed in three different senses:

(1). It is often used to denote human activity or a physical condition that is harmful or annoying to others. Thus it is often said that indecent conduct or a rubbish heap or the smoking chimney of a factory is a nuisance.

(2). It is often used to denote the harm caused by the human conduct or physical condition described in the first meaning. Thus it may be said that the annoyance caused by loud noises or by objectionable odors is a nuisance to the person affected by them.

When the word is used in either of these two senses it does not necessarily connote tort liability. The courts that use the word in either sense will often proceed to discuss whether the particular "nuisance" is actionable and may conclude that it is not.

(3). Often, however, the term has been used to denote both the conduct or condition and the resulting harm with the addition of the legal liability that arises from the combination of the two. Thus the courts may say that a person is maintaining a nuisance, meaning that he is engaged in an activity or is creating a condition that is harmful or annoying to others and for which he is legally liable; or they may distinguish between a "nuisance per se," meaning harmful conduct of a kind that always results in liability and a "nuisance per accidens," meaning harmful conduct that results in liability only under particular circumstances.

§ 821B. Public Nuisance

(1) A public nuisance is an unreasonable interference with a right common to the general public.

(2) Circumstances that may sustain a holding that an interference with a public right is unreasonable include the following:

(a) Whether the conduct involves a significant interference with the public health, the public safety, the public peace, the public comfort or the public convenience, or

(b) whether the conduct is proscribed by a statute, ordinance or administrative regulation, or

(c) whether the conduct is of a continuing nature or has produced a permanent or long-lasting effect, and, as the actor knows or has reason to know, has a significant effect upon the public right.

§ 821C. Who Can Recover for Public Nuisance

(1) In order to recover damages in an individual action for a public nuisance, one must have suffered harm of a kind different from that suffered by other members of the public exercising the right common to the general public that was the subject of interference.

(2) In order to maintain a proceeding to enjoin to abate a public nuisance, one must

(a) have the right to recover damages, as indicated in Subsection (1), or

(b) have authority as a public official or public agency to represent the state or a political subdivision in the matter, or

(c) have standing to sue as a representative of the general public, as a citizen in a citizen's action or as a member of a class in a class action.

§ 821D. Private Nuisance

A private nuisance is a nontrespassory invasion of another's interest in the private use and enjoyment of land.

§ 821F. Significant Harm

There is liability for a nuisance only to those to whom it causes significant harm, of a kind that would be suffered by a normal person in the community or by property in normal condition and used for a normal purpose.

Comment:

a. The rule stated in this Section is applicable to both public and private nuisances.

b. Liability—Damages—Injunction. The rule stated in this Section applies only to tort liability in an action for damages. A public nuisance may be prosecuted criminally although it has not yet resulted in any significant harm, or indeed any harm to anyone. Its tendency to cause harm may make it a sufficient interference with the public right to be a public nuisance and so a crime. Again, either a public or a private nuisance may be enjoined because harm is threatened that would be significant if it occurred, and that would make the nuisance actionable under the rule here stated, although no harm has yet resulted. (See §§ 933–951). The recovery of damages in a tort action is, however, limited to those who have in fact suffered significant harm of the kind stated in this Section.

c. Significant harm. By significant harm is meant harm of importance, involving more than slight inconvenience or petty annoyance. The law does not concern itself with trifles, and therefore there must be a real and appreciable invasion of the plaintiff's interests before he can have an action for either a public or a private nuisance. In the case of a public nuisance, he can maintain his action for damages only if he has suffered particular harm, of a kind different from that suffered by other members of the public exercising the public right. (See § 821C). This particular harm must be significant in character or, even though it is different in kind, the action cannot be maintained. Likewise in the case of a private nuisance, there must be a real and appreciable interference with the plaintiff's use or enjoyment of his land before he can have a cause of action.

d. Hypersensitive persons or property. When an invasion involves a detrimental change in the physical condition of land, there is seldom any doubt as to the significant character of the invasion. When, however, it involves only personal discomfort or annoyance, it is sometimes difficult to determine whether the invasion is significant. The standard for the determination of significant character is the standard of normal persons or property in the particular locality. If normal persons living in the community would regard the invasion in question as definitely offensive, seriously annoying or intolerable, then the invasion is significant. If normal persons in that locality would not be substantially annoyed or disturbed by the situation, then the invasion is not a significant one, even though the idiosyncrasies of the particular plaintiff may make it unendurable to him. Rights and privileges as to the use and enjoyment of land are based on the general standards of normal persons in the community and not on the standards of the individuals who happen to be there at the time.

Thus a hypersensitive nervous invalid cannot found an action for a private nuisance upon the normal ringing of a church bell across the street from his house, on the ground that the noise has become so unbearable to him that it throws him into convulsions and threatens his health or even his life, if a normal member of the community would regard the sound as unobjectionable or at most a petty annoyance. This is true also when the harm to the plaintiff results only because of the hypersensitive condition of his land or chattels or his abnormal use of them. Thus an ordinary power line supplying electric current for household use does not create a nuisance when it interferes by induction with highly sensitive electrical instruments operating in the vicinity.

On the other hand, when the invasion is of a kind that the normal individual in the community would find definitely annoying or offensive, the fact that those who live in the neighborhood are hardened to it and have no objection will not prevent the plaintiff from maintaining his action. For example, the noise of a boiler factory next door may be a private nuisance even though the plaintiff and others who live in the vicinity are stone deaf and cannot hear it. The deafness of the plaintiff himself will affect the damages that he can recover, but it does not prevent the existence of a genuine interference with the use and enjoyment of his land as, for example, for the purpose of entertaining guests.

Illustrations:

1. A and his friends customarily play croquet on A's front lawn, making a moderate amount of noise by conversation and the impact of croquet balls, which the normal individual in the community would not find to be objectionable. B, a nervous invalid who lives next door, is driven to distraction by the noise and made seriously ill. B cannot recover from A for a private nuisance.

2. A operates a race track, which is illuminated at night by flood lights directed downward. B operates next door an open-air motion picture theater, screened off from the highway. The reflection of A's lights, equivalent to the light of the full moon, would be harmless and unobjectionable to anyone making a normal use of adjoining land, but so seriously interferes with the operation of B's motion pictures that B loses customers. B cannot recover from A for a private nuisance.

3. A operates a slaughterhouse, which gives off highly offensive odors, sufficient to make life unendurable for any normal person living near it. B, who lives next door is without any sense of smell, and is not personally troubled by the odors. B can recover from A for a private nuisance.

e. Particular community. The location, character and habits of the particular community are to be taken into account in determining what is offensive or annoying to a normal individual living in it. Thus the odors of a hen house, which would be highly objectionable in a residential area in a city, may be acceptable and normally regarded as harmless and inoffensive in a rural district.

f. Normal mental reactions. In determining whether the harm would be suffered by a normal member of the community, fears and other mental reactions common to the community are to be taken into account, even though they may be without scientific foundation or other support in fact. Thus the presence of a leprosy sanatarium in the vicinity of a group of private residences may seriously interfere with the use and enjoyment of land because of the normal fear that it creates of possible contagion, even though leprosy is in fact so rarely transmitted through normal contacts that there is no practical possibility of communication of the disease.

g. Duration or frequency of invasion. It is often said by the courts and commentators that in order to constitute a nuisance the interference must continue or recur over some period of time. These statements usually are true for the particular facts or issue giving rise to them. Significant harm is necessary for a private nuisance or to a private action for a public nuisance and continuance or recurrence of the interference is often necessary to make the harm significant.

Likewise, if the harm was not foreseeable in the first instance, some continuance or recurrence may be required to establish the defendant's intent to invade the plaintiff's interests or his negligence regarding those interests. (See § 822). So also, the duration or frequency of the invasion is a factor to be considered in determining the gravity of the harm in comparison with the utility of the conduct of the defendant. (See §§ 826–831). Finally, the suit frequently is one for injunction against the continuance of the nuisance, and some continuance or recurrence is normally required as a basis for the injunction.

The decisions do not, however, support a categoric requirement of continuance or recurrence in all cases as an established rule of law. If the defendant's interference with the public right or with the use and enjoyment of land causes significant harm and his conduct is otherwise sufficient to subject him to liability for a nuisance, liability will result, however brief in duration the interference or the harm may be. Thus when a magazine of explosives, which has caused no harm, explodes and shakes the plaintiff's adjoining building to pieces, liability may be based on the ground of a private nuisance; and the same is true when the defendant, spraying his land with insecticide for five minutes, ruins the plaintiff's adjoining crops. So likewise, a public nuisance may consist of a single unlawful prize fight or indecent exposure or a two-minute obstruction of the public highway that causes particular harm such as personal injury to the plaintiff.

TOPIC 2. PRIVATE NUISANCE: ELEMENTS OF LIABILITY

§ 822. General Rule

One is subject to liability for a private nuisance if, but only if, his conduct is a legal cause of an invasion of another's interest in the private use and enjoyment of land, and the invasion is either

(a) intentional and unreasonable, or

(b) unintentional and otherwise actionable under the rules controlling liability for negligent or reckless conduct, or for abnormally dangerous conditions or activities.

§ 826. Unreasonableness of Intentional Invasion

An intentional invasion of another's interest in the use and enjoyment of land is unreasonable if

(a) the gravity of the harm outweighs the utility of the actor's conduct, or

(b) the harm caused by the conduct is serious and the financial burden of compensating for this and similar harm to others would not make the continuation of the conduct not feasible.

TOPIC 5. DEFENSES

§ 840D. Coming to the Nuisance

The fact that the plaintiff has acquired or improved his land after a nuisance interfering with it has come into existence is not in itself sufficient to bar his action, but it is a factor to be considered in determining whether the nuisance is actionable.

Comment:

a. The question involved in this Section arises when the plaintiff acquires land or moves onto it or improves the land, after a nuisance that interferes with the use or enjoyment of the land has come into existence. Prescriptive rights do not run in favor of the defendant until the nuisance has caused actual interference with the use and enjoyment of the land for the required period. When this has not occurred, the question becomes one of whether the defendant's priority in time and the plaintiff's voluntary choice to move in or to make improvements in the face of the existing nuisance will bar his recovery for it. There is some analogy here to assumption of risk as a defense. (Cf. § 840C).

b. The rule generally accepted by the courts is that in itself and without other factors, the "coming to the nuisance" will not bar the plaintiff's recovery. Otherwise the defendant by setting up an activity or a condition that results in the nuisance could condemn all the land in his vicinity to a servitude without paying any compensation, and so could arrogate to himself a good deal of the value of the adjoining land. The defendant is required to contemplate and expect the possibility that the adjoining land may be settled, sold or otherwise transferred and that a condition originally harmless may result in an actionable nuisance when there is later development.

Illustration:

1. A operates a brick kiln on his own land, which is adjacent to vacant land owned by B. The smoke, gas and fumes from the kiln do no harm to the vacant land. Before a prescriptive period has run, C buys the vacant land from B, moves in upon it and erects a dwelling and plants trees, vines and shrubbery. The operation of the brick kiln renders the occupation of the dwelling

uncomfortable and kills the planted vegetation. C is not barred from recovery by the fact that he has acquired and improved the land after the defendant's activity was already in existence.

c. Although it is not conclusive in itself, the fact that the plaintiff has "come to the nuisance" is still a factor of importance to be considered in cases where other factors are involved.

Illustrations:

2. A operates a copper smelter near the land of B. Smoke, fumes and gases from the smelter create a private nuisance interfering with the use and enjoyment of the land of B. For the sole purpose of bringing a lawsuit and forcing A to buy him out at a high price, C buys the land from B and moves in upon it. In his action for the private nuisance, the fact that C has acquired the land with the nuisance in existence, together with his purpose, will prevent his recovery.

3. A operates a brewery in a former residential area in which industrial plants are beginning to appear. The brewery noises, odors and smoke interfere with the use and enjoyment of the land of B adjoining it. C buys the land from B, moves in upon it and brings an action for the private nuisance. The fact that C has come to the nuisance, together with the changing character of the locality, may be sufficient to prevent recovery.

4. X City discharges its sewage into a slough connecting with a river. Plaintiff purchases land on the bank of the slough, sets up a shingle mill and rafts logs through the slough. With the growth of the city, the logs become increasingly coated with sewage, and the shingles are unfit for sale or use. The only other possible method of sewage disposal on the part of the city would involve prohibitive expense, out of all proportion to the harm done. This fact, together with the fact that plaintiff has come to the nuisance, may be held to prevent plaintiff's recovery for the public or the private nuisance.

DIVISION THIRTEEN

REMEDIES

Chapter 47

DAMAGES

TOPIC 1. GENERAL STATEMENTS

904.   General and Special Damages
905.   Compensatory Damages for Nonpecuniary Harm

TOPIC 2. DIMINUTION OF DAMAGES

TOPIC 1. GENERAL STATEMENTS

§ 904. General and Special Damages

(1) "General damages" are compensatory damages for a harm so frequently resulting from the tort that is the basis of the action that the existence of the damages is normally to be anticipated and hence need not be alleged in order to be proved.

(2) "Special damages" are compensatory damages for a harm other than one for which general damages are given.

§ 905. Compensatory Damages for Nonpecuniary Harm

Compensatory damages that may be awarded without proof of pecuniary loss include compensation

(a) for bodily harm, and

(b) for emotional distress.

§ 906. Compensatory Damages for Pecuniary Harm

Compensatory damages that will not be awarded without proof of pecuniary loss include compensation for

(a) harm to property,

(b) harm to earning capacity, and

(c) the creation of liabilities.

§ 908. Punitive Damages

(1) Punitive damages are damages, other than compensatory or nominal damages, awarded against a person to punish him for his outrageous conduct and to deter him and others like him from similar conduct in the future.

(2) Punitive damages may be awarded for conduct that is outrageous, because of the defendant's evil motive or his reckless indifference to the rights of others. In assessing punitive damages, the trier of fact can properly consider the character of the defendant's act, the nature and extent of the harm to the plaintiff that the defendant caused or intended to cause and the wealth of the defendant.

§ 910. Damages for Past, Present and Prospective Harms

One injured by the tort of another is entitled to recover damages from the other for all harm, past, present and prospective, legally caused by the tort.

§ 914. Expense of Litigation

(1) The damages in a tort action do not ordinarily include compensation for attorney fees or other expenses of the litigation.

(2) One who through the tort of another has been required to act in the protection of his interests by bringing or defending an action against a third person is entitled to recover reasonable compensation for loss of time, attorney fees and other expenditures thereby suffered or incurred in the earlier action.

§ 914A. Effect of Taxation

(1) The amount of an award of tort damages is not augmented or diminished because of the fact that the award is or is not subject to taxation.

(2) The amount of an award of tort damages is ordinarily not diminished because of the fact that although the award is not itself taxed, all or a part of it is to compensate for the loss of future benefits that would have been subject to taxation.

TOPIC 2. DIMINUTION OF DAMAGES

§ 918. Avoidable Consequences

(1) Except as stated in Subsection (2), one injured by the tort of another is not entitled to recover damages for any harm that he could have avoided by the use of reasonable effort or expenditure after the commission of the tort.

(2) One is not prevented from recovering damages for a particular harm resulting from a tort if the tortfeasor intended the harm or was aware of it and was recklessly disregardful of it, unless the injured person with knowledge of the danger of the harm intentionally or heedlessly failed to protect his own interests.

§ 920. Benefit to Plaintiff Resulting From Defendant's Tort

When the defendant's tortious conduct has caused harm to the plaintiff or to his property and in so doing has conferred a special benefit to the interest of the plaintiff that was harmed, the value of the benefit conferred is considered in mitigation of damages, to the extent that this is equitable.

Comment:

a. The rule stated in this Section normally requires that the damages allowable for an interference with a particular interest be diminished by the amount to which the same interest has been benefited by the defendant's tortious conduct. Thus if a surgeon performs an unprivileged operation resulting in pain and suffering, it may be shown that the operation averted future suffering. (See Illustration 1). If a surgeon has destroyed an organ of the body, it may be shown in mitigation that the operation improved other bodily functions. (See Illustration 2). Likewise one who has interfered with the physical condition of land can show in mitigation, except in cases like those dealt with in Comments c, d and f, that the change resulted in an improvement to the land. (See Illustration 3).

Illustrations:

1. A, a surgeon, having been directed to examine but not to operate upon B's ear, performs an operation that is painful but that averts future pain and suffering. The diminution in future pain is a factor to be considered in determining the amount of damages for the pain caused by the operation.

2. A, a surgeon, without B's consent, operates upon B's eye, causing B to lose the sight in that eye. In an action of battery, it may be shown in mitigation of damages for the loss of the eye that had A not operated, the sight of the other eye would have been lost.

3. A tortiously digs a channel through B's land, thereby making it impossible to grow crops upon the land through which the channel runs. It may be shown in mitigation that the digging

of the channel drains the remainder of B's land, making it more valuable.

§ 920A.   Effect of Payments Made to Injured Party

(1) A payment made by a tortfeasor or by a person acting for him to a person whom he has injured is credited against his tort liability, as are payments made by another who is, or believes he is, subject to the same tort liability.

(2) Payments made to or benefits conferred on the injured party from other sources are not credited against the tortfeasor's liability, although they cover all or a part of the harm for which the tortfeasor is liable.

RESTATEMENT OF THE LAW THIRD

TORTS

PRODUCTS LIABILITY

[*Editorial Note*: Restatement Third, Torts: Products Liability, promulgated in 1997, superseded the Institute's previous formulation of products-liability law, found primarily in the influential § 402A of Restatement Second, Torts, supra].

Chapter 1

LIABILITY OF COMMERCIAL PRODUCT SELLERS BASED ON PRODUCT DEFECTS AT TIME OF SALE

TOPIC 1. LIABILITY RULES APPLICABLE TO PRODUCTS GENERALLY

TOPIC 1. LIABILITY RULES APPLICABLE
TO PRODUCTS GENERALLY

§ 1. Liability of Commercial Seller or Distributor for Harm Caused by Defective Products

One engaged in the business of selling or otherwise distributing products who sells or distributes a defective product is subject to liability for harm to persons or property caused by the defect.

Comment:

a. History. This Section states a general rule of tort liability applicable to commercial sellers and other distributors of products generally. Rules of liability applicable to special products such as prescription drugs and used products are set forth in separate Sections in Topic 2 of this Chapter.

The liability established in this Section draws on both warranty law and tort law. Historically, the focus of products liability law was on manufacturing defects. A manufacturing defect is a physical departure from a product's intended design. See § 2(a). Typically, manufacturing defects occur in only a small percentage of units in a product line. Courts early began imposing liability without fault on product sellers for harm caused by such defects, holding a seller liable for harm caused by manufacturing defects even though all possible care had been exercised by the seller in the preparation and distribution of the product. In doing so, courts relied on the concept of warranty, in connection with which fault has never been a prerequisite to liability.

The imposition of liability for manufacturing defects has a long history in the common law. As early as 1266, criminal statutes imposed liability upon victualers, vintners, brewers, butchers, cooks, and other persons who supplied contaminated food and drink. In the late 1800s, courts in many states began imposing negligence and strict warranty liability on commercial sellers of defective goods. In the early 1960s, American courts began to recognize that a commercial seller of any product having a manufacturing defect should be liable in tort for harm caused by the defect regardless of the plaintiff's ability to maintain a traditional negligence or warranty action. Liability attached even if the manufacturer's quality control in producing the defective product was reasonable. A plaintiff was not required to be in direct privity with the defendant seller to bring an action. Strict liability in tort for defectively manufactured products merges the concept of implied warranty, in which negligence is not required, with the tort concept of negligence, in which contractual privity is not required. See § 2(a).

Questions of design defects and defects based on inadequate instructions or warnings arise when the specific product unit conforms to the intended design but the intended design itself, or its sale without adequate instructions or warnings, renders the product not reasonably safe. If these forms of defect are found to exist, then every unit in the same product line is potentially defective. See § 2, Comments *d, f,* and *i.* Imposition of liability for design defects and for defects based on inadequate instructions or warnings was relatively infrequent until the late 1960s and early 1970s. A number of restrictive rules made recovery for such defects, especially design defects, difficult to obtain. As these rules eroded, courts sought to impose liability without fault for design defects and defects due to inadequate instructions or warnings under the general principles of § 402A of the Restatement, Second, of Torts. However, it soon became evident that § 402A, created to deal with liability for manufacturing defects, could not appropriately be applied to cases of design defects or defects based on inadequate instructions or warnings. A product unit that fails to meet the manufacturer's design specifications thereby fails to perform its intended function and is, almost by definition, defective. However, when the product unit meets the manufacturer's own design specifications, it is necessary to go outside those specifications to determine whether the product is defective.

Sections 2(b) and 2(c) recognize that the rule developed for manufacturing defects is inappropriate for the resolution of claims of defective design and defects based on inadequate instructions or warnings. These latter categories of cases require determinations that the product could have reasonably been made safer by a better design or instruction or warning. Sections 2(b) and 2(c) rely on a reasonableness test traditionally used in determining whether an actor has been negligent. See Restatement, Second, Torts §§ 291–293. Nevertheless, many courts insist on speaking of liability based on the standards described in §§ 2(b) and 2(c) as being "strict."

Several factors help to explain this rhetorical preference. First, in many design defect cases, if the product causes injury while being put to a reasonably foreseeable use, the seller is held to have known of the risks that foreseeably attend such use. See § 2, Comment *m.* Second, some courts have sought to limit the defense of comparative fault in certain products liability contexts. In furtherance of this objective, they have avoided characterizing the liability test as based in negligence, thereby limiting the effect of comparative or contributory fault. See § 17, Comment *d.* Third, some courts are concerned that a negligence standard might be too forgiving of a small manufacturer who might be excused for its ignorance of risk or for failing to take adequate precautions to avoid risk. Negligence, which focuses on the conduct of the defendant-manufacturer, might allow a finding that a defendant with meager resources was not negligent because it was too burdensome for such a defendant to discover risks or to design or warn against them. The concept of strict liability, which focuses on the product rather than the conduct of the manufacturer, may help make the point that a defendant is held to the expert standard of knowledge available to the relevant manufacturing community at the time the product was manufactured. Finally, the liability of nonmanufacturing sellers in the distributive chain is strict. It is no defense that they acted reasonably and did not discover a defect in the product, be it from manufacturing, design, or failure to warn. See Comment *e*.

Thus, "strict products liability" is a term of art that reflects the judgment that products liability is a discrete area of tort law which borrows from both negligence and warranty. It is not fully congruent with classical tort or contract law. Rather than perpetuating confusion spawned by existing doctrinal categories, §§ 1 and 2 define the liability for each form of defect in terms directly addressing the various kinds of defects. As long as these functional criteria are met, courts may utilize the terminology of negligence, strict liability, or the implied warranty of merchantability, or simply define liability in the terms set forth in the black letter. See § 2, Comment *n*.

b. Sale or other distribution. The rule stated in this Section applies not only to sales transactions but also to other forms of commercial product distribution that are the functional equivalent of product sales. See § 20.

c. One engaged in the business of selling or otherwise distributing. The rule stated in this Section applies only to manufacturers and other commercial sellers and distributors who are engaged in the business of selling or otherwise distributing the type of product that harmed the plaintiff. The rule does not apply to a noncommercial seller or distributor of such products. Thus, it does not apply to one who sells foodstuffs to a neighbor, nor does it apply to the private owner of an automobile who sells it to another.

It is not necessary that a commercial seller or distributor be engaged exclusively or even primarily in selling or otherwise distributing the type of product that injured the plaintiff, so long as the sale of the product is other than occasional or casual. Thus, the rule applies to a motion-picture theater's routine sales of popcorn or ice cream, either for consumption on the premises or in packages to be taken home. Similarly, a service station that does mechanical repair work on cars may also sell tires and automobile equipment as part of its regular business. Such sales are subject to the rule in this Section. However, the rule does not cover occasional sales (frequently referred to as "casual sales") outside the regular course of the seller's business. Thus, an occasional sale of surplus equipment by a business does not fall within the ambit of this rule. Whether a defendant is a commercial seller or distributor within the meaning of this Section is usually a question of law to be determined by the court.

d. *Harm to persons or property.* The rule stated in this Section applies only to harm to persons or property, commonly referred to as personal injury and property damage. For rules governing economic loss, see § 21.

e. *Nonmanufacturing sellers or other distributors of products.* The rule stated in this Section provides that all commercial sellers and distributors of products, including nonmanufacturing sellers and distributors such as wholesalers and retailers, are subject to liability for selling products that are defective. Liability attaches even when such nonmanufacturing sellers or distributors do not themselves render the products defective and regardless of whether they are in a position to prevent defects from occurring. See § 2, Comment o. Legislation has been enacted in many jurisdictions that, to some extent, immunizes nonmanufacturing sellers or distributors from strict liability. The legislation is premised on the belief that bringing nonmanufacturing sellers or distributors into products liability litigation generates wasteful legal costs. Although liability in most cases is ultimately passed on to the manufacturer who is responsible for creating the product defect, nonmanufacturing sellers or distributors must devote resources to protect their interests. In most situations, therefore, immunizing nonmanufacturers from strict liability saves those resources without jeopardizing the plaintiff's interests. To assure plaintiffs access to a responsible and solvent product seller or distributor, the statutes generally provide that the nonmanufacturing seller or distributor is immunized from strict liability only if: (1) the manufacturer is subject to the jurisdiction of the court of plaintiff's domicile; and (2) the manufacturer is not, nor is likely to become, insolvent.

In connection with these statutes, two problems may need to be resolved to assure fairness to plaintiffs. First, as currently structured, the statutes typically impose upon the plaintiff the risk of insolvency of the manufacturer between the time an action is brought and the time a judgment can be enforced. If a nonmanufacturing seller or distributor is dismissed from an action at the outset when it appears that the manufacturer will be able to pay a judgment, and the manufacturer subsequently becomes insolvent and is unable to pay the judgment, the plaintiff may be left to suffer the loss uncompensated. One possible solution could be to toll the statute of limitations against nonmanufacturers so that they may be brought in if necessary. Second, a nonmanufacturing seller or distributor occasionally will be responsible for the introduction of a defect in a product even though it exercised reasonable care in handling or supervising the product in its control. In such instances, liability for a § 2(a) defect should be imposed on the nonmanufacturing seller or distributor. See § 2, Illustration 2.

§ 2. Categories of Product Defect

A product is defective when, at the time of sale or distribution, it contains a manufacturing defect, is defective in design, or is defective because of inadequate instructions or warnings. A product:

(a) contains a manufacturing defect when the product departs from its intended design even though all possible care was exercised in the preparation and marketing of the product;

(b) is defective in design when the foreseeable risks of harm posed by the product could have been reduced or avoided by the adoption of a reasonable alternative design by the seller or other distributor, or a predecessor in the commercial chain of distribution, and the omission of the alternative design renders the product not reasonably safe;

(c) is defective because of inadequate instructions or warnings when the foreseeable risks of harm posed by the product could have been reduced or avoided by the provision of reasonable instructions or warnings by the seller or other distributor, or a predecessor in the commercial chain of distribution, and the omission of the instructions or warnings renders the product not reasonably safe.

Comment:

a. Rationale. The rules set forth in this Section establish separate standards of liability for manufacturing defects, design defects, and defects based on inadequate instructions or warnings. They are generally applicable to most products. Standards of liability applicable to special product categories such as prescription drugs and used products are set forth in separate sections in Topic 2 of this Chapter.

The rule for manufacturing defects stated in Subsection (a) imposes liability whether or not the manufacturer's quality control efforts satisfy standards of reasonableness. Strict liability without fault in this context is generally believed to foster several objectives. On the premise that tort law serves the instrumental function of creating safety incentives, imposing strict liability on manufacturers for harm caused by manufacturing defects encourages greater investment in product safety than does a regime of fault-based liability under which, as a practical matter, sellers may escape their appropriate share of responsibility. Some courts and commentators also have said that strict liability discourages the consumption of defective products by causing the purchase price of products to reflect, more than would a rule of negligence, the costs of defects. And by eliminating the issue of manufacturer fault from plaintiff's case, strict liability reduces the transaction costs involved in litigating that issue.

Several important fairness concerns are also believed to support manufacturers' liability for manufacturing defects even if the plaintiff is unable to show that the manufacturer's quality control fails to meet risk-utility norms. In many cases manufacturing defects are in fact caused by manufacturer negligence but plaintiffs have difficulty proving it. Strict liability therefore performs a function similar to the concept of res ipsa loquitur, allowing deserving plaintiffs to succeed notwithstanding what would otherwise be difficult or insuperable problems of proof. Products that malfunction due to manufacturing defects disappoint reasonable expectations of product performance. Because manufacturers invest in quality control at consciously chosen levels, their knowledge that a predictable number of flawed products will enter the marketplace entails an element of deliberation about the amount of injury that will result from their activity. Finally, many believe that consumers who benefit from products without suffering harm should share, through increases in the prices charged for those products, the burden of unavoidable injury costs that result from manufacturing defects.

An often-cited rationale for holding wholesalers and retailers strictly liable for harm caused by manufacturing defects is that, as between them and innocent victims who suffer harm because of defective products, the product sellers as business entities are in a better position than are individual users and consumers to insure against such losses. In most instances, wholesalers and retailers will be able to pass liability costs up the chain of product distribution to the manufacturer. When joining the manufacturer in the tort action presents the plaintiff with procedural difficulties, local retailers can pay damages to the victims and then seek indemnity from manufacturers. Finally, holding retailers and wholesalers strictly liable creates incentives for them to deal only with reputable, financially responsible manufacturers and distributors, thereby helping to protect the interests of users and consumers. For considerations relevant to reducing nonmanufacturers' liability, see § 1, Comment *e*.

In contrast to manufacturing defects, design defects and defects based on inadequate instructions or warnings are predicated on a different concept of responsibility. In the first place, such defects cannot be determined by reference to the manufacturer's own design or marketing standards because those standards are the very ones that plaintiffs attack as unreasonable. Some sort of independent assessment of advantages and disadvantages, to which some attach the label "risk-utility balancing," is necessary. Products are not generically defective merely because they are dangerous. Many product-related accident costs can be eliminated only by excessively sacrificing product features that make products useful and desirable. Thus, the various trade-offs need to be considered in determining whether accident costs are more fairly and efficiently borne by accident victims, on the one hand, or, on the other hand, by consumers generally through the mechanism of higher product prices attributable to liability costs imposed by courts on product sellers.

Subsections (b) and (c), which impose liability for products that are defectively designed or sold without adequate warnings or instructions and are thus not reasonably safe, achieve the same general objectives as does liability predicated on negligence. The emphasis is on creating incentives for manufacturers to achieve optimal levels of safety in designing and marketing products. Society does not benefit from products that are excessively safe—for example, automobiles designed with maximum speeds of 20 miles per hour—any more than it benefits from products that are too risky. Society benefits most when the right, or optimal, amount of product safety is achieved. From a fairness perspective, requiring individual users and consumers to bear appropriate responsibility for proper product use prevents careless users and consumers from being subsidized by more careful users and consumers, when the former are paid damages out of funds to which the latter are forced to contribute through higher product prices.

In general, the rationale for imposing strict liability on manufacturers for harm caused by manufacturing defects does not apply in the context of imposing liability for defective design and defects based on inadequate instruction or warning. Consumer expectations as to proper product design or warning are typically more difficult to discern than in the case of a manufacturing defect. Moreover, the element of deliberation in setting appropriate levels of design safety is not directly analogous to the setting of levels of quality control by the manufacturer. When a manufacturer sets its quality control at a certain level, it is aware that a given number of products may leave the assembly line in a defective condition and cause injury to innocent victims who can generally do nothing to avoid injury. The implications of deliberately drawing lines with respect to product design safety are different. A reasonably designed product still carries with it elements of risk that must be protected against by the user or consumer since some risks cannot be designed out of the product at reasonable cost.

Most courts agree that, for the liability system to be fair and efficient, the balancing of risks and benefits in judging product design and marketing must be done in light of the knowledge of risks and risk-avoidance techniques reasonably attainable at the time of distribution. To hold a manufacturer liable for a risk that was not foreseeable when the product was marketed might foster increased manufacturer investment in safety. But such investment by definition would be a matter of guesswork. Furthermore, manufacturers may persuasively ask to be judged by a normative behavior standard to which it is reasonably possible for manufacturers to conform. For these reasons, Subsections (b) and (c) speak of products being defective only when risks are reasonably foreseeable.

b. *The nonexclusiveness of the definitions of defect in this Section.* When a plaintiff seeks recovery under the general rule of liability in § 1, in most instances the plaintiff must establish a prima facie case of product defect by satisfying the requirements of § 2. Section 2 is not, however, the exclusive means by which the plaintiff may establish liability in a products case based on the general rule in § 1. Some courts, for example, while recognizing that in most cases involving defective design the plaintiff must prove the availability of a reasonable alternative design, also observe that such proof is not necessary in every case involving design defects. Sections 3 and 4 and Comment *e* to § 2 provide approaches to the establishment of defective design other than that provided in § 2(b).

c. *Manufacturing defects.* As stated in Subsection (a), a manufacturing defect is a departure from a product unit's design specifications. More distinctly than any other type of defect, manufacturing defects disappoint consumer expectations. Common examples of manufacturing defects are products that are physically flawed, damaged, or incorrectly assembled. In actions against the manufacturer, under prevailing rules concerning allocation of burdens of proof the plaintiff ordinarily bears the burden of establishing that such a defect existed in the product when it left the hands of the manufacturer.

d. *Design defects: general considerations.* Whereas a manufacturing defect consists of a product unit's failure to meet the manufacturer's design specifications, a product asserted to have a defective design meets the manufacturer's design specifications but raises the question whether the specifications themselves create unreasonable risks. Answering that question requires reference to a standard outside the specifications. Subsection (b) adopts a reasonableness ("risk-utility balancing") test as the standard for judging the defectiveness of product designs. More specifically, the test is whether a reasonable alternative design would, at reasonable cost, have reduced the foreseeable risks of harm posed by the product and, if so, whether the omission of the alternative design by the seller or a predecessor in the distributive chain rendered the product not reasonably safe. (This is the primary, but not the exclusive, test for defective design. See Comment *b*.) Under prevailing rules concerning allocation of burden of proof, the plaintiff must prove that such a reasonable alternative was, or reasonably could have been, available at time of sale or distribution. See Comment *f*.

Assessment of a product design in most instances requires a comparison between an alternative design and the product design that caused the injury, undertaken from the viewpoint of a reasonable person. That approach is also used in administering the traditional reasonableness standard in negligence. See Restatement, Second, Torts § 283, Comment *c*. The policy reasons that support use of a reasonable-person perspective in connection with the general negligence standard also support its use in the products liability context.

How the defendant's design compares with other, competing designs in actual use is relevant to the issue of whether the defendant's design is defective. Defendants often seek to defend their product designs on the ground that the designs conform to the "state of the art." The term "state of the art" has been variously defined to mean that the product design conforms to industry custom, that it reflects the safest and most advanced technology developed and in commercial use, or that it reflects technology at the cutting edge of scientific knowledge. The confusion brought about by these various definitions is unfortunate. This Section states that a design is defective if the product could have been made safer by the adoption of a reasonable alternative design. If such a design could have been practically adopted at time of sale and if the omission of such a design rendered the product not reasonably safe, the plaintiff establishes defect under Subsection (b). When a defendant demonstrates that its product design was the safest in use at the time of sale, it may be difficult for the plaintiff to prove that an alternative design could have been practically adopted. The defendant is thus allowed to introduce evidence with regard to industry practice that bears on whether an alternative design was practicable. Industry practice may also be relevant to whether the omission of an alternative design rendered the product not reasonably safe. While such evidence is admissible, it is not necessarily dispositive. If the plaintiff introduces expert testimony to establish that a reasonable alternative design could practically have been adopted, a trier of fact may conclude that the product was defective notwithstanding that such a design was not adopted by any manufacturer, or even considered for commercial use, at the time of sale.

Early in the development of products liability law, courts held that a claim based on design defect could not be sustained if the dangers presented by the product were open and obvious. Subsection (b) does not recognize the obviousness of a design-related risk as precluding a finding of defectiveness. The fact that a danger is open and obvious is relevant to the issue of defectiveness, but does not necessarily preclude a plaintiff from establishing that a reasonable alternative design should have been adopted that would have reduced or prevented injury to the plaintiff.

The requirement in Subsection (b) that the plaintiff show a reasonable alternative design applies in most instances even though the plaintiff alleges that the category of product sold by the defendant is so dangerous that it should not have been marketed at all. See Comment *e*. Common and widely distributed products such as alcoholic beverages, firearms, and above-ground swimming pools may be found to be defective only upon proof of the requisite conditions in Subsection (a), (b), or (c). If such products are defectively manufactured or sold without reasonable warnings as to their danger when such warnings are appropriate, or if reasonable alternative designs could have been adopted, then liability under §§ 1 and 2 may attach. Absent proof of defect under those Sections, however, courts have not imposed liability for categories of products that are generally available and widely used and consumed, even if they pose substantial risks of harm. Instead, courts generally have concluded that legislatures and administrative agencies can, more appropriately than courts, consider the desirability of commercial distribution of some categories of widely used and consumed, but nevertheless dangerous, products.

Illustrations:

3. ABC Co. manufactured and sold a high-speed printing press to XYZ Printers, by whom Robert is employed. The press includes a circular plate cylinder that spins at a very high speed. On occasion, a foreign object, known in the trade as a "hickie," finds its way onto the plate of the unit, causing a blemish or imperfection on the printed page. To remove a hickie, it is customary practice for an employee to apply a piece of plastic to the printing plate while it is spinning. Robert performed this practice, known as "chasing the hickie," and while doing so suffered serious injuries to his hand. All employees, including Robert, knew that chasing the hickie was a dangerous procedure. Plaintiff's expert testifies that a safety-guard at the point of operation, which could have prevented Robert's injury, was both

technologically and economically feasible and is utilized in similar machinery without causing difficulty. The fact that the danger is open and obvious does not bar the design claim against ABC.

4. XYZ Co. manufactures above-ground swimming pools that are four feet deep. Warnings are embossed on the outside of the pools in large letters stating "DANGER—DO NOT DIVE—SHALLOW WATER." In disregard of the warnings, Mary, age 21, dove head first into an XYZ pool and suffered serious injury. Expert testimony establishes that when Mary's outstretched hands hit the pool's slippery vinyl bottom her hands slid apart, causing her to strike her head against the bottom of the pool. For the purposes of this Illustration it is assumed that the warnings were adequate and that the only issue is whether the above-ground pool was defectively designed because the bottom was too slippery. All the expert witnesses agree that the vinyl pool liner that XYZ utilized was the best and safest liner available and that no alternative, less slippery liner was feasible. Mary has failed to establish defective design under Subsection (b).

e. Design defects: possibility of manifestly unreasonable design. Several courts have suggested that the designs of some products are so manifestly unreasonable, in that they have low social utility and high degree of danger, that liability should attach even absent proof of a reasonable alternative design. In large part the problem is one of how the range of relevant alternative designs is described. For example, a toy gun that shoots hard rubber pellets with sufficient velocity to cause injury to children could be found to be defectively designed within the rule of Subsection (b). Toy guns unlikely to cause injury would constitute reasonable alternatives to the dangerous toy. Thus, toy guns that project ping-pong balls, soft gelatin pellets, or water might be found to be reasonable alternative designs to a toy gun that shoots hard pellets. However, if the realism of the hard-pellet gun, and thus its capacity to cause injury, is sufficiently important to those who purchase and use such products to justify the court's limiting consideration to toy guns that achieve realism by shooting hard pellets, then no reasonable alternative will, by hypothesis, be available. In that instance, the design feature that defines which alternatives are relevant—the realism of the hard-pellet gun andthus its capacity to injure—is precisely the feature on which the user places value and of which the plaintiff complains. If a court were to adopt this characterization of the product, and deem the capacity to cause injury an egregiously unacceptable quality in a toy for use by children, it could conclude that liability should attach without proof of a reasonable alternative design. The court would declare the product design to be defective and not reasonably safe because the extremely high degree of danger posed by its use or consumption so substantially outweighs its negligible social utility that no rational, reasonable person, fully aware of the relevant facts, would choose to use, or to allow children to use, the product.

Illustration:

> 5. ABC Co. manufactures novelty items. One item, an exploding cigar, is made to explode with a loud bang and the emission of smoke. Robert purchased the exploding cigar and presented it to his boss, Jack, at a birthday party arranged for him at the office. Jack lit the cigar. When it exploded, the heat from the explosion lit Jack's beard on fire causing serious burns to his face. If a court were to recognize the rule identified in this Comment, the finder of fact might find ABC liable for the defective design of the exploding cigar even if no reasonable alternative design was available that would provide similar prank characteristics. The utility of the exploding cigar is so low and the risk of injury is so high as to warrant a conclusion that the cigar is defective and should not have been marketed at all.

f. Design defects: factors relevant in determining whether the omission of a reasonable alternative design renders a product not reasonably safe. Subsection (b) states that a product is defective in design if the omission of a reasonable alternative design renders the product not reasonably safe. A broad range of factors may be considered in determining whether an alternative design is reasonable and whether its omission renders a product not reasonably safe. The factors include, among others, the magnitude and probability of the foreseeable risks of harm, the instructions and warnings accompanying the product, and the nature and strength of consumer expectations regarding the product, including expectations arising from product portrayal and marketing. See Comment *g.* The relative advantages and disadvantages of the product as designed and as it alternatively could have been designed may also be considered. Thus, the likely effects of the alternative design on production costs; the effects of the alternative design on product longevity, maintenance, repair, and esthetics; and the range of consumer choice among products are factors that may be taken into account. A plaintiff is not necessarily required to introduce proof on all of these factors; their relevance, and the relevance of other factors, will vary from case to case. Moreover, the factors interact with one another. For example, evidence of the magnitude and probability of foreseeable harm may be offset by evidence that the proposed alternative design would reduce the efficiency and the utility of the product. On the other hand, evidence that a proposed alternative design would increase production costs may be offset by evidence that product portrayal and marketing created substantial expectations of performance or safety, thus increasing the probability of foreseeable harm. Depending on the mix of these factors, a number of variations in the design of a given product may meet the test in Subsection (b). On the other hand, it is not a factor under Subsection (b) that the imposition of liability would have a negative effect on corporate earnings or would reduce employment in a given industry.

When evaluating the reasonableness of a design alternative, the overall safety of the product must be considered. It is not sufficient that the alternative design would have reduced or prevented the harm suffered by the plaintiff if it would also have introduced into the product other dangers of equal or greater magnitude.

While a plaintiff must prove that a reasonable alternative design would have reduced the foreseeable risks of harm, Subsection (b) does not require the plaintiff to produce expert testimony in every case. Cases arise in which the feasibility of a reasonable alternative design is obvious and understandable to laypersons and therefore expert testimony is unnecessary to support a finding that the product should have been designed differently and more safely. For example, when a manufacturer sells a soft stuffed toy with hard plastic buttons that are easily removable and likely to choke and suffocate a small child who foreseeably attempts to swallow them, the plaintiff should be able to reach the trier of fact with a claim that buttons on such a toy should be an integral part of the toy's fabric itself (or otherwise be unremovable by an infant) without hiring an expert to demonstrate the feasibility of an alternative safer design. Furthermore, other products already available on the market may serve the same or very similar function at lower risk and at comparable cost. Such products may serve as reasonable alternatives to the product in question.

In many cases, the plaintiff must rely on expert testimony. Subsection (b) does not, however, require the plaintiff to produce a prototype in order to make out a prima facie case. Thus, qualified expert testimony on the issue suffices, even though the expert has produced no prototype, if it reasonably supports the conclusion that a reasonable alternative design could have been practically adopted at the time of sale.

The requirements in Subsection (b) relate to what the plaintiff must prove in order to prevail at trial. This Restatement takes no position regarding the requirements of local law concerning the adequacy of pleadings or pretrial demonstrations of genuine issues of fact. It does, however, assume that the plaintiff will have the opportunity to conduct reasonable discovery so as to ascertain whether an alternative design is practical.

A test that considers such a broad range of factors in deciding whether the omission of an alternative design renders a product not reasonably safe requires a fair allocation of proof between the parties. To establish a prima facie case of defect, the plaintiff must prove the availability of a technologically feasible and practical alternative design that would have reduced or prevented the plaintiff's harm. Given inherent limitations on access to relevant data, the plaintiff is not required to establish with particularity the costs and benefits associated with adoption of the suggested alternative design.

In sum, the requirement of Subsection (b) that a product is defective in design if the foreseeable risks of harm could have been reduced by a reasonable alternative design is based on the common-sense notion that liability for harm caused by product designs should attach only when harm is reasonably preventable. For justice to be achieved, Subsection (b) should not be construed to create artificial and unreasonable barriers to recovery.

The necessity of proving a reasonable alternative design as a predicate for establishing design defect is, like any factual element in a case, addressed initially to the courts. Sufficient evidence must be presented so that reasonable persons could conclude that a reasonable alternative could have been practically adopted. Assuming that a court concludes that sufficient evidence on this issue has been presented, the issue is then for the trier of fact. This Restatement takes no position regarding the specifics of how a jury should be instructed. So long as jury instructions are generally consistent with the rule of law set forth in Subsection (b), their specific form and content are matters of local law.

g. *Consumer expectations: general considerations.* Under Subsection (b), consumer expectations do not constitute an independent standard for judging the defectiveness of product designs. Courts frequently rely, in part, on consumer expectations when discussing liability based on other theories of liability. Some courts, for example, use the term "reasonable consumer expectations" as an equivalent of "proof of a reasonable, safer design alternative," since reasonable consumers have a right to expect product designs that conform to the reasonableness standard in Subsection (b). Other courts, allowing an inference of defect to be drawn when the incident is of a kind that ordinarily would occur as a result of product defect, observe that products that fail when put to their manifestly intended use disappoint reasonable consumer expectations. See § 3. However, consumer expectations do not play a determinative role in determining defectiveness.

See Comment *h*. Consumer expectations, standing alone, do not take into account whether the proposed alternative design could be implemented at reasonable cost, or whether an alternative design would provide greater overall safety. Nevertheless, consumer expectations about product performance and the dangers attendant to product use affect how risks are perceived and relate to foreseeability and frequency of the risks of harm, both of which are relevant under Subsection (b). See Comment *f*. Such expectations are often influenced by how products are portrayed and marketed and can have a significant impact on consumer behavior. Thus, although consumer expectations do not constitute an independent standard for judging the defectiveness of product designs, they may substantially influence or even be ultimately determinative on risk-utility balancing in judging whether the omission of a proposed alternative design renders the product not reasonably safe.

Subsection (b) likewise rejects conformance to consumer expectations as a defense. The mere fact that a risk presented by a product design is open and obvious, or generally known, and that the product thus satisfies expectations, does not prevent a finding that the design is defective. But the fact that a product design meets consumer expectations may substantially influence or even be ultimately determinative on risk-utility balancing in judging whether the omission of a proposed alternative design renders the product not reasonably safe. It follows that, while disappointment of consumer expectations may not serve as an independent basis for allowing recovery under Subsection (b), neither may conformance with consumer expectations serve as an independent basis for denying recovery. Such expectations may be relevant in both contexts, but in neither are they controlling.

i. Inadequate instructions or warnings. Commercial product sellers must provide reasonable instructions and warnings about risks of injury posed by products. Instructions inform persons how to use and consume products safely. Warnings alert users and consumers to the existence and nature of product risks so that they can prevent harm either by appropriate conduct during use or consumption or by choosing not to use or consume. In most instances the instructions and warnings will originate with the manufacturer, but sellers down the chain of distribution must warn when doing so is feasible and reasonably necessary. In any event, sellers down the chain are liable if the instructions and warnings provided by predecessors in the chain are inadequate. See Comment *o*. Under prevailing rules concerning allocation of burdens of proof, plaintiff must prove that adequate instructions or warnings were not provided. Subsection (c) adopts a reasonableness test for judging the adequacy of product instructions and warnings. It thus parallels Subsection (b), which adopts a similar standard for judging the safety of product designs. Although the liability standard is formulated in essentially identical terms in Subsections (b) and (c), the defectiveness concept is more difficult to apply in the warnings context. In evaluating the adequacy of product warnings and instructions, courts must be sensitive to many factors. It is impossible to identify anything approaching a perfect level of detail that should be communicated in product disclosures. For example, educated or experienced product users and consumers may benefit from inclusion of more information about the full spectrum of product risks, whereas less-educated or unskilled users may benefit from more concise warnings and instructions stressing only the most crucial risks and safe-handling practices. In some contexts, products intended for special categories of users, such as children, may require more vivid and unambiguous warnings. In some cases, excessive detail may detract from the ability of typical users and consumers to focus on the important aspects of the warnings, whereas in others reasonably full disclosure will be necessary to enable informed, efficient choices by product users. Product warnings and instructions can rarely communicate all potentially relevant information, and the ability of a plaintiff to imagine a hypothetical better warning in the aftermath of an accident does not establish that the warning actually accompanying the product was inadequate. No easy guideline exists for courts to adopt in assessing the adequacy of product warnings and instructions. In making their assessments, courts must focus on various factors, such as content and comprehensibility, intensity of expression, and the characteristics of expected user groups.

Depending on the circumstances, Subsection (c) may require that instructions and warnings be given not only to purchasers, users, and consumers, but also to others who a reasonable seller should know will be in a position to reduce or avoid the risk of harm. There is no general rule as to whether one supplying a product for the use of others through an intermediary has a duty to warn the ultimate product user directly or may rely on the intermediary to relay warnings. The standard is one of reasonableness in the circumstances. Among the factors to be considered are the gravity of the risks posed by the product, the likelihood that the intermediary will convey the information to the ultimate user, and the feasibility and effectiveness of giving a warning directly to the user. Thus, when the purchaser of machinery is the owner of a workplace who provides the machinery to employees for their use, and there is reason to doubt that the employer will pass warnings on to employees, the seller is required to reach the employees directly with necessary instructions and warnings if doing so is reasonably feasible.

In addition to alerting users and consumers to the existence and nature of product risks so that they can, by appropriate conduct during use or consumption, reduce the risk of harm, warnings also may be needed to inform users and consumers of nonobvious and not generally known risks that unavoidably inhere in using or consuming the product. Such warnings allow the user or consumer to avoid the risk warned against by making an informed decision not to purchase or use the product at all and hence not to encounter the risk. In this context, warnings must be provided for inherent risks that reasonably foreseeable product users and consumers would reasonably deem material or significant in deciding whether to use or consume the product. Whether or not many persons would, when warned, nonetheless decide to use or consume the product, warnings are required to protect the interests of those reasonably foreseeable users or consumers who would, based on their own reasonable assessments of the risks and benefits, decline product use or consumption. When such warnings are necessary, their omission renders the product not reasonably safe at time of sale. Notwithstanding the defective condition of the product in the absence of adequate warnings, if a particular user or consumer would have decided to use or consume even if warned, the lack of warnings is not a legal cause of that plaintiff's harm. Judicial decisions supporting the duty to provide warnings for informed decisionmaking have arisen almost exclusively with regard to those toxic agents and pharmaceutical products with respect to which courts have recognized a distinctive need to provide risk information so that recipients of the information can decide whether they wish to purchase or utilize the product. See § 6, Comment d.

j. Warnings: obvious and generally known risks. In general, a product seller is not subject to liability for failing to warn or instruct regarding risks and risk-avoidance measures that should be obvious to, or generally known by, foreseeable product users. When a risk is obvious or generally known, the prospective addressee of a warning will or should already know of its existence. Warning of an obvious or generally known risk in most instances will not provide an effective additional measure of safety. Furthermore, warnings that deal with obvious or generally known risks may be ignored by users and consumers and may diminish the significance of warnings about non-obvious, not-generally-known risks. Thus, requiring warnings of obvious or generally known risks could reduce the efficacy of warnings generally. When reasonable minds may differ as to whether the risk was obvious or generally known, the issue is to be decided by the trier of fact. The obviousness of risk may bear on the issue of design defect rather than failure to warn. See Comments *d* and *g*.

k. Warnings: adverse allergic or idiosyncratic reactions. Cases of adverse allergic or idiosyncratic reactions involve a special subset of products that may be defective because of inadequate warnings. Many of these cases involve nonprescription drugs and cosmetics. However, virtually any tangible product can contain an ingredient to which some persons may be allergic. Thus, food, nonprescription drugs, toiletries, paint, solvents, building materials, clothing, and furniture have all been involved in litigation to which this Comment is relevant. Prescription drugs and medical devices are also capable of causing allergic reactions, but they are governed by § 6.

The general rule in cases involving allergic reactions is that a warning is required when the harm-causing ingredient is one to which a substantial number of persons are allergic. The degree of substantiality is not precisely quantifiable. Clearly the plaintiff in most cases must show that the allergic predisposition is not unique to the plaintiff. In determining whether the plaintiff has carried the burden in this regard, however, the court may properly consider the severity of the plaintiff's harm. The more severe the harm, the more justified is a conclusion that the number of persons at risk need not be large to be considered "substantial" so as to require a warning. Essentially, this reflects the same risk-utility balancing undertaken in warnings cases generally. But courts explicitly impose the requirement of substantiality in cases involving adverse allergic reactions.

The ingredient that causes the allergic reaction must be one whose danger or whose presence in the product is not generally known to consumers. When both the presence of an allergenic ingredient in the product and the risks presented by such ingredient are widely known, instructions and warnings about that danger are unnecessary. When the presence of the allergenic ingredient would not be anticipated by a reasonable user or consumer, warnings concerning its presence are required. Similarly, when the presence of the ingredient is generally known to consumers, but its dangers are not, a warning of the dangers must be given.

Finally, as required in Subsection (c), warnings concerning risks of allergic reactions that are not reasonably foreseeable at the time of sale need not be provided. See Comment *m.*

l. Relationship between design and instruction or warning. Reasonable designs and instructions or warnings both play important roles in the production and distribution of reasonably safe products. In general, when a safer design can reasonably be implemented and risks can reasonably be designed out of a product, adoption of the safer design is required over a warning that leaves a significant residuum of such risks. For example, instructions and warnings may be ineffective because users of the product may not be adequately reached, may be likely to be inattentive, or may be insufficiently motivated to follow the instructions or heed the warnings. However, when an alternative design to avoid risks cannot reasonably be implemented, adequate instructions and warnings will normally be sufficient to render the product reasonably safe. Compare Comment *e*. Warnings are not, however, a substitute for the provision of a reasonably safe design.

The fact that a risk is obvious or generally known often serves the same function as a warning. See Comment *j*. However, obviousness of risk does not necessarily obviate a duty to provide a safer design. Just as warnings may be ignored, so may obvious or generally known risks be ignored, leaving a residuum of risk great enough to require adopting a safer design. See Comment *d*.

m. Reasonably foreseeable uses and risks in design and warning claims. Subsections (b) and (c) impose liability only when the product is put to uses that it is reasonable to expect a seller or distributor to foresee. Product sellers and distributors are not required to foresee and take precautions against every conceivable mode of use and abuse to which their products might be put. Increasing the costs of designing and marketing products in order to avoid the consequences of unreasonable modes of use is not required.

In cases involving a claim of design defect in a mechanical product, foreseeability of risk is rarely an issue as a practical matter. Once the plaintiff establishes that the product was put to a reasonably foreseeable use, physical risks of injury are generally known or reasonably knowable by experts in the field. It is not unfair to charge a manufacturer with knowledge of such generally known or knowable risks.

The issue of foreseeability of risk of harm is more complex in the case of products such as prescription drugs, medical devices, and toxic chemicals. Risks attendant to use and consumption of these products may, indeed, be unforeseeable at the time of sale. Unforeseeable risks arising from foreseeable product use or consumption by definition cannot specifically be warned against. Thus, in connection with a claim of inadequate design, instruction, or warning, plaintiff should bear the burden of establishing that the risk in question was known or should have been known to the relevant manufacturing community. The harms that result from unforeseeable risks—for example, in the human body's reaction to a new drug, medical device, or chemical—are not a basis of liability. Of course, a seller bears responsibility to perform reasonable testing prior to marketing a product and to discover risks and risk-avoidance measures that such testing would reveal. A seller is charged with knowledge of what reasonable testing would reveal. If testing is not undertaken, or is performed in an inadequate manner, and this failure results in a defect that causes harm, the seller is subject to liability for harm caused by such defect.

Illustration:

15. ABC Adhesives Inc. manufactures a chemical adhesive for use in laying ceramic tile. Recently it has become known that prolonged use of its ceramic adhesive over many years by diabetics can cause severe aggravation of the diabetic condition. Diabetics who have been using the ABC adhesive and have suffered serious aggravation of their condition bring an action against ABC for failing to warn about the risks of prolonged product use. However, it cannot be established that, at the time ABC's product was distributed, special risks to diabetics were reasonably foreseeable or that reasonable testing of the product would have led to the discovery of the risks. ABC is not liable since the risks attendant to such product use were not reasonably foreseeable.

o. Liability of nonmanufacturing sellers for defective design and defects due to inadequate instructions or warnings. Nonmanufacturing sellers such as wholesalers and retailers often are not in a good position feasibly to adopt safer product designs or better instructions or warnings. Nevertheless, once it is determined that a reasonable alternative design or reasonable instructions or warnings could have been provided at or before the time of sale by a predecessor in the chain of distribution and would have reduced plaintiff's harm, it is no defense that a nonmanufacturing seller of such a product exercised due care. Thus, strict liability is imposed on a wholesale or retail seller who neither knew nor should have known of the relevant risks, nor was in a position to have taken action to avoid them, so long as a predecessor in the chain of distribution could have acted reasonably to avoid the risks. See Comment *a.* For exceptions to the general rule regarding the liability of a nonmanufacturer seller, see § 1, Comment *e.*

p. Misuse, modification, and alteration. Product misuse, modification, and alteration are forms of post-sale conduct by product users or others that can be relevant to the determination of the issues of defect, causation, or comparative responsibility. Whether such conduct affects one or more of the issues depends on the nature of the conduct and whether the manufacturer should have adopted a reasonable alternative design or provided a reasonable warning to protect against such conduct.

Under the rule in Subsection (b), liability for defective design attaches only if the risks of harm related to foreseeable product use could have been reduced by the adoption of a reasonable alternative design. Similarly, under the rule in Subsection (c), liability for failure to instruct or warn attaches only if the risks presented by the product could have been reduced by the adoption of reasonable instructions or warnings. Foreseeable product misuse, alteration, and modification must also be considered in deciding whether an alternative design should have been adopted. The post-sale conduct of the user may be so unreasonable, unusual, and costly to avoid that a seller has no duty to design or warn against them. When a court so concludes, the product is not defective within the meaning of Subsection (b) or (c).

A product may, however, be defective as defined in Subsection (b) or (c) due to the omission of a reasonable alternative design or the omission of an adequate warning, yet the risk that eventuates due to misuse, modification, or alteration raises questions whether the extent or scope of liability under the prevailing rules governing legal causation allow for the imposition of liability. See § 15.

Moreover, a product may be found to be defective and causally responsible for plaintiff's harm but the plaintiff may have misused, altered, or modified the product in a manner that calls for the reduction of plaintiff's recovery under the rules of comparative responsibility. Thus, an automobile may be defectively designed so as to provide inadequate protection against harm in the event of a collision, and the plaintiff's negligent modification of the automobile may have caused the collision eventuating in plaintiff's harm. See § 17.

It follows that misuse, modification, and alteration are not discrete legal issues. Rather, when relevant, they are aspects of the concepts of defect, causation, and plaintiff's fault. Jurisdictions differ on the question of who bears the burden of raising and introducing proof regarding conduct that constitutes misuse, modification, and alteration. The allocation of burdens in this regard is not addressed in this Restatement and is left to local law.

Illustration:

20. The ABC Chair Co. manufactures and sells oak chairs. The backs of the chairs have five horizontal wooden bars shaped to the contour of the human back. John, a college student, climbed up to the top bar of an ABC chair to reach the top shelf of a bookcase. The chair tipped and John fell, suffering serious harm. John brings an action against ABC, alleging that the chair should either have had the stability to support him when standing on the top bar or have had a differently designed back so that he could not use the bars for that purpose. The ABC chair is not defectively designed. John's misuse of the product is so unreasonable that the risks it entails need not be designed against.

q. Causation. Under § 1, the product defect must have caused harm to the plaintiff. See §§ 17 and 18.

r. Warranty. Liability for harm caused by product defects imposed by the rules stated in this Chapter is tort liability, not liability for breach of warranty under the Uniform Commercial Code (U.C.C.). Courts may characterize claims under this Chapter as claims for breaches of the implied warranty of merchantability. But in cases involving defect-caused harm to persons or property, a well-coordinated body of law dealing with liability for such harm arising out of the sale of defective products would adopt the tort definition of product defect. See Comment *n*.

§ 3. Circumstantial Evidence Supporting Inference of Product Defect

It may be inferred that the harm sustained by the plaintiff was caused by a product defect existing at the time of sale or distribution, without proof of a specific defect, when the incident that harmed the plaintiff:

(a) was of a kind that ordinarily occurs as a result of product defect; and

(b) was not, in the particular case, solely the result of causes other than product defect existing at the time of sale or distribution.

§ 4. Noncompliance and Compliance with Product Safety Statutes or Regulations

In connection with liability for defective design or inadequate instructions or warnings:

(a) a product's noncompliance with an applicable product safety statute or administrative regulation renders the product defective with respect to the risks sought to be reduced by the statute or regulation; and

(b) a product's compliance with an applicable product safety statute or administrative regulation is properly considered in determining whether the product is defective with respect to the risks sought to be reduced by the statute or regulation, but such compliance does not preclude as a matter of law a finding of product defect.

TOPIC 2. LIABILITY RULES APPLICABLE TO SPECIAL PRODUCTS OR PRODUCT MARKETS

§ **6.** Liability of Commercial Seller or Distributor for Harm Caused by Defective Prescription Drugs and Medical Devices

(a) A manufacturer of a prescription drug or medical device who sells or otherwise distributes a defective drug or medical device is subject to liability for harm to persons caused by the defect. A prescription drug or medical device is one that may be legally sold or otherwise distributed only pursuant to a health-care provider's prescription.

(b) For purposes of liability under Subsection (a), a prescription drug or medical device is defective if at the time of sale or other distribution the drug or medical device:

(1) contains a manufacturing defect as defined in § 2(a); or

(2) is not reasonably safe due to defective design as defined in Subsection (c); or

(3) is not reasonably safe due to inadequate instructions or warnings as defined in Subsection (d).

(c) A prescription drug or medical device is not reasonably safe due to defective design if the foreseeable risks of harm posed by the drug or medical device are sufficiently great in relation to its foreseeable therapeutic benefits that reasonable health-care providers, knowing of such foreseeable risks and therapeutic benefits, would not prescribe the drug or medical device for any class of patients.

(d) A prescription drug or medical device is not reasonably safe due to inadequate instructions or warnings if reasonable instructions or warnings regarding foreseeable risks of harm are not provided to:

(1) prescribing and other health-care providers who are in a position to reduce the risks of harm in accordance with the instructions or warnings; or

(2) the patient when the manufacturer knows or has reason to know that health-care providers will not be in a position to reduce the risks of harm in accordance with the instructions or warnings.

215

(e) A retail seller or other distributor of a prescription drug or medical device is subject to liability for harm caused by the drug or device if:

(1) at the time of sale or other distribution the drug or medical device contains a manufacturing defect as defined in § 2(a); or

(2) at or before the time of sale or other distribution of the drug or medical device the retail seller or other distributor fails to exercise reasonable care and such failure causes harm to persons.

Comment:

a. History. Subsections (b)(1) and (d)(1) state the traditional rules that drug and medical-device manufacturers are liable only when their products contain manufacturing defects or are sold without adequate instructions and warnings to prescribing and other health-care providers. Until recently, courts refused to impose liability based on defective designs of drugs and medical devices sold only by prescription. However, consistent with recent trends in the case law, two limited exceptions from these traditional rules are generally recognized. Subsection (d)(2) sets forth situations when a prescription-drug or medical-device manufacturer is required to warn the patient directly of risks associated with consumption or use of its product. And Subsection (c) imposes liability for a drug or medical device whose risks of harm so far outweigh its therapeutic benefits that reasonable, properly informed health-care providers would not prescribe it.

b. Rationale. The obligation of a manufacturer to warn about risks attendant to the use of drugs and medical devices that may be sold only pursuant to a health-care provider's prescription traditionally has required warnings directed to health-care providers and not to patients. The rationale supporting this "learned intermediary" rule is that only health-care professionals are in a position to understand the significance of the risks involved and to assess the relative advantages and disadvantages of a given form of prescription-based therapy. The duty then devolves on the health-care provider to supply to the patient such information as is deemed appropriate under the circumstances so that the patient can make an informed choice as to therapy. Subsection (d)(1) retains the "learned intermediary" rule. However, in certain limited therapeutic relationships the physician or other health-care provider has a much-diminished role as an evaluator or decisionmaker. In these instances it may be appropriate to impose on the manufacturer the duty to warn the patient directly. See Subsection (d)(2).

The traditional refusal by courts to impose tort liability for defective designs of prescription drugs and medical devices is based on the fact that a prescription drug or medical device entails a unique set of risks and benefits. What may be harmful to one patient may be beneficial to another. Under Subsection (c) a drug is defectively designed only when it provides no net benefit to any class of patients. Courts have concluded that as long as a drug or medical device provides net benefits to some persons under some circumstances, the drug or device manufacturer should be required to instruct and warn health-care providers of the foreseeable risks and benefits. Courts have also recognized that the regulatory system governing prescription drugs is a legitimate mechanism for setting the standards for drug design. In part, this deference reflects concerns over the possible negative effects of judicially imposed liability on the cost and availability of valuable medical technology. This deference also rests on two further assumptions: first, that prescribing health-care providers, when adequately informed by drug manufacturers, are able to assure that the right drugs and medical devices reach the right patients; and second, that governmental regulatory agencies adequately review new prescription drugs and devices, keeping unreasonably dangerous designs off the market.

Nevertheless, unqualified deference to these regulatory mechanisms is considered by a growing number of courts to be unjustified. An approved prescription drug or medical device can present significant risks without corresponding advantages. At the same time, manufacturers must have ample discretion to develop useful drugs and devices without subjecting their design decisions to the ordinary test applicable to products generally under § 2(b). Accordingly, Subsection (c) imposes a more rigorous test for defect than does § 2(b), which does not apply to prescription drugs and medical devices. The requirement for establishing defective design of a prescription drug or medical device under Subsection (c) is that the drug or device have so little merit compared with its risks that reasonable health-care providers, possessing knowledge of risks that were known or reasonably should have been known, would not have prescribed the drug or device for any class of patients. Thus, a prescription drug or medical device that has usefulness to any class of patients is not defective in design even if it is harmful to other patients. Because of the special nature of prescription drugs and medical devices, the determination of whether such products are not reasonably safe is to be made under Subsections (c) and (d) rather than under §§ 2(b) and 2(c).

The rules imposing liability on a manufacturer for inadequate warning or defective design of prescription drugs and medical devices assume that the federal regulatory standard has not preempted the imposition of tort liability under state law. When such preemption is found, liability cannot attach if the manufacturer has complied with the applicable federal standard. See § 4, Comment *e*.

The doctrine of preemption based on supremacy of federal law should be distinguished from the proposition that compliance with statutory and regulatory standards satisfies the state's requirement for product safety. Subsections (c) and (d) recognize common-law causes of action for defective drug design and for failure to provide reasonable instructions or warnings, even though the manufacturer complied with governmental standards. For the rules governing compliance with governmental standards generally, see § 4(b).

c.   Manufacturers' liability for manufacturing defects. Limitations on the liability for prescription drug and medical-device designs do not support treating drug and medical-device manufacturers differently from commercial sellers of other products with respect to manufacturing defects. Courts have traditionally subjected manufacturers of prescription products to liability for harm caused by manufacturing defects.

d.   Manufacturers' liability for failure adequately to instruct or warn prescribing and other health-care providers. Failure to instruct or warn is the major basis of liability for manufacturers of prescription drugs and medical devices. When prescribing health-care providers are adequately informed of the relevant benefits and risks associated with various prescription drugs and medical devices, they can reach appropriate decisions regarding which drug or device is best for specific patients. Sometimes a warning serves to inform health-care providers of unavoidable risks that inhere in the drug or medical device. By definition, such a warning would not aid the health-care provider in reducing the risk of injury to the patient by taking precautions in how the drug is administered or the medical device is used. However, warnings of unavoidable risks allow the health-care provider, and thereby the patient, to make an informed choice whether to utilize the drug or medical device. Beyond informing prescribing health-care providers, a drug or device manufacturer may have a duty under the law of negligence to use reasonable measures to supply instructions or warnings to nonprescribing health-care providers who are in positions to act on such information so as to reduce or prevent injury to patients.

e.   Direct warnings to patients. Warnings and instructions with regard to drugs or medical devices that can be sold legally only pursuant to a prescription are, under the "learned intermediary" rule, directed to health-care providers. Subsection (d)(2) recognizes that direct warnings and instructions to patients are warranted for drugs that are dispensed or administered to patients without the personal intervention or evaluation of a health-care provider. An example is the administration of a vaccine in clinics where mass inoculations are performed. In many such programs, health-care providers are not in a position to evaluate the risks attendant upon use of the drug or device or to relate them to patients. When a manufacturer supplies prescription drugs for distribution to patients in this type of unsupervised environment, if a direct warning to patients is feasible and can be effective, the law requires measures to that effect.

Although the learned intermediary rule is generally accepted and a drug manufacturer fulfills its legal obligation to warn by providing adequate warnings to the health-care provider, arguments have been advanced that in two other areas courts should consider imposing tort liability on drug manufacturers that fail to provide direct warnings to consumers. In the first, governmental regulatory agencies have mandated that patients be informed of risks attendant to the use of a drug. A noted example is the FDA requirement that birth control pills be sold to patients accompanied by a patient package insert. In the second, manufacturers have advertised a prescription drug and its indicated use in the mass media. Governmental regulations require that, when drugs are so advertised, they must be accompanied by appropriate information concerning risk so as to provide balanced advertising. The question in both instances is whether adequate warnings to the appropriate health-care provider should insulate the manufacturer from tort liability.

Those who assert the need for adequate warnings directly to consumers contend that manufacturers that communicate directly with consumers should not escape liability simply because the decision to prescribe the drug was made by the health-care provider. Proponents of the learned intermediary rule argue that, notwithstanding direct communications to the consumer, drugs cannot be dispensed unless a health-care provider makes an individualized decision that a drug is appropriate for a particular patient, and that it is for the health-care provider to decide which risks are relevant to the particular patient. The Institute leaves to developing case law whether exceptions to the learned intermediary rule in these or other situations should be recognized.

When the content of the warnings is mandated or approved by a governmental agency regulation and a court finds that compliance with such regulation federally preempts tort liability, then no liability under this Section can attach. For the rules governing compliance with governmental standards generally, see § 4(b).

f. Manufacturers' liability for defectively designed prescription drugs and medical devices. Subsection (c) reflects the judgment that, as long as a given drug or device provides net benefits for a class of patients, it should be available to them, accompanied by appropriate warnings and instructions. Learned intermediaries must generally be relied upon to see that the right drugs and devices reach the right patients. However, when a drug or device provides net benefits to no class of patients—when reasonable, informed health-care providers would not prescribe it to any class of patients—then the design of the product is defective and the manufacturer should be subject to liability for the harm caused.

A prescription drug or device manufacturer defeats a plaintiff's design claim by establishing one or more contexts in which its product would be prescribed by reasonable, informed health-care providers. That some individual providers do, in fact, prescribe defendant's product does not in itself suffice to defeat the plaintiff's claim. Evidence regarding the actual conduct of health-care providers, while relevant and admissible, is not necessarily controlling. The issue is whether, objectively viewed, reasonable providers, knowing of the foreseeable risks and benefits of the drug or medical device, would prescribe it for any class of patients. Given this very demanding objective standard, liability is likely to be imposed only under unusual circumstances. The court has the responsibility to determine when the plaintiff has introduced sufficient evidence so that reasonable persons could conclude that plaintiff has met this demanding standard.

Illustration:

1. ABC Pharmaceuticals manufactures and distributes D, a prescription drug intended to prolong pregnancy and thus to reduce the risks associated with premature birth. Patricia, six months pregnant with a history of irregular heart beats, was given D during a hospital stay in connection with her pregnancy. As a result, she suffered heart failure and required open-heart surgery. In Patricia's action against ABC, her expert testifies that, notwithstanding FDA approval of D five years prior to Patricia's taking the drug, credible studies published two years prior to Patricia's taking the drug concluded that D does not prolong pregnancy for any class of patients. Notwithstanding a finding by the trier of fact that ABC gave adequate warnings to the prescribing physician regarding the serious risks of heart failure in patients with a history of irregular heart beats, the trier of fact can find that reasonably informed health-care providers would not prescribe D for any class of patients, thus rendering ABC subject to liability.

g. Foreseeability of risks of harm in prescription drug and medical device cases. Duties concerning the design and marketing of prescription drugs and medical devices arise only with respect to risks of harm that are reasonably foreseeable at the time of sale. Imposing liability for unforeseeable risks can create inappropriate disincentives for the development of new drugs and therapeutic devices. Moreover, because actuaries cannot accurately assess unknown and unknowable risks, insuring against losses due to unknowable risks would be problematic. Drug and medical device manufacturers have the responsibility to perform reasonable testing prior to marketing a product and to discover risks and risk-avoidance measures that such testing would reveal. See § 2, Comments *a* and *m*.

Illustrations:

2. DEF Pharmaceuticals, Inc., manufactures and distributes prescription drugs. Seven years ago DEF, after years of research and testing, received permission from the FDA to market X, a drug prescribed for the treatment of low-grade infections. Three years later, Jim, age 12, began taking X on his physician's prescription for a recurring respiratory-tract infection. Jim took X for approximately one year. Two years after Jim had stopped taking X, medical research discovered that X causes loss of vision in adolescents. Prior to this discovery DEF had not warned of this risk. Jim has begun to manifest symptoms of the sort caused by the drug. No evidence suggests that DEF's testing of X was substandard, or that any reasonable drug company should have discovered the side effects sooner than they were discovered. In a failure-to-warn action by Jim against DEF, the court should direct a verdict in favor of the defendant.

3. The same facts as Illustration 2, except that two years before Jim began taking X, medical researchers published a credible study in a leading medical journal concerning the possibility that a drug with toxicological effects very similar to X adversely affects vision in adolescents. After publication of the study suggesting a possible link between X and loss of vision in adolescents, DEF did not conduct further research or provide warnings to physicians of the risk of X causing loss of vision. Jim's expert witness testifies that a reasonable manufacturer would have tested further and that such testing would have revealed that X causes vision loss in time to have warned Jim's physician. In Jim's failure-to-warn action against DEF, the trial court should submit the issue of DEF's failure to warn to the trier of fact on appropriate instructions.

h. Liability of retail seller of prescription drugs and medical devices for defective designs and defects due to inadequate instructions or warnings. The rule governing most products imposes liability on wholesalers and retailers for selling a defectively designed product, or one without adequate instructions or warnings, even though they have exercised reasonable care in marketing the product. See § 1, Comment *e*, and § 2, Comment *o*. Courts have refused to apply this general rule to nonmanufacturing retail sellers of prescription drugs and medical devices and, instead, have adopted the rule stated in Subsection (e). That rule subjects retailers to liability only if the product contains a manufacturing defect or if the retailer fails to exercise reasonable care in connection with distribution of the drug or medical device. In so limiting the liability of intermediary parties, courts have held that they should be permitted to rely on the special expertise of manufacturers, prescribing and treating health-care providers, and governmental regulatory agencies. They have also emphasized the needs of medical patients to have ready access to prescription drugs at reasonable prices.

Illustration:

4. ABC Pharmaceuticals manufactures and distributes a prescription drug to reduce blood pressure. ABC supplies pharmacies with pamphlets explaining the risks and warning patients against drinking alcohol while taking the drug. ABC asks the pharmacies to give the pamphlets to patients when dispensing the drug. The P Pharmacy received the pamphlets but negligently failed to give them to patients. P is subject to liability to those patients suffering injury for whom the pamphlets would have been effective in avoiding risks of usage.

§ 7. Liability of Commercial Seller or Distributor for Harm Caused by Defective Food Products

One engaged in the business of selling or otherwise distributing food products who sells or distributes a food product that is defective under § 2, § 3, or § 4 is subject to liability for harm to persons or property caused by the defect. Under § 2(a), a harm-causing ingredient of the food product constitutes a defect if a reasonable consumer would not expect the food product to contain that ingredient.

Comment:

a. General applicability of §§ 2, 3, and 4 to food products. Except for the special problems identified in Comment *b*, liability for harm caused by defects in commercially distributed food products are determined under the same rules generally applicable to non-food products. A food product may contain a manufacturing defect under § 2(a), as when a can of peas contains a pebble; may be defectively designed under § 2(b), as when the recipe for potato chips contains a dangerous chemical preservative; or may be sold without adequate warnings under § 2(c), as when the seller fails to inform consumers that the dye applied to the skins of oranges contains a well-known allergen. Section 3 may allow a plaintiff to reach the trier of fact when, unable to identify the specific defect, the plaintiff becomes violently ill immediately after consuming the defendant's food product and other causes are sufficiently eliminated. And § 4 may apply when a commercially distributed food product fails to conform to applicable safety statutes or administrative regulations.

   b. *The special problem under § 2(a).* When a plaintiff suffers harm due to the presence in food of foreign matter clearly not intended by the product seller, such as a pebble in a can of peas or the pre-sale spoilage of a jar of mayonnaise, the claim is readily treated under § 2(a), which deals with harm caused by manufacturing defects. Food product cases, however, sometimes present unique difficulties when it is unclear whether the ingredient that caused the plaintiff's harm is an unanticipated adulteration or is an inherent aspect of the product. For example, is a one-inch chicken bone in a chicken enchilada, or a fish bone in fish chowder, a manufacturing defect or, instead, an inherent aspect of the product? The analytical problem stems from the circumstance that food products in many instances do not have specific product designs that may be used as a basis for determining whether the offending product ingredient constitutes a departure from design, and is thus a manufacturing defect. Food recipes vary over time, within the same restaurant or other commercial food-preparation facility, from facility to facility, and from locale to locale.

   Faced with this indeterminacy, some courts have attempted to rely on a distinction between "foreign" and "natural" characteristics of food products to determine liability. Under that distinction, liability attaches only if the alleged adulteration is foreign rather than natural to the product. Most courts have found this approach inadequate, however. Although a one-inch chicken bone may in some sense be "natural" to a chicken enchilada, depending on the context in which consumption takes place, the bone may still be unexpected by the reasonable consumer, who will not be able to avoid injury, thus rendering the product not reasonably safe. The majority view is that, in this circumstance of uncertainty, the issue of whether a food product containing a dangerous but arguably natural component is defective under § 2(a) is to be determined by reference to reasonable consumer expectations within the relevant context of consumption. A consumer expectations test in this context relies upon culturally defined, widely shared standards that food products ought to meet. Although consumer expectations are not adequate to supply a standard for defect in other contexts, assessments of what consumers have a right to expect in various commercial food preparations are sufficiently well-formed that judges and triers of fact can sensibly resolve whether liability should be imposed using this standard.

Chapter 4

PROVISIONS OF GENERAL APPLICABILITY

TOPIC 2. AFFIRMATIVE DEFENSES

TOPIC 2. AFFIRMATIVE DEFENSES

§ 17. Apportionment of Responsibility Between or Among Plaintiff, Sellers and Distributors of Defective Products, and Others

(a) A plaintiff's recovery of damages for harm caused by a product defect may be reduced if the conduct of the plaintiff combines with the product defect to cause the harm and the plaintiff's conduct fails to conform to generally applicable rules establishing appropriate standards of care.

(b) The manner and extent of the reduction under Subsection (a) and the apportionment of plaintiff's recovery among multiple defendants are governed by generally applicable rules apportioning responsibility.

Comment:

a. History. The rule stated in this Section recognizes that the fault of the plaintiff is relevant in assessing liability for product-caused harm. Section 402A of the Restatement, Second, of Torts, recognizing strict liability for harm caused by defective products, was adopted in 1964 when the overwhelming majority rule treated contributory negligence as a total bar to recovery. Understandably, the Institute was reluctant to bar a plaintiff's products liability claim in tort based on conduct that was not egregious. Thus, § 402A, Comment *n*, altered the general tort defenses by narrowing the applicability of contributory negligence and emphasizing assumption of risk as the primary defense. Since then, comparative fault has swept the country. Only a tiny minority of states retain contributory fault as a total bar.

A strong majority of jurisdictions apply the comparative responsibility doctrine to products liability actions. Courts today do not limit the relevance of plaintiff's fault as did the Restatement, Second, of Torts to conduct characterized as voluntary assumption of the risk. See Comment *d*.

Certain forms of consumer behavior—product misuse and product alteration or modification—have been the subject of much confusion and misunderstanding. Early decisions treated product misuse, alteration, and modification, whether by the plaintiff or a third party, as a total bar to recovery against a product seller. Today misuse, alteration, and modification relate to one of three issues in a products liability action. In some cases, misuse, alteration, and modification are important in determining whether the product is defective. In others, they are relevant to the issue of legal cause. Finally, when the plaintiff misuses, alters, or modifies the product, such conduct may constitute contributory fault and reduce the plaintiff's recovery under the rules of comparative responsibility. See Comment *c*.

§ 18. Disclaimers, Limitations, Waivers, and Other Contractual Exculpations as Defenses to Products Liability Claims for Harm to Persons

Disclaimers and limitations of remedies by product sellers or other distributors, waivers by product purchasers, and other similar contractual exculpations, oral or written, do not bar or reduce otherwise valid products liability claims against sellers or other distributors of new products for harm to persons.

Comment:

a. Effects of contract defenses on products liability tort claims for harm to persons. A commercial seller or other distributor of a new product is not permitted to avoid liability for harm to persons through limiting terms in a contract governing the sale of a product. It is presumed that the ordinary product user or consumer lacks sufficient information and bargaining power to execute a fair contractual limitation of rights to recover. For a limited exception to this general rule, see Comment *d*. The rule in this Section applies only to "sellers or other distributors of new products." For rules governing commercial sellers of used products, including whether they may rely on disclaimers, waivers, and other contractual defenses, see § 8. Nothing in this Section is intended to constrain parties within the commercial chain of distribution from contracting inter se for indemnity agreements or save-harmless clauses.

d. *Waiver of rights in contractual settings in which product purchasers possess both adequate knowledge and sufficient economic power.* The rule in this Section applies to cases in which commercial product sellers attempt unfairly to disclaim or otherwise limit their liability to the majority of users and consumers who are presumed to lack information and bargaining power adequate to protect their interests. This Section does not address whether consumers, especially when represented by informed and economically powerful consumer groups or intermediaries, with full information and sufficient bargaining power, may contract with product sellers to accept curtailment of liability in exchange for concomitant benefits, or whether such consumers might be allowed to agree to substitute alternative dispute resolution mechanisms in place of traditional adjudication. When such contracts are accompanied by alternative nontort remedies that serve as an adequate quid pro quo for reducing or eliminating rights to recover in tort, arguments may support giving effect to such agreements. Such contractual arrangements raise policy questions different from those raised by this Section and require careful consideration by the courts.

RESTATEMENT OF THE LAW THIRD

TORTS

APPORTIONMENT OF LIABILITY

TOPIC 1. BASIC RULES OF COMPARATIVE RESPONSIBILITY

TOPIC 2. LIABILITY OF MULTIPLE TORTFEASORS FOR INDIVISIBLE HARM

TOPIC 3. CONTRIBUTION AND INDEMNITY

TOPIC 5. APPORTIONMENT OF LIABILITY WHEN DAMAGES CAN BE DIVIDED BY CAUSATION

INTRODUCTION

This Restatement addresses apportionment of liability when more than one person is legally liable for an injury. The Restatement Second Torts contained a rule that a plaintiff's contributory negligence was an absolute bar to recovery. Since then, all but four states and the District of Columbia have adopted comparative responsibility. That change raises a host of new issues, which are the subject of this Restatement.

Topic 1 covers the basic issues raised when a plaintiff's negligent conduct is a legal cause of the injury. Section 1 identifies the claims to which this Restatement applies. Section 7 reflects the rule, now widely accepted, that a plaintiff's negligence reduces recovery by the plaintiff's comparative share of responsibility. Section 8 addresses the difficult question of how to assign responsibility to a plaintiff and other parties, including those who are liable based on differing theories. Plaintiff's negligence is defined in § 3. The burden of proving plaintiff's negligence is addressed in § 4. Contractual assumption of risk is covered in § 2, which also eliminates implied assumption of risk as an independent defense.

Topic 2 addresses joint and several liability. its five parallel, alternative Tracks (A–E) reflect the fact that there is no majority rule on this question. After initially defining joint and several liability and several liability in two preliminary sections, Topic 2 proceeds in §§ 12–16 to provide universal rules for intentional tortfeasors, parties vicariously liable, parties who engage in concerted action, parties who negligently fail to protect a plaintiff from an intentional tortfeasor, and the effect of a partial settlement. Section 17 states that the institute takes no position on whether, or in which form, joint and several liability, several liability, or some hybrid of the two should be employed. The remainder of Topic 2 provides five different alternative systems of joint and several, several, and hybrid liability. Track "A" reflects a pure joint-and-several-liability system and would be useful in those jurisdictions that retain joint and several liability. Track "B" contains a pure several-liability provision. Three hybrid systems are reflected in Tracks "C" (insolvent parties' shares reallocated to other solvent parties), "D" (defendants whose comparative responsibility exceeds a threshold are jointly and severally liable, while those below the threshold are severally liable), and "E" (defendants are jointly and severally liable for economic damages and severally liable for noneconomic damages).

The next three Topics are considerably briefer: Topic 3 covers contribution and indemnity, Topic 4 covers partial settlements and satisfaction of claims, and Topic 5 covers divisible damages and

228

apportioning liability based on causation rather than comparative responsibility.

Throughout this Restatement, the provisions of the Restatement Second of Torts that are superseded, modified, or readopted have been identified. A list of affected sections in the Restatement Second of Torts is contained in § 1, Comment *a* and Parallel Tables showing the relationship between the sections or their Restatement and their counterparts in Restatement Second appears at the end of this volume.

At the time that this Restatement was completed, Restatement Third, Torts: General Principles, was still being drafted. Consequently, this Restatement refers to Restatement Second, Torts, for general principles of tort law, such as negligence, intent, and causation. When Restatement Third, Torts: General Principles, is completed, its provisions should be understood to replace the references herein to Restatement Second.

TOPIC 1. BASIC RULES OF COMPARATIVE RESPONSIBILITY

§ 1. Issues and Causes of Action Addressed by This Restatement

This Restatement addresses issues of apportioning liability among two or more persons. It applies to all claims (including lawsuits and settlements) for death, personal injury (including emotional distress or consortium), or physical damage to tangible property, regardless of the basis of liability.

Comment:

a. Nomenclature and issues addressed by this Restatement. The term "this Restatement," whenever used in Topics 1–5, refers to Restatement Third, Torts: Apportionment of Liability. It does not refer generally to Restatement Third, Torts.

This Restatement addresses issues that arise in apportioning liability among two or more persons, including the plaintiff. Some of its topics, such as comparative responsibility, were not addressed in the Restatement Second of Torts. Other topics, such as joint and several liability, were addressed in the Restatement Second of Torts. Even for topics that were addressed in the Restatement Second of Torts, the nearly universal adoption of comparative responsibility by American courts and legislatures has had a dramatic impact. This Restatement reflects changes in the law since the publication of the Restatement Second of Torts.

Comparative responsibility has a potential impact on almost all areas of tort law. Sometimes comparative responsibility directly affects apportionment, such as when it determines the *effect* of a plaintiff's negligence on his or her recovery. At other times, comparative responsibility can affect rules of apportionment, which in turn can affect other rules of tort law. For example, rules about joint and several liability can affect rules concerning fault or causation, because a court might be willing to relax liability rules when a defendant is liable only for a portion of the harm. Thus, the impact of comparative responsibility on American tort law is profound.

Comparative responsibility requires courts to coordinate liability rules and defenses in ways that transcend the traditional boundaries between various torts. Tort law generally reflects two variables: the nature of the defendant's conduct and the nature of the plaintiff's injury. Apportionment issues cut across this structure. Several defendants might be subject to liability under different tort theories, but apportionment among them requires coordination. A single defendant can be liable under several tort theories. Therefore, a plaintiff's conduct can be relevant in different ways, depending on the theory of recovery. It would be difficult to compare a plaintiff's conduct with a defendant's conduct if different apportionment rules govern different bases of liability in the same lawsuit.

Applying different apportionment rules to different parts of a multi-party, multi-theory lawsuit poses important practical problems, but it also highlights conceptual tensions. The intellectual underpinning of having subcategories in substantive tort law—that is, of having separate torts—is that various torts raise different policy concerns. The intellectual underpinning of comparative responsibility is that a single injury is more or less unitary. Consequently, this Restatement must address the resulting tensions between maintaining distinctions based on the different torts and a common comparison of the parties' responsibility in a single lawsuit.

REPORTERS' NOTE

Comment a. Nomenclature and issues addressed by this Restatement. Defining the scope of this Restatement has been one of the most important and difficult tasks of this project. The basic idea is to leave "first-order" questions involving the basic rules of liability, causation, and defenses to the applicable substantive law. Instead, this Restatement addresses "second-order" questions about apportioning liability among two or more persons, including the plaintiff, taking as a given the underlying substantive law about liability. These second-order issues have been most directly affected by the widespread adoption of comparative negligence (now comparative responsibility) and by widespread judicial and legislative activity on the issue of joint and several liability. The line between first-order and second-order issues has been difficult to maintain, however. Some first-order issues, such as what constitutes plaintiff's negligence, have been so dramatically affected by the shift to comparative responsibility that they have been included. Nevertheless, the distinction between first-order and second-order issues is a strong organizing principle for this Restatement.

Comment b. Bases of liability addressed by this Restatement. The bases of liability in this Comment are illustrative, not exhaustive.

Causes of action other than those for death, personal injury, or physical damage to tangible property are not part of the core to which comparative responsibility is directed. See Comment *d.* There is one exception, however. Some jurisdictions allow recovery for negligently caused economic harm in certain situations. See, e.g., People Express Airlines, Inc. v. Consolidated Rail Corp., 495 A.2d 107 (N.J.1985); Mattingly v. Sheldon Jackson College, 743 P.2d 356 (Alaska 1987); Union Oil Co. v. Oppen, 501 F.2d 558 (9th Cir.1974). See generally Powers & Niver, *Negligence, Breach of Contract, and the Economic Loss Rule,* 23 Tex. Tech. L. Rev. 477, 485 (1992). When such harm is caused by an accidental injury, the claim is similar to a claim for negligently caused tangible property damage. Moreover, such a claim may arise in a suit that also includes claims for death, personal injury, or tangible property damage. Under those circumstances, the claims probably should be governed by the rules stated in this Restatement. Other types of claims involving purely intangible economic loss, however, may raise different policy issues. Courts should be careful in those cases to determine whether the rules stated in this Restatement are appropriate.

Before comparative responsibility, most courts did not apply contributory negligence as a defense in strict products liability. Comment *n* of Restatement Second, Torts § 402A provided that assumption of risk was a defense to strict products liability, but that a plaintiff's mere negligent failure to discover or guard against the possible existence of a product defect was not a defense. Comment *n* was silent about a plaintiff's negligence that was more than a mere failure to discover or guard against the possibility of a product defect, but that did not rise to the level of assumption of risk. Some courts held that this type of negligence was not a defense to strict products liability. See, e.g., McCown v. Int'l Harvester Co., 342 A.2d 381 (Pa.1975).

Most states now apply their comparative-responsibility system to strict products liability. See, e.g., Daly v. General Motors Corp., 144

Cal.Rptr. 380, 575 P.2d 1162 (1978); Butaud v. Suburban Marine & Sporting Goods, Inc., 555 P.2d 42 (Alaska 1976); Colo. Rev. Stat. § 13–21–111 (1987); Tex. Civ. Prac. & Rem. Code, ch. 33 (1987). See also Morales v. American Honda Motor Co., 151 F.3d 500 (6th Cir.1998) (breach of warranty). Most states at least hold that a plaintiff's negligence that constitutes more than a mere failure to discover or guard against the possibility of a product defect supports the factfinder's assigning a percentage of responsibility to the plaintiff. See, e.g., Daly v. General Motors Corp., 144 Cal.Rptr. 380, 575 P.2d 1162 (1978); General Motors Corp. v. Sanchez, 997 S.W.2d 584 (Tex.1999). Other jurisdictions have gone further to hold that all forms of a plaintiff's negligence are relevant for a factfinder's assigning a percentage of responsibility to the plaintiff. See, e.g., Pan–Alaska Fisheries, Inc. v. Marine Const. & Design Co., 565 F.2d 1129 (9th Cir.1977). The latter position is now the rule in Restatement Third, Torts: Products Liability § 13.

When most courts or legislatures adopted comparative responsibility, the systems did not apply to intentional torts. See, e.g., Tex. Civ. Prac. & Rem. Code, ch. 33 (1987). Nevertheless, leaving intentional torts out of a comparative-responsibility system can create problems. In a multiparty lawsuit involving negligent tortfeasors and intentional tortfeasors, it would be cumbersome to have different apportionment systems apply to different parts of the same case. Consider a case in which one tortfeasor shoots the plaintiff at a convenience store, the convenience store is negligent for not having proper security, and a doctor aggravates the injury through malpractice. All three tortfeasors jointly caused the aggravated portion of the injury. It would be difficult to allocate responsibility for either the initial injury or the aggravated part of the injury without using the same comparative-responsibility system for all of the tortfeasors.

Comparative responsibility has a different underlying logic than the classical structure of tort law. Tort law traditionally has been structured along lines defined primarily by the type of injury the plaintiff suffers and the defendant's state of mind or culpability. The intellectual underpinning of this compartmentalized, tort-by-tort approach is that, when types of injuries change and states of mind or culpability change, the policy concerns of tort law also change. When a defendant intentionally invades a plaintiff's rights, it makes sense to have different defenses, different rules about damages, and so forth, than when a defendant is merely negligent or, in strict liability, is innocent. Historical reasons and pure fortuity also have influenced the structure of tort law and the available defenses, but the structure can be justified only by an argument that different torts—different types of injuries and different states of mind—evoke different policy concerns.

Comparative responsibility and comparative contribution raise a somewhat different set of concerns. When several actors cause a single injury, comparative responsibility asks a court to treat the injury as a unit and compare the contributions of the various actors. This creates tension with the compartmentalized structure of tort law, which divides cases according to causes of action. To the extent that courts compare all of the actors in a single set of percentages, they often have to forego applying different apportionment rules to parties who commit different torts.

The difference in policy concerns surrounding different causes of action remains important, especially for causes of action that differ according to the defendant's state of mind. Courts should not merely rely on ease of administration, in the sense of judicial time and effort, to disregard important policy differences among different torts. Nevertheless, a litigation system must be workable. It does little to advance underlying policy goals to have a system that is too complex for trial courts and jurors—who in the last analysis are linchpins in our litigation system—to implement. Thus, the rules stated in this Restatement often reflect compromises between the particular policy goals of the individual torts and the general goal of workability.

Comment c. Special issues involving intentional torts. There is an intuitive sense that a plaintiff's own failure to use reasonable care should not affect a plaintiff's recovery against an intentional tortfeasor. This intuition draws on the image of a mugger who claims that the victim was negligent for being out too late at night or for wearing too much jewelry. In other situations, however, the intuition to reject a plaintiff's negligence as a comparative defense might not be as strong, such as when a defendant who otherwise batters a plaintiff honestly but unreasonably believes the conduct was privileged or that it was not harmful or offensive (such as when a defendant intentionally exposes a plaintiff to a pollutant that the defendant honestly but unreasonably believes is not harmful). Sometimes the plaintiff's own conduct is intentional. Moreover, the factfinder can take the degree of intentionality or even deliberateness of the tortfeasor's conduct into account when assigning percentages of responsibility to the various parties. See § 8.

Courts can also develop substantive liability rules, often called "no duty" rules, to cover certain types of plaintiff conduct, such as a claim that a victim of a sexual assault dressed provocatively, a claim involving domestic violence, or a claim by the mugging victim mentioned above. See §§ 3, 8. Courts have spent a great deal of time and energy developing similar rules with respect to a defendant's conduct in negligence. Because most courts have not applied comparative responsibility to intentional torts, they have not had the opportunity to develop similar rules for plaintiffs who encounter a defendant's intentional conduct. Courts can even adopt substantive rules of liability to protect against having a plaintiff's conduct reduce his or her recovery from intentional tortfeasors, but nevertheless have the same conduct reduce the plaintiff's recovery against other, nonintentional tortfeasors.

Applying comparative responsibility to intentional torts is not the majority rule, but it commands significant support among courts that have addressed the question, especially in cases apportioning damages among defendants. Much of this growing support is in cases involving a comparison of *defendants'* responsibility, not a comparison of a *defendant* with a *plaintiff.* See Rosh v. Cave Imaging Sys., Inc., 32 Cal.Rptr.2d 136 (Ct.App.1994), review denied (Oct. 13, 1994) (comparing negligent security guards with assailant); Bhinder v. Sun Co., Inc., 717 A.2d 202 (Conn.1998) (permitting negligent convenience store to have responsibility assigned to robber who killed plaintiff-employee); Blazovic v. Andrich, 590 A.2d 222 (N.J.1991) (comparing negligence of plaintiff in provoking fight with negligent bar owner for failure to provide adequate lighting and intentional tortfeasors who started fight); Veazey v. Elmwood Plantation Associates, Ltd., 650 So.2d 712 (La.1994) (leaving application of comparative responsibility to intentional and negligent defendants to trial court's discretion and affirming the trial court's decision not to do so; later superseded by statute, La. Civil Code Ann. art. 2323 (West 1996)); Reichert v. Atler, 875 P.2d 379 (N.M.1994) (comparing negligence of defendant bar owner in failing to provide adequate security with assailant); Scott v. County of Los Angeles, 32 Cal.Rptr.2d 643 (Ct.App.1994) (comparing intentional tortfeasor with negligence of defendant social-care worker), review denied (Oct. 20, 1994); Pamela B. v. Hayden, 31 Cal.Rptr.2d 147 (Ct.App.1994) (comparing negligence of property owner and landlord with intentional rape by nondefendant), review granted, 33 Cal.Rptr.2d 568 (1994), review dismissed, 38 Cal.Rptr.2d 345 (1995); Weidenfeller v. Star & Garter, 2 Cal.Rptr.2d 14 (Ct.App.1991) (comparing defendant's negligence with fault of intentional tortfeasor); Martin v. United States, 984 F.2d 1033 (9th Cir.1993) (applying California law) (comparing negligent day-camp supervisor with rapist); Torres v. New Mexico, 894 P.2d 386 (N.M.1995) (holding that if policeman found negligent his fault should be compared with assailant); Field v. Boyer, 952 P.2d 1078 (Utah 1998) (comparison of negligent and intentional parties is acceptable, but only with those parties named in the suit or immune from suit); Steele v. Kerrigan, 689 A.2d 685 (N.J.1997) (comparing negligent defendant with intentional assailant); Hutcherson v. City of Phoenix, 961 P.2d 449 (Ariz.1998) (comparing negligent and intentional defendants); McKillip v. Smitty's Super Valu, Inc., 945 P.2d 372 (Ariz.Ct. App.1997), review denied (allowing comparison of negligent defendant store and customer who intentionally threw object on the floor, causing plaintiff to fall); Muse v. Dunbar, 716 So.2d 110 (La.Ct.App. 1998), writ denied (comparison of fault between negligent and intentional tortfeasors); Ozaki v. Ass'n of Apartment Owners of Discovery Bay, 954 P.2d 644 (Haw.1998) (comparison of negligent property owner and intentional tortfeasor); Roman Catholic Diocese of Covington v. Secter, 966 S.W.2d 286 (Ky.Ct.App.1998) (comparing negligent and intentional tortfeasors); Siler v. 146 Montague Associates, 228 A.D.2d 33, 652 N.Y.S.2d 315 (1997), appeal dismissed on jurisdictional grounds (Sept. 18, 1997) (allowing comparison of negligent property owner and intentional assailant); Ortiz v. New York City Housing Authority, 22 F.Supp.2d 15 (E.D.N.Y.1998) (negligent landlord and assailant); Harvey v. Farmers Insurance Exchange, 983 P.2d 34 (Colo.Ct.App.1998) (permitting apportionment between sexual assaulter and negligent defendant). But see Turner v. Jordan, 957 S.W.2d 815 (Tenn.1997) (holding that negligence of defendant should not be compared with intentional tortfeasor if defendant had a duty to prevent the intentional acts); Kansas State Bank & Trust Co. v. Specialized Transp. Serv., Inc., 819 P.2d 587 (Kan.1991) (preventing comparison of negligent defendant to intentional tortfeasor when defendant had duty to prevent intentional harm); White v. Hansen, 837 P.2d 1229 (Colo.1992) (interpreting statute); Slawson v. Fast Food Enters., 671 So.2d 255 (Fla.Dist.Ct.App.1996) (interpreting a statute and refusing to compare intentional tortfeasor and negligent property owner when property owner had duty to prevent rape); Stellas v. Alamo Rent–A–Car, Inc., 702 So.2d 232 (Fla.1997) (holding that it was error to compare negligence of defendant with intentional assailants); Prime Hospitality Corp. v. Simms, 700 So.2d 167 (Fla.Dist.Ct.App.1997), review dismissed, 707 So.2d 1126 (Fla.1998) (refusing to compare negligent defendant and perpetrator); Merrill Crossings Assocs. v. McDonald, 705 So.2d 560 (Fla.1997) (refusing to apply comparative fault when the suit is "based on an intentional tort"); Whitehead v. Food Max of Mississippi, 163 F.3d 265 (5th Cir.1998) (Mississippi comparative-fault statute, which explicitly excludes intentional tortfeasors, bars assignment of comparative responsibility to such tortfeasors); Bencivenga v. J.J.A.M.M., Inc., 609 A.2d 1299 (N.J.Sup.Ct.1992) (negligence of defendant dance club may not be compared with *unknown* intentional tortfeasor); Cortez v. University Mall Shopping Ctr., 941 F.Supp. 1096 (D.Utah 1996), overruled by Field v. Boyer, 952 P.2d 1078 (Utah 1998); Welch v. Southland Corp., 952 P.2d 162 (Wash.1998) (interpreting statute to limit assignment of comparative responsibility to unintentional tortfeasors); McLean v. Kirby Co., 490 N.W.2d 229 (N.D.1992) (comparative-negligence statute applicable at time of rape barred assignment of responsibility to rapist; subsequent revision of statute may change outcome in future cases); Will v. United States, 152 F.3d 932 (9th Cir.1998) (deciding, based on Washington law, that an intentional tortfeasor may not be submitted for apportionment of responsibility); Uniform Contribution Among Tortfeasors Act, § 1(c).

Some of the support, however, is in cases comparing a *plaintiff's* responsibility with an intentional *defendant's* responsibility. See N.D.Cent. Code § 32–03.2–02 (1996) ("under this section, fault includes ... reckless or willful conduct...."); Comeau v. Lucas, 455 N.Y.S.2d 871 (N.Y.App.Div.1982) (comparing disruptive behavior of plaintiff with intentional assault by defendant); Bisaillon v. Casares, 798 P.2d 1368 (Ariz.Ct.App.1990) (comparing defendant's intentional tort, other defendant's negligence, and plaintiff's fault), review denied, Oct. 23, 1990; Bonpua v. Fagan, 602 A.2d 287 (N.J.Super.Ct.App.Div.1992) (comparing negligence of plaintiff in provoking fight with defendant's intentional battery); Barth v. Coleman, 878 P.2d 319 (N.M.1994) (comparing negligence of plaintiff with negligence of defendant and intentional assault by other); Morris v. Yogi Bear's Jellystone Park Camp Resort, 539 So.2d 70 (La.Ct.App.1989) (comparing intentional rapist with negligence of 13–year-old victim). But see McLain v. Training and Dev. Corp., 572 A.2d 494 (Me.1990) (refusing to compare defendant's responsibility for assault and battery with contributory negligence of plaintiff); Honegger v. Yoke's Washington Foods, Inc., 921 P.2d 1080 (Wash.App.1996); Kelzer v. Wachholz, 381 N.W.2d 852 (Minn.Ct.App.1986) (refusing to compare fault of plaintiff with intentional trespasser); Tratchel v. Essex Group, Inc., 452 N.W.2d 171 (Iowa 1990) (refusing to compare negligence of plaintiff with intentional tort of fraud); Cartwright v. Equitable Life Assurance Soc'y, 914 P.2d 976 (Mont.1996) (refusing to compare plaintiff's negligence with defendant's fraud); Hattori v. Peairs, 662 So.2d 509 (La.Ct.App.1995) (refusing to compare negligence of the victim with intentional tort of defendant). See also Hickey v. Zezulka, 487 N.W.2d 106 (Mich.1992) (comparing intentional plaintiff with negligent defendant); Wijngaarde v. Parents of Guy, 720 So.2d 6 (La.Ct.App.1998) (plaintiff, who was assaulted by fellow student, was assigned comparative responsibility for provoking assault, but intentional tortfeasor liable for plaintiff's share of comparative responsibility as well). There is also scholarly support for applying comparative responsibility to intentional torts. See Sisk, *Comparative Fault and Common Sense*, 30 Gonz. L. Rev. 29 (1994–95); McNichols, *Should Comparative Responsibility Ever Apply to Intentional Torts*, 37 Okla. L. Rev. 641 (1984); Dear & Zipperstein, *Comparative Fault and Intentional Torts: Doctrinal Barriers and*

Policy Considerations, 24 Santa Clara L. Rev. 1 (1984); Sobelsohm, *Comparing Fault,* 60 Ind. L.J. 413, 442 (1985).

Some courts that have applied comparative responsibility to cases involving intentional tortfeasors have hedged by giving trial courts or appellate courts discretion to decline doing so when it would produce an unfair result. See, e.g., Veazey v. Elmwood Plantation Associates, Ltd., 650 So.2d 712 (La.1994); Green v. USAA Casualty Ins. Co., 668 So.2d 397 (La.Ct.App.1996). But see Morrison v. Kappa Alpha PSI Fraternity, 738 So.2d 1105 (La.Ct.App.1999) (noting that *Veazey* has been overturned by statute, La. Civil Code Ann. art. 2323 (1996)). Other courts have used their normal power to set aside unreasonable verdicts to guard against unfair results. See Scott v. County of Los Angeles, 32 Cal.Rptr.2d 643 (Ct.App.1994). Moreover, the problem of an unfair result is most acute when the intentional tortfeasor is insolvent, the negligent tortfeasor was supposed to protect the plaintiff against the intentional tortfeasor, and the negligent tortfeasor is not jointly and severally liable. That problem is addressed in § 14.

Notwithstanding this development, however, this Restatement does not take a position on whether a plaintiff's negligence is a comparative defense to intentional torts. That issue is left to substantive law. This Restatement does, however, apply its system of comparative responsibility to apportion liability among intentional and negligent defendants.

Comment d. Exceptions. The policies underlying certain statutory causes of action may be incompatible with applying plaintiff's negligence as a percentage defense or with other rules stated in this Restatement. See, e.g., Boyles v. Hamilton, 45 Cal.Rptr. 399 (1965) (child-labor statute); Zerby v. Warren, 210 N.W.2d 58 (Minn.1973) (sale of dangerous product to minors); Soronen v. Olde Milford Inn, 202 A.2d 208 (N.J.Super.Ct.App.Div.1964), appeal after remand 218 A.2d 630 (sale of dangerous product to minors); Gowins v. Pennsylvania R.R. Co., 299 F.2d 431 (6th Cir.), cert. denied, 371 U.S. 824, 83 S.Ct. 44, 9 L.Ed.2d 64 (1962) (Federal Safety Appliance and Boiler Inspection Act); Wells v. Coulter Sales, Inc., 306 N.W.2d 411 (Mich.Ct. App.1981) (workplace-safety statute). But see McGovern v. Koza's Bar & Grill, 604 A.2d 226 (N.J.Super.1991) (noting that *Soronen* has been overturned by statute).

Comment e. Other types of injuries. The rules and principles in this Restatement should influence the resolution of similar issues for other bases of liability. This is especially true when a statutory cause of action calls for courts to develop common-law principles to fill in unanswered questions about apportionment of liability among multiple parties. See, e.g., Comerica Bank—Detroit v. Allen Indus., 769 F.Supp.

1408 (E.D.Mich.1991) (CERCLA contribution); United States v. Western Processing Co., 756 F.Supp. 1424 (W.D.Wash.1990) (CERCLA contribution); Lyncott Corp. v. Chemical Waste Management, Inc., 690 F.Supp. 1409 (E.D.Pa.1988) (CERCLA contribution); Franklin v. Kaypro Corp., 884 F.2d 1222, 1229–32 (9th Cir.1989), cert. denied, 498 U.S. 890, 111 S.Ct. 232, 112 L.Ed.2d 192 (1990) (Securities Exchange Act); Singer v. Olympia Brewing Co., 878 F.2d 596 (2d Cir.1989), cert. denied, 493 U.S. 1024, 110 S.Ct. 729, 107 L.Ed.2d 748 (1990) (Securities Exchange Act); Dobson v. Camden, 705 F.2d 759 (5th Cir.1983) (Civil Rights Act), rev'd on other grounds, 725 F.2d 1003 (5th Cir.1984); Miller v. Apartments & Homes, Inc., 646 F.2d 101 (3d Cir.1981) (Civil Rights Act); In re Masters Mates, 957 F.2d 1020 (2d Cir.1992) (ERISA); Donovan v. Robbins, 752 F.2d 1170 (7th Cir.1985) (ERISA); FDIC v. Geldermann, Inc., 975 F.2d 695 (10th Cir.1992) (Federal Deposit Insurance Act); Resolution Trust Corp. v. Gallagher, 815 F.Supp. 1107 (N.D.Ill.1993). See generally Kornhauser & Revesz, *Settlements Under Joint and Several Liability,* 68 N.Y.U. L. Rev. 427, 430–32 (1993); Di Cola, *Fairness and Efficiency: Allowing Contribution Under ERISA,* 80 Calif. L. Rev. 1543, 1548–53 (1992); Adamski, *Contribution and Settlement in Multiparty Actions Under Rule* 10b–5, 66 Iowa L. Rev. 533 (1981); Davis, *Multiple Defendant Settlements in 10b–5: Good Faith Contribution Bar,* 40 Hastings L.J. 1253 (1989); Boomgaarden & Breer, *Surveying the Superfund Settlement Dilemma,* 27 Land & Water L. Rev. 83 (1992); Cross, *Settlement Under the 1986 Superfund Amendments,* 66 Or. L. Rev. 517 (1987); Mason, *Contribution, Contribution Protection, and Nonsettlor Liability Under CERCLA: Following Laskin's Lead,* 19 B.C. Envtl. Aff. L. Rev. 73 (1991); Boston, *Toxic Apportionment: A Causation and Risk Contribution Model,* 25 Envtl. L. 549 (1995); Hall, Harris & Reinsdorf, *Superfund Response Cost Allocations: The Law, The Science and The Practice,* 49 Bus. Law. 1489 (1994); Note, *Superfund Settlements: The Failed Promise of the 1986 Amendments,* 74 Va. L. Rev. 123 (1988).

Nevertheless, special policy considerations may affect statutory causes of action and other common-law causes of action. Moreover, some of these causes of action may not often be presented in the same lawsuit with other causes of action, so the need for a uniform system of apportionment is not as important. For these reasons, courts should be cautious when borrowing from this Restatement for these other statutory or other common-law claims.

One area of apportionment that has received considerable attention in statutory causes of action is joint and several liability. For example, the vast majority of courts interpret the Comprehensive Environmental Response, Compensation and Liability Act of 1980, as amended, 42 U.S.C. §§ 9601–75 (1995) ("CERCLA"), to impose joint and several liability for indivisible harm when the United States is the plaintiff, despite any explicit statutory language addressing the matter. See O'Neil v. Picillo, 883 F.2d 176, 178–80 (1st Cir.1989); B.F. Goodrich v. Betkoski, 99 F.3d 505, 514 (2d Cir.1996); United States v. Alcan Aluminum Corp., 990 F.2d 711, 721–22 (2d Cir.1993); United States v. Monsanto Co., 858 F.2d 160, 171–73 & n.23 (4th Cir.1988) ("While CERCLA does not mandate the imposition of joint and several liability, it permits it in cases of indivisible harm."); United States v. R.W. Meyer, Inc., 889 F.2d 1497 (6th Cir.1989); United States v. Chem–Dyne Corp., 572 F.Supp. 802, 808 (S.D.Ohio 1983) (scope of liability under CERCLA to be determined according to "traditional and evolving principles of common law"). Most courts rely on Restatement Second, Torts § 433A(1)(b) to determine whether there is a reasonable basis to divide the costs of clean up based on the contribution of each liable party, thereby permitting apportionment on the basis of causation. See United States v. Township of Brighton, 153 F.3d 307 (6th Cir.1998) (discussing what constitutes a "reasonable basis" for causal apportionment); United States v. Alcan Aluminum Corp., 990 F.2d 711 (2d Cir.1993); United States v. R.W. Meyer, Inc., 889 F.2d 1497, 1507 (6th Cir.1989). A few courts have adopted a more liberal, equitable apportionment rule. See United States v. A & F Materials Co., 578 F.Supp. 1249 (S.D.Ill.1984). See generally Oswald, *New Directions in Joint and Several Liability under CERCLA?*, 28 U.C. Davis L. Rev. 299 (1995) (surveying cases imposing joint and several liability and decisions on apportionment based on causation). In addition to CERCLA, a number of courts have adopted joint and several liability for other federal environmental statutes. See United States v. Valentine, 856 F.Supp. 627, 633 (D.Wyo.1994) (Resource Recovery and Conservation Act); United States v. Hollywood Marine, Inc., 519 F.Supp. 688, 692 (S.D.Tex.1981) (Clean Water Act).

Comment f. Claims against employers for workplace injuries. Suits under workers' compensation statutes to recover from an employer for workplace injuries are an example of a special cause of action that implicates distinct policies. Moreover, claims based on workers' compensation statutes do not often occur in hybrid cases involving other causes of action. Claims based on workers' compensation statutes typically are adjudicated in a separate lawsuit or administrative proceeding and are governed by rules that do not consider the culpability or responsibility of the parties. Thus, they are not governed by the rules stated in this Restatement. In the infrequent cases in which suits against employers for workplace injuries are governed by common-law causes of action or ordinary wrongful-death statutes, the rules stated in this Restatement are applicable.

§ 2. Contractual Limitations on Liability

When permitted by contract law, substantive law governing the claim, and applicable rules of construction, a contract between the plaintiff and another person absolving the person from liability for future harm bars the plaintiff's recovery from that person for the harm. Unlike a plaintiff's negligence, a valid contractual limitation on liability does not provide an occasion for the factfinder to assign a percentage of responsibility to any party or other person.

Comment:

a. Nomenclature and history. Contractual limitations on liability are often called "express assumption of risk." This Section uses the term "contractual limitations on liability" to refer more directly to contract law on issues of validity and construction. This Section is drawn from and replaces the rule for express assumption of risk in Restatement Second, Torts § 496B.

b. Rationale and effect. In appropriate situations, the parties to a transaction should be able to agree which of them should bear the risk of injury, even when the injury is caused by a party's legally culpable conduct. That policy is not altered or undermined by the adoption of comparative responsibility. Consequently, a valid contractual limitation on liability, within its terms, creates an absolute bar to a plaintiff's recovery from the other party to the contract. A valid contractual limitation on liability does not provide an occasion for the factfinder to assign a percentage of responsibility to any party or other person. In these respects, a valid contractual limitation on liability differs from a plaintiff's negligence, which merely reduces a plaintiff's recovery by the percentage of responsibility the factfinder assigns to the plaintiff. See § 7.

c. Method of forming contractual limitations on liability. A contractual limitation on liability may occur by written agreement, express oral agreement, or conduct that creates an implied-in-fact contract. See Comment *d*. Whether there is such a contract is determined by the applicable rules of contract law. The essential element of a contractual limitation on liability is that each party agrees that the defendant is under no obligation to protect the plaintiff and shall not be liable to the plaintiff for the consequences of conduct that would otherwise be tortious. The agreement may be general, relieving all obligation to protect the plaintiff, or limited to specific conduct and risks. The agreement may absolve liability entirely, or it may limit liability to a specific amount. A contractual limitation on liability is related to contractual indemnity and is governed by similar rules. See § 22 and Comment *f*.

§ 3. Ameliorative Doctrines for Defining Plaintiff's Negligence Abolished

Plaintiff's negligence is defined by the applicable standard for a defendant's negligence. Special ameliorative doctrines for defining plaintiff's negligence are abolished.

Comment:

a. Standard for plaintiff's negligence same as standard for defendant's negligence. This Section draws on and replaces Restatement Second, Torts § 463. It does not define the standard under which a party is judged to be negligent. That question is addressed in Restatement Second, Torts §§ 281–429. This Section applies the standard of negligence, however defined, to plaintiffs. It also abolishes certain ameliorative doctrines that were designed to avoid the harsh effects of contributory negligence as an absolute bar to a plaintiff's recovery. These doctrines are no longer appropriate when, under comparative responsibility, a plaintiff's negligence only reduces his or her recovery.

The standard of negligence employed to evaluate a plaintiff's conduct is the same as the standard of negligence employed to evaluate a defendant's conduct. See Restatement Second, Torts §§ 282–328. It applies to conduct that imposes risks on the plaintiff or on other persons to the same extent that the standard employed to evaluate a defendant also applies to conduct that imposes risks on the defendant and on others. A plaintiff's conduct that imposes risks on other persons may be valued differently from conduct that imposes risks only on the plaintiff. See § 8. Plaintiff's negligence can include conduct that is reckless, grossly negligent, or intentional.

b. Timing of the plaintiff's and defendant's conduct: last clear chance, mitigation of damages, and avoidable consequences. Subject to the rule stated in § 7, Comment *k*, this Section applies to all types of plaintiff's conduct, regardless of the relative timing of the defendant's conduct, the plaintiff's conduct, and the accident. Thus, this Section replaces Restatement Second, Torts § 478 (Time of Plaintiff's Negligence in Relation to That of Defendant). No last-clear-chance rule categorically forgives a plaintiff for conduct that would otherwise constitute negligence. See Restatement Second, Torts §§ 479–480.

This Section applies to a plaintiff's unreasonable conduct that aggravates the plaintiff's injuries. No rule about mitigation of damages or avoidable consequences categorically forgives a plaintiff of this type of conduct or categorically excludes recovery. See Restatement Second, Torts § 918. Topic 5 addresses apportionment of liability among parties whose conduct causes divisible portions of a plaintiff's injuries, such as when a defendant causes all of a plaintiff's injuries but the plaintiff's conduct merely aggravates the injuries.

The timing of the plaintiff's and defendant's conduct may be relevant to the degree of responsibility the factfinder assigns to a plaintiff. See § 8. It may also be relevant to whether the plaintiff's injury was within the scope of liability of either the plaintiff's or defendant's conduct. See Restatement Second, Torts §§ 440–453.

c. Relationship to implied assumption of risk and defendant's negligence. This Section applies to a plaintiff's negligence even when the plaintiff is actually aware of a risk and voluntarily undertakes it. See § 2; Restatement Second, Torts §§ 496A, 496C–496G. Except as provided in § 2, no jury instruction is given on assumption of risk.

A plaintiff who is actually aware of a *reasonable* risk and voluntarily undertakes it, as when a parent tries to rescue a child from a fire, is not negligent. The parent may, however, be negligent for other reasons, such as the manner of the rescue. When a plaintiff is negligent, the plaintiff's awareness of a risk is relevant to the plaintiff's degree of responsibility. See § 8.

Whether the defendant reasonably believes that the plaintiff is aware of a risk and voluntarily undertakes it may be relevant to whether the defendant acted reasonably. The defendant might reasonably have relied on the plaintiff to avoid the known risk, or other policy considerations may dictate that the defendant has no duty or a limited duty to the plaintiff. See § 2, Comment *j*; Restatement Second, Torts § 282. Whether the plaintiff is aware of a risk and voluntarily assumes it may also be relevant to whether the plaintiff's conduct is a superseding cause. See Restatement Second, Torts § 442. Comparative responsibility may affect what constitutes a superseding cause, but that issue is beyond the scope of this Restatement.

§ 4. Proof of Plaintiff's Negligence and Legal Causation

The defendant has the burden to prove plaintiff's negligence, and may use any of the methods a plaintiff may use to prove defendant's negligence. Except as otherwise provided in Topic 5, the defendant also has the burden to prove that the plaintiff's negligence, if any, was a legal cause of the plaintiff's damages.

§ 7. Effect of Plaintiff's Negligence When Plaintiff Suffers an Indivisible Injury

Plaintiff's negligence (or the negligence of another person for whose negligence the plaintiff is responsible) that is a legal cause of an indivisible injury to the plaintiff reduces the plaintiff's recovery in proportion to the share of responsibility the factfinder assigns to the plaintiff (or other person for whose negligence the plaintiff is responsible).

§ 8. Factors for Assigning Shares of Responsibility

Factors for assigning percentages of responsibility to each person whose legal responsibility has been established include

(a) the nature of the person's risk-creating conduct, including any awareness or indifference with respect to the risks created by the conduct and any intent with respect to the harm created by the conduct; and

(b) the strength of the causal connection between the person's risk-creating conduct and the harm.

Comment:

a. Assigning shares of responsibility. The factfinder assigns comparative percentages of "responsibility" to parties and other relevant persons whose negligence or other legally culpable conduct was a legal cause of the plaintiff's injury. See § 7, Comment *g*. The factfinder does not assign percentages of "fault," "negligence," or "causation."

"Responsibility" is a general and neutral term. Assigning shares of "fault" or "negligence" can be misleading because some causes of action are not based on negligence or fault. Assigning shares of "causation" wrongly suggests that indivisible injuries jointly caused by two or more actors can be divided on the basis of causation. Assigning shares of "culpability" could be misleading if it were not made clear that "culpability" refers to "legal culpability," which may include strict liability.

Of course, it is not possible to precisely compare conduct that falls into different categories, such as intentional conduct, negligent conduct, and conduct governed by strict liability, because the various theories of recovery are incommensurate. However, courts routinely compare seemingly incommensurate values, such as when they balance safety and productivity in negligence or products liability law. "Assigning shares of responsibility" may be a less confusing phrase because it

243

suggests that the factfinder, after considering the relevant factors, *assigns* shares of responsibility rather than *compares* incommensurate quantities. Nevertheless, the term "comparative responsibility" is used pervasively by courts and legislatures to describe percentage-allocation systems.

b. Causation and scope of liability. Conduct is relevant for determining percentage shares of responsibility only when it caused the harm and when the harm is within the scope of the person's liability. See § 7, Comment *f.*

Illustration:

1. A rear-ends B's automobile when B is stopped at a red light at night. B sues A, alleging that A was not watching the road. A claims that B was negligent for failing to have working taillights and for being drunk. In assigning a percentage of responsibility to B, the factfinder considers B's failure to have working taillights if the factfinder finds that the absence of working taillights was a legal cause of the collision; the factfinder does not consider B's drunkenness if the factfinder concludes that the same accident would have happened even if B had been sober and thus that B's drunkenness was not a legal cause of the collision.

c. Factors in assigning shares of responsibility. The relevant factors for assigning percentages of responsibility include the nature of each person's risk-creating conduct and the comparative strength of the causal connection between each person's risk-creating conduct and the harm. The nature of each person's risk-creating conduct includes such things as how unreasonable the conduct was under the circumstances, the extent to which the conduct failed to meet the applicable legal standard, the circumstances surrounding the conduct, each person's abilities and disabilities, and each person's awareness, intent, or indifference with respect to the risks. The comparative strength of the causal connection between the conduct and the harm depends on how attenuated the causal connection is, the timing of each person's conduct in causing the harm, and a comparison of the risks created by the conduct and the actual harm suffered by the plaintiff.

One or more of these factors may be relevant for assigning percentages of responsibility, even though they may not be a necessary element proving a particular claim or defense. However, these factors are irrelevant even to apportionment if there is no causal connection between the referenced conduct and the plaintiff's injuries. See Comment *b.* It should be noted that the mental-state factors in this Section may be considered for apportioning responsibility even if they are not themselves causally connected to the plaintiff's injury, as long as the risk-creating conduct to which they refer is causally connected to the injury.

Courts have power to admit evidence that is relevant and material in light of these factors. They also have discretion to exclude otherwise relevant evidence that is tangential, confusing, or prejudicial. See, e.g., Fed. Rules Evid. 401, 403, 404. The admission of liability by a party does not prevent another party from introducing evidence relevant to the factors for assigning percentages of responsibility unless the admission is of 100 percent of the liability. When evidence is relevant to apportioning responsibility but not to the existence of an underlying claim or defense, the court should consider giving a limiting instruction to focus the jury on the proper use of the evidence.

Illustrations:

2. A is injured when A's and B's automobiles collide at an intersection with a four-way stop. In A's lawsuit against B, A is found negligent for taking his eyes off the road to attend to a child in the back seat, and B is found negligent for purposefully trying to beat A's automobile across the intersection after seeing it approaching. A's conduct and B's conduct are each found to have caused A's indivisible injury. The factfinder would be justified in assigning a higher percentage of responsibility to B because, between A and B, (a) B's conduct deviated more significantly from the legally required norm, (b) B had a more culpable state of mind, and (c) the other circumstances surrounding A's conduct were more forgivable.

TOPIC 2. LIABILITY OF MULTIPLE TORTFEASORS FOR INDIVISIBLE HARM

§ 10. Effect of Joint and Several Liability

When, under applicable law, some persons are jointly and severally liable to an injured person, the injured person may sue for and recover the full amount of recoverable damages from any jointly and severally liable person.

§ 11. Effect of Several Liability

When, under applicable law, a person is severally liable to an injured person for an indivisible injury, the injured person may recover only the severally liable person's comparative-responsibility share of the injured person's damages.

§ 12. Intentional Tortfeasors

Each person who commits a tort that requires intent is jointly and severally liable for any indivisible injury legally caused by the tortious conduct.

§ 14. Tortfeasors Liable for Failure to Protect the Plaintiff from the Specific Risk of an Intentional Tort

A person who is liable to another based on a failure to protect the other from the specific risk of an intentional tort is jointly and severally liable for the share of comparative responsibility assigned to the intentional tortfeasor in addition to the share of comparative responsibility assigned to the person.

Comment:

a. Scope. The rule in this Section applies only when a person is negligent *because* of the failure to take reasonable precautions to protect against the specific risk created by an intentional tortfeasor. Negligence (or strict liability) is determined in accordance with governing rules about tortious conduct, but this Section only applies if the risk that makes the tortfeasor negligent or strictly liable is the failure to take precautions against an intentional tort. When a person's unrelated tortious conduct and an intentional tortfeasor's acts concur to cause harm to another, the rules of joint and several liability provided in the applicable Track (A–E) govern. For reasons explained in Comment *b*, this Section is limited to instances in which the person is liable because of the risk of an intentional tort and does not extend to duties to protect against another's negligence. This Section does not determine when a party who fails to protect against the risk of an intentional tort is liable for failing to do so. Rather, the rule in this Section applies only when the governing law provides for such liability.

Illustration:

1. A is a guest at a hotel operated by B. B neglects to provide adequate door locks on A's room, as a result of which C, an intruder, gains access to A's room, assaults A, and steals A's property. B is liable for the shares of comparative responsibility assigned both to B and to C, because the risk that made B's conduct negligent was specifically the risk that someone would assault A and steal A's property. C is jointly and severally liable for all of A's damages. See § 12 (intentional tortfeasors). B's right to contribution from C is governed by § 23, Comment *e*. C's right to contribution from B is governed by § 23 and Comment *l*.

The rule stated in this Section includes tortious acts of commission as well as omission. Thus, if in Illustration 1, B had provided adequate door locks, but negligently repaired the lock on A's room, thereby enabling C to gain access to A's room, B would also be liable for C's share of comparative responsibility.

b.   Rationale. The modification of joint and several liability and the application of comparative responsibility to intentional tortfeasors create a difficult problem. When a person is injured by an intentional tort and another person negligently failed to protect against the risk of an intentional tort, the great culpability of the intentional tortfeasor may lead a factfinder to assign the bulk of responsibility for the harm to the intentional tortfeasor, who often will be insolvent. This would leave the person who negligently failed to protect the plaintiff with little liability and the injured plaintiff with little or no compensation for the harm. Yet when the risk of an intentional tort is the specific risk that required the negligent tortfeasor to protect the injured person, that result significantly diminishes the purpose for requiring a person to take precautions against this risk.

A number of courts therefore have concluded that persons who negligently fail to protect against the specific risk of an intentional tort should bear the risk that the intentional tortfeasor is insolvent. The rule stated in this Section similarly makes such persons liable for the intentional tortfeasor's share of comparative responsibility. The negligent person may assert a contribution claim against the intentional tortfeasor, as provided in § 23, Comment *e.*

The method that most courts have employed to impose the risk of insolvency of an intentional tortfeasor on a person who negligently fails to protect the plaintiff is to refuse to permit assignment of a share of comparative responsibility to the intentional tortfeasor in a suit against the negligent party. While this method accomplishes the same goal, it is a less desirable means than the rule provided in this Section, which makes the negligent party liable for both that party's share as well as the intentional tortfeasor's share of comparative responsibility. Including intentional tortfeasors in the assignment of comparative responsibility provides a system for resolving all claims in a single proceeding, including any contribution or indemnity claims that may exist among negligent, strictly liable, and intentional tortfeasors. See § 1, Comment *c.* Including intentional tortfeasors also permits appropriate crediting of the judgment in the case of partial settlements. See § 16. In addition, coupling a rule permitting assignment of comparative responsibility to intentional tortfeasors with the rule provided in this Section avoids the unfairness of holding a party whose negligence is wholly unrelated to the intentional tortfeasor liable for the share of comparative responsibility assigned to the intentional tortfeasor. See Illustration 2.

Because § 12 (intentional tortfeasors) already provides that an intentional tortfeasor is jointly and severally liable for all harm legally caused by the intentional tort, this Section is unnecessary when the person with a duty to protect commits an intentional tort. Thus, if the law-enforcement officer in Illustration 6 took no action because of a grudge against A and a desire to see A harmed by B, § 12 (intentional tortfeasors) would make the law-enforcement officer jointly and severally liable for the injury suffered by A, regardless of this Section. More significantly, in jurisdictions that retain full joint and several liability (Track A), the rule provided in this Section is unnecessary because joint and several liability applies to every tortfeasor who is a legal cause of the plaintiff's injury. However, in jurisdictions that have adopted some modification of joint and several liability (Tracks B–E), this Section makes the person who tortiously fails to protect against an intentional tort liable not only for that person's own share of comparative responsibility but also for the intentional tortfeasor's share of comparative responsibility.

Arguably, the rule provided in this Section might logically apply even when a person negligently fails to protect another from risks created by a negligent tortfeasor. Thus, a person who negligently entrusts a handgun to a child, who then negligently shoots a third party, might be held liable for any share of comparative responsibility assigned to the child. However, the breadth of circumstances in which a person might be found negligent for failing to act based on the risk created by the foreseeable negligence of a third person is so great that a categorical extension of the rule stated in this Section could undermine the policies embodied in a jurisdiction's decision to abrogate joint and several liability.

When the third party's actions are merely negligent, rather than intentional, there are less likely to be great disparities between the share of comparative responsibility assigned to each party. When a jurisdiction has made a judgment to modify joint and several liability for unintentional tortfeasors who act independently, extending the rule provided in this Section to all those who negligently fail to protect against another's negligent conduct appears inconsistent with the basic judgment made by the jurisdiction that adopted several liability for the purpose of limiting each tortfeasor's liability to his or her comparative share of responsibility. Thus, while the rule stated in this Section is limited to a specific duty to protect against intentional torts, whether there are other limited circumstances in which the rule should be extended to those who fail to protect against nonintentional tortfeasors is a matter on which this Restatement takes no position.

§ 15. Persons Acting in Concert

When persons are liable because they acted in concert, all persons are jointly and severally liable for the share of comparative responsibility assigned to each person engaged in concerted activity.

§ 16. Effect of Partial Settlement on Jointly and Severally Liable Tortfeasors' Liability

The plaintiff's recoverable damages from a jointly and severally liable tortfeasor are reduced by the comparative share of damages attributable to a settling tortfeasor who otherwise would have been liable for contribution to jointly and severally liable defendants who do not settle. The settling tortfeasor's comparative share of damages is the percentage of comparative responsibility assigned to the settling tortfeasor multiplied by the total damages of the plaintiff.

Comment:

b. History. Restatement Second, Torts § 885(3) provided for a credit based on a settlement with one tortfeasor of at least the amount paid by the settling tortfeasor to the plaintiff. This Section replaces § 885(3).

c. Rationale. When joint and several liability applies, it is important to assure that the settling tortfeasor not be subject to any further liability arising out of plaintiff's claim. That condition can be satisfied by barring any contribution claims against a settling tortfeasor by other responsible parties, as § 23 does. Fairness in loss allocation, however, requires that nonsettling tortfeasors receive a credit against the judgment for the settling tortfeasor's share of responsibility. This Section provides nonsettling tortfeasors with a credit equal to the percentage share of plaintiff's damages assigned to the settling tortfeasor. If the factfinder later determines that the settling tortfeasor bore no responsibility or on some other basis determined that the settling tortfeasor was not liable to the nonsettling tortfeasor for contribution (e.g., because of an immunity), the nonsettling tortfeasor receives no credit for that nonliable settling tortfeasor. Since the statute of limitations for a contribution claim generally begins to run after that on the plaintiff's claim, the fact that the plaintiff's claim against the settling tortfeasor was barred by the statute of limitations would not affect whether the defendant was entitled to a credit.

Illustration:

    1. A, a passenger in B's car, sues B for negligence in going through a stop sign and C, who also went through a stop sign at the same intersection, resulting in a collision that injured A. A settles with B for $20,000. The factfinder assigns 20 percent responsibility to A for distracting B and 45 percent and 35 percent responsibility respectively to B and C and determines that A suffered $100,000 in damages. C receives a $45,000 credit (B's 45% share of comparative responsibility x $100,000 damages) due to A's settlement with B that is applied to the total damage award by the jury, thereby reducing C's liability to $35,000.

No perfect method exists for apportioning liability among a plaintiff, a settling tortfeasor, and a nonsettling tortfeasor. Each of the available options has its advantages and disadvantages. Nevertheless, the rule adopted in this Section provides the nonsettling tortfeasor with a credit against the judgment in the amount of the comparative share of the settling tortfeasor. The comparative-share credit is adopted rather than its primary alternative, a credit in the amount of the settlement with the settling tortfeasor, also known as a pro tanto credit because on balance it better provides for fairness in loss allocation and has administrability advantages. First, the comparative-share credit obviates the need for courts to review the bona fides of partial settlements and contributes to an equitable distribution of liability among the plaintiff, settling tortfeasors, and nonsettling tortfeasors. Second, it is more easily applied and avoids the complications of determining whether the settlement should be credited against the total damages before or after the plaintiff's share of the damages is subtracted from the total damages. Third, it has the benefit of being consistent with the treatment of partial settlements when there is only several liability. Fourth, a percentage-share credit avoids the need to value assets for which there is no ready market valuation. The United States Supreme Court, after thoroughly canvassing the respective advantages and disadvantages of these two systems, chose a comparative-share credit for Admiralty cases.

The major advantage of a pro tanto credit system is that it encourages early partial settlements, because the plaintiff is assured that all damages can be recovered from the remaining tortfeasors if the plaintiff prevails at trial. Early settlement is especially attractive to a plaintiff who needs financing for his suit or who needs funds promptly to pay for medical rehabilitation or to replace lost income. However, there is no empirical evidence nor any theoretical reason to believe that a pro tanto credit is more conducive to complete settlement of a case once a partial settlement has occurred. Thus, to the extent that facilitating the complete voluntary resolution of a suit before trial for the sake of judicial efficiency is the goal, there is no reason to believe that either a pro tanto or a comparative-share credit is preferable.

A pro tanto regime is preferable in a joint and several liability jurisdiction when a defendant has insufficient assets to satisfy a judgment, so as to facilitate settlement with such a defendant. If a comparative-share credit is employed, the plaintiff must obtain a judgment against the partially insolvent defendant in order to have other solvent defendants pay the share of the partially solvent defendant that is not covered by liability insurance or other assets of that defendant. This disadvantage is partially ameliorated by Comment g, which permits the parties to seek a pretrial determination of partial insolvency by a defendant. Once such a determination is made, the nonsettling tortfeasor would be provided a credit in the amount that the partially insolvent settling tortfeasor had available to satisfy the judgment or the amount of the comparative share of the settling tortfeasor, whichever is less. Such a rule would permit the plaintiff to settle with a partially insolvent tortfeasor and still retain the benefits of joint and several liability. Similarly, the provisions of § C21 for reallocation could, if employed at an early stage in the case, ameliorate this disadvantage of a proportionate-share-credit system. This could be done by providing the same reallocated result as would be reached if there were no settlement and the partially insolvent party remained in the case throughout the trial.

A pro tanto credit has the disadvantage of imposing any inadequacy in a partial settlement between the plaintiff and a settling tortfeasor on nonsettling tortfeasors against whom the plaintiff prevails at trial. Of course, if the plaintiff does not prevail at trial against the nonsettling tortfeasor, the plaintiff will bear the inadequacy in the settlement. Nevertheless, most settlements are discounted by the estimated probability of liability of the settling tortfeasor and, to some extent, for the costs and fees saved; hence, a pro tanto credit usually will increase the potential liability of a nonsettling tortfeasor. In effect, the plaintiff and settling tortfeasor can externalize a portion of the settling tortfeasor's responsibility to a nonsettling tortfeasor, which results in an inequitable apportionment of liability. While a pro tanto credit encourages early settlement, it does so at the risk of producing an unfair allocation of liability. Employing a pro tanto credit also creates valuation problems in cases in which the settlement amount is contingent or to be paid in the future.

Some jurisdictions with a pro-tanto-credit rule attempt to restrict the possibility of inadequate settlements by reviewing the settlement to assure that it is reasonable or entered into in good faith. See Uniform Contribution Among Tortfeasors Act § 4. Court determination of good faith necessarily requires a satellite legal proceeding to assess the settlement, and there is reason to question the capacity of courts to make a determination on this matter. If the "good faith" requirement is taken seriously, the hearing on the matter will require consideration of a number of factors and may consume significant party and judicial resources, and, if courts do not take this requirement seriously, fairness in loss allocation is compromised.

By contrast, a comparative-share credit tends to produce a fairer ultimate allocation of responsibility among all parties—plaintiff, settling tortfeasors, and nonsettling tortfeasors. A nonsettling tortfeasor's liability is not dependent on the outcome of negotiations between other parties to the suit, negotiations that exclude the nonsettling tortfeasor. Its disadvantage is that it, as discussed above, makes partial settlements more difficult. The comparative-share credit also requires the factfinder to determine the comparative share of a nonparty. This results in administrative costs, that, while probably not as substantial as those required by the pro tanto "good faith" hearing, nevertheless exist. Determining the comparative share of a nonparty settling tortfeasor may also, in some cases, introduce confusion to the fact-finding process.

On balance, the comparative-share credit appears preferable and is generally the rule in jurisdictions that retain joint and several liability. The comparative-share credit has a number of administrative advantages over the pro tanto rule.

The comparative-share credit does not require that the settling tortfeasor remain as a party in the case. Since settling tortfeasors have no continuing interest in the outcome of the case, they should be dismissed. Evidence bearing on their responsibility would be introduced by the plaintiff and the nonsettling defendants, and, because of their opposing interests in the assignment of responsibility to the settling tortfeasor, the evidence will be presented in an adversarial context. Moreover, because settlements often do not take place until after substantial discovery has been conducted, the nonsettling parties will often already have the benefit of discovery that bears on the settling party's responsibility. In those cases in which the plaintiff believes that the settling tortfeasor's cooperation is critical to the plaintiff's interests at trial (i.e., by being present at trial to explain the settling tortfeasor's role and minimize the responsibility assigned to it), the settlement could include a cooperation provision requiring such participation. In any case, courts should be sensitive to the change in incentives that may occur with a partial settlement. Plaintiff's interest will be in minimizing the comparative responsibility of the settling tortfeasor. The defendant's interest will be in maximizing it, although before settlement there may have been an agreement among defendants not to pursue each other. When appropriate and when excessive delay would not be occasioned, the court should consider seriously a request to afford the parties additional discovery.

§ 17. Joint and Several or Several Liability for Independent Tortfeasors

If the independent tortious conduct of two or more persons is a legal cause of an indivisible injury, the law of the applicable jurisdiction determines whether those persons are jointly and severally liable, severally liable, or liable under some hybrid of joint and several and several liability.

Comment:

a. Alternative versions of joint and several or several liability. The Institute takes no position on whether joint and several liability, several liability, or some combination of the two should be adopted for independent tortfeasors who cause an indivisible injury. As noted in § 10, Comment *a*, there is currently no majority rule on this question, although joint and several liability has been substantially modified in most jurisdictions both as a result of the adoption of comparative fault and tort reform during the 1980s and 1990s. Nevertheless, five different versions of joint and several, several, and combinations of the two are presented in the five separate and independent Tracks that follow this Section. These five Tracks are mutually exclusive, although modifications (or combinations of some) of them are possible.

The first Track—the "A" series—presents a rule of pure joint and several liability. The "A" Track then proceeds to resolve subsidiary issues implicated by this premise. These issues include identifying those who may be submitted to the jury for assignment of a percentage of comparative responsibility and the treatment of claims against an employer who is immune from tort liability because of the exclusive remedy bar of workers' compensation. The second Track—the "B" series—presents a pure several-liability scheme and addresses the subsidiary questions posed by that premise.

The first hybrid Track—the "C" series—begins with a rule of joint and several liability for independent tortfeasors who cause an indivisible injury to a plaintiff. However, it places the risk of a tortfeasor's insolvency on all parties who bear responsibility for the plaintiff's damages, including the plaintiff. An insolvent tortfeasor's comparative share of responsibility is reallocated to the other parties in proportion to their comparative responsibility. A very similar result is obtained by starting with a rule of several liability but then providing for reallocation in the event of insolvency. This Track also addresses which persons should be subject to an assignment of comparative responsibility and the effect of that allocation on the apportionment of liability among the parties. This Track is theoretically the most appealing in that it apportions the risk of insolvency to the remaining parties in the case in proportion to their responsibility, thereby providing an equitable mechanism for coping with insolvency. There may be administrative and practical difficulties with the reallocation provisions that are contained in this Track.

The "D" Track is another hybrid system in which joint and several liability is imposed on independent tortfeasors whose percentage of comparative responsibility exceeds a specified threshold. Thus, tortfeasors assigned a modest percentage of comparative responsibility below the threshold are severally liable, while those at or above the threshold are jointly and severally liable. The "D" Track reflects legislation in approximately a dozen states and responds to the concern that many tortfeasors whose responsibility for a plaintiff's injury is quite minimal are held liable for the entirety of the recoverable damages under a pure joint-and-several-liability scheme. However, any threshold is an imperfect way to screen out tangential tortfeasors, and often the threshold is set too high (50 percent) to serve this function well. When there are many tortfeasors, this Track does not perform well, as it virtually guarantees that several liability will be imposed, regardless of the role of any given tortfeasor in the plaintiff's injuries. This threshold series also imposes the risk of insolvency on an entirely innocent plaintiff whenever all solvent defendants are below the specified threshold. To the extent that the justification for modifying joint and several liability is the adoption of comparative responsibility so that the plaintiff may also be legally culpable, imposing the risk of insolvency on an innocent plaintiff is unwarranted.

The "E" Track represents yet another hybrid system, in which the variable that determines joint and several liability or several liability is the type of harm suffered by the plaintiff. Independent tortfeasors are jointly and severally liable for damages for certain harms (often termed "economic" or "pecuniary" harms) but are severally liable for compensatory damages for the remainder of harm (referred to as "noneconomic" or "nonpecuniary" harm). Apportioning the risk of insolvency in this fashion (i.e., defendants bear it with regard to economic harm and plaintiffs bear it with regard to noneconomic harms) thus treats the recovery of economic loss as more important to a plaintiff. In addition, damages for economic harm, being susceptible to objective proof, are subject to considerably less variance in their determination by the factfinder. The "E" Track reflects legislation in about a half-dozen states. Some critics contend that this

Track works an injustice to those who are not wage earners and
thereby suffer a greater proportion of noneconomic damages in a
lawsuit. Others, including those that focus on deterrence, would also
dispute the proposition that noneconomic damages are less important
than economic damages. This Track also treats unfairly the plaintiff
who is not comparatively responsible for the injury by imposing the
risk of insolvency for noneconomic loss on the innocent plaintiff rather
than the culpable defendants. Finally, this Track creates some administrative and practical difficulties in its operation.

REPORTERS' NOTE

*Comment a. Alternative versions of joint and several or several
liability.* The clear trend over the past several decades has been a
move away from pure joint and several liability. Most jurisdictions
have adopted some hybrid form of joint and several and several
liability. As of the time this Restatement was published, pure joint and
several liability was employed in 15 jurisdictions. However, only nine
of those states had adopted comparative responsibility; five of the
remaining joint-and-several-liability jurisdictions still retain contributory negligence and one uses a slight/gross rule to determine is a
plaintiff can recover. Fifteen jurisdictions have adopted several liability. More jurisdictions have some form of a hybrid system than have
either pure joint and several or pure several-liability systems.

TOPIC 3. CONTRIBUTION AND INDEMNITY

§ 23. Contribution

(a) **When two or more persons are or may be liable
for the same harm and one of them discharges the liability of another by settlement or discharge of judgment, the
person discharging the liability is entitled to recover
contribution from the other, unless the other previously
had a valid settlement and release from the plaintiff.**

(b) **A person entitled to recover contribution may
recover no more than the amount paid to the plaintiff in
excess of the person's comparative share of responsibility.**

(c) **A person who has a right of indemnity against
another person under § 22 does not have a right of contribution against that person and is not subject to liability
for contribution to that person.**

Comment:

e. Proportionate shares. If a person is otherwise entitled to
contribution, the amount of contribution is determined by the percent-

ages of responsibility the factfinder assigns to each person. See §§ 7, 8.

Illustration:

> 5. A sues B and C. The factfinder finds that B and C are liable, finds that A's damages are $100,000, and assigns 10 percent responsibility to A, 30 percent responsibility to B, and 60 percent responsibility to C. In a jurisdiction that uses joint and several liability, A is entitled to collect $90,000 from B. See § 7, Topic 2. If A collects $90,000 from B, B is entitled to recover $60,000 ($100,000 x .60) in contribution from C.

f. Contribution limited to amount above the percentage share of the person seeking contribution. If a person is otherwise entitled to recover contribution, contribution is limited to the amount that person pays to the plaintiff above that person's percentage of responsibility. In a jurisdiction where a defendant is only severally liable under Topic 2, a defendant normally would pay no more than its own percentage share and would not be entitled to contribution. Even in a jurisdiction that does not use joint and several liability, however, a severally liable defendant might be sued with less than all of the relevant persons and be liable for more than its own percentages of responsibility, and therefore be entitled to contribution. See Comment *c* and Illustration 4.

Illustrations:

> 10. A sues B and C. The factfinder finds that B and C are liable, finds that A's damages are $100,000, and assigns 40 percent responsibility to B and 60 percent responsibility to C. B pays A $40,000, either because the jurisdiction does not use joint and several liability, see Topic 2, or because A chooses to recover only $40,000 from B. B cannot recover contribution from C because B did not pay more than B's percentage share of responsibility. See also Comment *b.*

> 11. Same facts as Illustration 10, except that B pays A $50,000. B can recover $10,000 in contribution from C. See also Comment *b.*

g. Contribution for more than the percentage share of the person against whom contribution is sought. In a jurisdiction that uses joint and several liability, see Topic 2, and subject to Comments *f* and *j,* a person who otherwise is entitled to contribution is entitled to recover the percentage share of liability of the person against whom contribution is sought plus that person's proportionate share of any other person's percentage share of liability.

Illustration:

     12. A sues B, C, and D. The factfinder finds that B, C, and D are liable, finds that A's damages are $100,000, and assigns 10 percent responsibility to A, 50 percent responsibility to B, 25 percent responsibility to C, and 15 percent responsibility to D. B pays the entire $90,000 judgment and sues C for contribution. B can recover $30,000 contribution from C ($25,000 plus 25/75ths of $15,000). See Comment *e*. After C pays B $30,000 in contribution, B can recover $10,000 and C can recover $5,000 in contribution from D.

    h. Contribution in favor of a settlor. A person who is otherwise entitled to contribution can recover contribution even though the person extinguished the liability of another by settlement rather than payment of judgment. A settlor need not prove that he would have been found liable to the plaintiff. A settlor must show only that the settlement was reasonable.

    i. Contribution against a settlor. A person who settles with the plaintiff before final judgment is not liable for contribution to others for the injury. In contrast, settlement after final judgment, or after settlement between the plaintiff and the person seeking contribution, does not protect the settlor from contribution. The effect of settlement on nonsettling persons is determined by § 15.

TOPIC 5. APPORTIONMENT OF LIABILITY WHEN DAMAGES CAN BE DIVIDED BY CAUSATION

§ 26. Apportionment of Liability When Damages Can Be Divided by Causation

    (a) When damages for an injury can be divided by causation, the factfinder first divides them into their indivisible component parts and separately apportions liability for each indivisible component part under Topics 1 through 4.

    (b) Damages can be divided by causation when the evidence provides a reasonable basis for the factfinder to determine:

       (1) that any legally culpable conduct of a party or other relevant person to whom the factfinder assigns a percentage of responsibility was a legal cause of less than the entire damages for which the plaintiff seeks recovery and

       (2) the amount of damages separately caused by that conduct.

Otherwise, the damages are indivisible and thus the injury
is indivisible. Liability for an indivisible injury is apportioned under Topics 1 through 4.

Comment:

a. *Scope.* This Section addresses apportionment of liability when
damages can be divided by causation. Damages can be divided by
causation when any person or group of persons to whom the factfinder
assigns a percentage of responsibility (or any tortious act of such a
person) was a legal cause of less than the entire damages. See
Comment *f.* Divisible damages are first divided by causation into
indivisible parts, and then each indivisible part is apportioned by
responsibility. This Section addresses how these two processes work in
the same case.

Dividing damages by causation and apportioning liability by responsibility in the same case has not been widely addressed by statute
or case law. Most rules about dividing damages by causation were
developed before comparative responsibility. See Restatement Second,
Torts §§ 433A, 433B, 434, 879, 881. Most rules about comparative
responsibility were developed in the context of indivisible injuries. Few
courts have addressed the interaction between these two processes.
Thus, this Section is designed to leave room for future development.

The policies underlying division by causation and apportionment
by responsibility suggest solutions to these issues. No party should be
liable for harm it did not cause, and an injury caused by two or more
persons should be apportioned according to their respective shares of
comparative responsibility. Sometimes these policies converge, but
sometimes they conflict. They must be tempered with two additional
considerations. A working system must be capable of being understood
and applied by courts and juries in a reasonably efficient manner, and
available evidence sometimes leaves uncertainty that the legal regime
must accommodate. These considerations, along with existing case law
and statutory guidance, support the rules in this Section.

b. *History.* Division of damages by causation was addressed in
Restatement Second, Torts §§ 433A (Apportionment of Harm to
Causes), 433B (Burden of Proof), 434 (Functions of Court and Jury),
879 (Concurring and Consecutive Independent Acts), and 881 (Distinct
or Divisible Harms). This Section replaces §§ 433A, 433B, 879, 881,
and the portion of § 434 that addresses division of damages by
causation. Division of damages by causation is also addressed in
Restatement Third, Torts: Products Liability § 16.

c. *Employing the two-step process in Subsection (a).* Under
Subsection (a), the factfinder divides divisible damages into their

indivisible component parts. The factfinder then apportions liability for each indivisible component part under Topics 1–4. For each indivisible component part, the factfinder assigns a percentage of comparative responsibility to each party or other relevant person. See §§ 7, 8. The percentages of comparative responsibility for each component part add to 100 percent. See § 7, Comment *g*. The other rules in Topics 1–4 are applied to each component part as though the suit involved that part alone. The plaintiff is entitled to judgment in an amount that aggregates the judgments for each component part.

Illustrations:

1.   A negligently parks his automobile in a dangerous location. B negligently crashes his automobile into A's automobile, damaging it. When B is standing in the road inspecting the damage, B is hit by C, causing personal injury to B. B sues A and C for personal injury and property damage. B's negligent driving and A's negligent parking caused damage to B's automobile. A's negligent parking, B's negligent driving, B's negligent standing in the road, and C's negligent driving caused B's personal injuries. The factfinder determines damages separately for B's automobile and B's person. The factfinder assigns separate percentages of responsibility to A and B for damage to B's automobile, considering A's parking and B's driving. A's and B's percentages add to 100 percent. The factfinder assigns a separate percentage of responsibility to A, B, and C for B's personal injury, considering A's parking, B's driving, B's standing in the road, and C's driving. A's, B's, and C's percentages add to 100 percent. After applying the rules in Topics 1–4 to each component injury, the court determines A's and C's liability to B by adding each party's liability for each component injury.

2.   Same facts as Illustration 1. The factfinder finds that damages for B's automobile are $1,000 and that damages for B's personal injury are $10,000. For the damage to B's automobile, the factfinder assigns 70 percent responsibility to A and 30 percent responsibility to B. For B's personal injuries, the factfinder assigns 20 percent responsibility to A, 40 percent responsibility to B, and 40 percent responsibility to C. A is liable to B for $2,700: $700 ($1,000 x .70) for damage to B's automobile plus $2,000 ($10,000 x .20) for B's personal injuries. C is liable to B for $4,000 ($10,000 x .40) for B's personal injury. Whether A and C are jointly and severally liable for B's personal injury is determined by Topic 2.

3.   Same facts as Illustration 2, except that, for B's personal injury, the factfinder assigns 20 percent responsibility to A, 60

percent responsibility to B, and 20 percent responsibility to C. Under pure comparative responsibility, A is liable to B for $2,700: $700 ($1,000 x .70) for damage to B's automobile and $2,000 ($10,000 x .20) for B's personal injuries. C is liable to B for $2,000 ($10,000 x .20) for B's personal injury. See § 7. Under modified comparative negligence, A is liable to B for $700 ($1,000 x .70) for damage to B's automobile. B is barred from recovering from A or C for B's personal injury. See § 7, Comment *n*.

4.   Same facts as Illustration 3, except that A settles with B before trial. C is liable to B for $2,000 ($10,000 x .20) for B's personal injuries, with no joint and several liability for A's 20 percent share. See § 16; § B19, Comment *k*; § E19, Comment *o*. (In a jurisdiction that employs a pro tanto credit for settlement, the settlement is credited proportionately to damage to B's automobile and B's personal injury.)

d.   Rationale for the two-step process in Subsection (a). Apportionment of liability under Subsection (a) requires two steps. The factfinder divides the plaintiff's damages by causation into their indivisible component parts and then apportions liability for each component part under Topics 1–4. See Comment *c*. This process effectuates the basic policies of causation and comparative responsibility. It does not make a plaintiff or a defendant responsible for damages that person did not cause, and it apportions liability among persons causing any component part according to that person's comparative share of responsibility.

Problems can arise when the evidence of who caused what part of the damages is uncertain or the number of component parts is in dispute. If the court cannot determine in advance of the jury submission who caused what part of the damages, it may be difficult to instruct the jury about who to compare for each component part. Even when it is not difficult to determine the indivisible component parts, the number of parties or the variety of conduct can create problems for submitting the case to a jury. See Comment *j*.

These administrative difficulties could be avoided by asking the jury to find the plaintiff's aggregate damages and then assigning a single set of percentages to all persons who caused at least part of the damages, taking into account evidence of causation and comparative responsibility. See Comment *j*. However, this solution can create problems of its own. A jury might assign a high percentage to a party who was highly culpable but who caused only a small part of the damages, resulting in that party's being held liable for more damage than it caused. Under modified comparative responsibility, a jury might assign a plaintiff more than 50 percent responsibility, barring the plaintiff from any recovery, even though the plaintiff's negligence caused only part of the damages. That result would frustrate a basic policy goal of causation for plaintiff's negligence. See § 7, Comment *f*. These problems are avoided by the two-step process in Subsection (a).

e.   Persons to whom the factfinder assigns a percentage of responsibility. Under Topic 2, percentages of comparative responsibility can be assigned to a plaintiff, the defendants, settling tortfeasors, and, depending on rules about joint and several or several liability, nonparty tortfeasors ("other relevant persons"). This Section incorporates the rules in Topic 2.

f.   Divisible damages. Whether damages can be divided by causation is a question of fact. The fact that the magnitude of each indivisible component part cannot be determined with precision does not mean that the damages are indivisible. All that is required is a reasonable basis for dividing the damages. See Comment *h*.

Divisible damages can occur in a variety of circumstances. They can occur when one person caused all of the damages and another person caused only part of the damages. They can occur when the parties caused one part of the damages and nontortious conduct caused another part. They can occur when the nontortious conduct occurred before or after the parties' tortious conduct. They can occur in cases involving serial injuries, regardless of the length of time between the injuries. They can occur when the plaintiff's own conduct caused part of the damages.

Dividing damages by causation among different tortious acts by the same person may be required. When a person commits two or more tortious acts that cause different parts of the damages, each tortious act is treated separately.

g.   Indivisible injuries. Damages are indivisible, and thus the injury is indivisible, when all legally culpable conduct of the plaintiff and every tortious act of the defendants and other relevant persons caused all the damages. Unless sufficient evidence permits the factfinder to determine that damages are divisible, they are indivisible.

h.   Burden of proof and sufficiency of evidence to permit damages to be divided by causation. This Section does not address whether, as a part of the prima facie case, a person caused the plaintiff any injury. For example, this Section does not address whether, in a crashworthiness case involving enhanced injury to a passenger, the defect caused any enhanced injury and, therefore, whether the plaintiff has made out a prima facie case. That question is governed by Restatement Third, Torts: Products Liability § 16. When the plaintiff has made out a prima facie case, this Section addresses apportionment

261

of liability among two or more persons who caused the divisible damages, including how much damage each person caused.

Whether damages are divisible is a question of fact. A party alleging that damages are divisible has the burden to prove that they are divisible. Whether there is sufficient evidence to prove divisibility is determined by each jurisdiction's applicable rules. The magnitude of each divisible part is also a question of fact. The burden to prove the magnitude of each part is on the party who seeks division.

Historically, courts required plaintiffs to prove with specificity the magnitude of the damages each defendant caused. This often resulted in the plaintiff's being unable to meet the burden of proof. The unfairness of this rule led several courts to either relax the evidence required or hold that, when a plaintiff could show that each defendant caused some of the damages, each was jointly and severally liable for the entire damages unless the defendants could prove the magnitude of each part. See Restatement Second, Torts § 433B. Shifting the burden of proof to defendants to prove the magnitude of the parts may be unfair to defendants because it can impose full liability on a defendant who caused only part of the damages. The justification for shifting the burden of proof was that a culpable defendant should bear the risk that evidence is unavailable to permit division.

Even before comparative responsibility, the rationale of placing the burden of proof on culpable rather than innocent parties did not always support placing the burden on defendants. Plaintiffs sometimes claim their negligence caused only a part of the damages. Before comparative responsibility, this would mean that the plaintiff was barred from recovering the damages caused by the plaintiff's negligence. Under comparative responsibility, this would mean that the plaintiff's negligence reduces the damages caused by the plaintiff's negligence. The rationale for shifting the burden of proof to the defendant—that the defendant is culpable but the plaintiff is innocent—does not apply to that case. Thus, this Comment places the burden to prove the magnitude of divisible damages on the party who seeks to avoid responsibility for the entire damages.

Comparative responsibility provides an alternative means for apportioning liability for divisible damages: dividing the damages according to each person's percentage of responsibility. This alternative has problems of its own. A party's culpability is different from the magnitude of damages the party caused. See Comment *a*. A party's comparative responsibility may have been minimal, but the party may have caused the majority of the damages. Comparative responsibility is ill-suited to apportioning damages for another reason. Under joint and several liability, a defendant may be liable for more than the defendant's own percentage share of the damages. If a defendant did not cause the damages, however, the defendant should not be liable, regardless of joint and several liability.

A more attractive solution is to place the burden of proof on the party seeking to avoid responsibility for the entire injury, along with relaxing the burden of production. This allows the factfinder to divide damages based on the available evidence. Ultimately, however, the sufficiency of the evidence is determined by applicable procedural rules.

i. Inconsistent jury findings. Having juries assign different sets of percentages for different parts of damages creates the possibility of inconsistent verdicts. A jury might find that specific conduct was legally culpable in one set of percentages but not in another. Similarly, a jury might compare specific conduct at different ratios of responsibility in different sets of percentages.

The problem of inconsistent jury findings is inherent in a decision to have the jury make two or more assignments of responsibility. The problem could be avoided by having the jury make only one assignment of responsibility for the plaintiff's entire injury. See Comment *j*. That solution has problems of its own, however, because it could make a defendant liable for damages the defendant did not cause or make a plaintiff bear more of the loss than the plaintiff caused. See Comment *d*. Sometimes that problem is unavoidable. See Comment *j*. When it is not, however, the problem of inconsistent verdicts is less serious than the problem of holding a party liable for injuries it did not cause.

Normally, small variations in responsibility in different sets of percentages is tolerable, especially when they do not affect thresholds for modified comparative responsibility or joint and several liability. See § 7, Comment *n*; § D18. These variations normally do not require correction or a new trial. Ultimately, however, the effect of inconsistent findings is determined by each jurisdiction's applicable law. It is not determined by the rules in this Restatement. Because any inconsistency will be apparent on the face of the verdict, courts can have the jury correct the inconsistency, thereby avoiding a new trial. See Fed. R. Civ. P. 49(b).

j. One-step apportionment. Sometimes a court may determine that the two-step process in Subsection (a) is administratively unsuitable because the case is too complex for a jury to find the requisite facts. The complexity of apportioning liability in a two-step process increases as the number of relevant causes increases. Thus, a court may decide to use a one-step process of apportionment. The factfinder determines the total recoverable damages and then assigns percentages of responsibility to each person who caused some of the damages.

These percentages add to 100 percent. See § 7, Comment *g*. When assigning percentages of responsibility, the factfinder takes into account evidence relevant to comparative responsibility, see § 8, and evidence relevant to causation.

The percentages of responsibility affect liability in the same way as for an indivisible injury. Thus, whether a plaintiff is barred from recovery depends on the applicable rule of pure or modified comparative responsibility. See § 7, Comment *n*. Whether defendants are jointly and severally liable depends on the applicable rules of joint and several liability. See Topic 2.

A problem with a one-step process is that it may result in a party's being held liable for more damages than the party caused. See Comment *d*. A party's comparative responsibility is distinct from the magnitude of the injury the party caused. When the factfinder is permitted to combine these two concepts to arrive at a single apportionment of liability, there is a risk that a party will be required to pay for damages it did not cause. Thus, the two-step process in Subsection (a) is used unless the court determines that it is administratively infeasible.

A second problem with a one-step process is that there is no clear standard for determining whether the two-step process in Subsection (a) is administratively infeasible. Nevertheless, some cases may be so complex that courts need leeway to depart from the two-step process. However, courts are properly mindful that the two-step process in Subsection (a) is preferable.

k. Apportionment of liability depends on legal rules about causation, damages, what constitutes a legally cognizable injury, and how the injury is characterized. This Topic and this Restatement depend on existing rules about legal causation, damages, what constitutes a legally cognizable injury, and how an injury is characterized. Whether a person is liable depends on those rules.

l. Apportionment of liability depends on factual determinations about causation and damages. In addition to depending on *legal* rules about legal cause, damages, and legally cognizable injuries, whether damages are divisible depends on *factual* determinations about the plaintiff's damages and the causal relationship between the tortious acts and those damages. When there is conflicting evidence about these causal relationships or damages, a determination of whether the damages are divisible depends on findings about these facts. That may require special interrogatories.

m. Apportionment of liability depends on findings of legally culpable conduct and legal causation. Apportionment of liability depends on findings that each person was legally culpable and was a legal cause of all or some of the damages. See § 7; Restatement Second, Torts § 431.

n.   Apportionment of liability when liability is based on market share. When several defendants act tortiously in manufacturing and selling the same or similar products, but the plaintiff cannot identify which defendant provided the product that caused injury, some jurisdictions use "market share" liability to impose liability on each manufacturer for a portion of the damages equivalent to the manufacturer's market share. This Restatement does not address whether market-share liability should be used.

When market-share liability is used, questions arise about apportioning liability. Whether the damages can be divided by causation depends on the particular theory of market-share liability. When a plaintiff has a claim against each defendant for the portion of the injury equivalent to that defendant's market share, the plaintiff has a separate claim against each defendant and there is no issue about apportioning liability. On the other hand, when a plaintiff has a claim against a single defendant to recover full damages, there may be a need to apportion liability among the defendants.

Because of variety in the conceptual underpinnings for market-share liability, there are a number of different systems for apportioning market-share liability among defendants. Some of these systems differ from the two-step process in Subsection (a). Courts that use market share as a surrogate for proof that the defendant caused the entire damages might not consider the plaintiff's damages to be divisible. On the other hand, courts that use market-share liability as a surrogate for dividing the aggregate damages to all consumers might use a two-step process for dividing damages similar to the process in Subsection (a). Courts concerned not just with the portion of aggregate damages each defendant caused, but also with each defendant's comparative responsibility, might apportion liability under the one-step process similar in Comment *j.*

Because of the substantial variation in market-share systems and the concomitant variation in methods for apportioning liability among defendants, this Restatement leaves the rules for such apportionment to the applicable jurisdiction's law.

*

APPENDICES

NOTE: While the main text of this book represents a collection of the most important Tort concepts assembled with a view to law school coursework on the subject, the underlying Restatements of the Law from which it was derived are much more expansive. In order to put the contents of the abridged text into its larger context and to provide a path to further research, these appendices display a full topical outline of the three contributing bodies of Resatatement material. In all, they reflect four volumes of the Restatement of Torts Second and the two volumes published to date of Torts Third. They are available in your law library, shelved and on line.

ANALYSIS

APPENDIX A

RESTATEMENT SECOND, TORTS

DIVISION ONE

INTENTIONAL HARMS TO PERSONS, LAND, AND CHATTELS

CHAPTER 1
MEANING OF TERMS USED THROUGHOUT THE RESTATEMENT OF TORTS

CHAPTER 2
INTENTIONAL INVASIONS OF INTERESTS IN PERSONALITY

TOPIC 1. THE INTEREST IN FREEDOM FROM HARMFUL BODILY CONTACT

TOPIC 2. THE INTEREST IN FREEDOM FROM OFFENSIVE BODILY CONTACT

***

CHAPTER 4
DEFENSES OF PERSON, LAND, AND CHATTELS—RECAPTION

TOPIC 1. SELF-DEFENSE AND DEFENSE OF THIRD PERSONS

TOPIC 2. DEFENSE OF ACTOR'S INTEREST IN HIS EXCLUSIVE POSSESSION OF LAND AND CHATTELS

CHAPTER 5

ARREST AND PREVENTION OF CRIME

TOPIC 1. ARREST
TITLE A. DEFINITIONS

Chapter 7

INVASIONS OF THE INTEREST IN THE EXCLUSIVE POSSESSION OF LAND AND ITS PHYSICAL CONDITION (TRESPASS ON LAND)

Chapter 8

PRIVILEGED ENTRIES ON LAND

CHAPTER 10
PRIVILEGES INTENTIONALLY TO INVADE INTERESTS IN PRESENT AND FUTURE POSSESSION OF CHATTELS

TOPIC 1. PRIVILEGES ARISING FROM CONSENT

TOPIC 2. PRIVILEGES ARISING IRRESPECTIVE OF CONSENT

DIVISION TWO
NEGLIGENCE

Chapter 12
GENERAL PRINCIPLES

***

CHAPTER 13

LIABILITY FOR CONDITION AND USE OF LAND

Chapter 14

LIABILITY OF PERSONS SUPPLYING CHATTELS
FOR THE USE OF OTHERS

TOPIC 1. RULES APPLICABLE TO ALL SUPPLIERS

CHAPTER 16
THE CAUSAL RELATION NECESSARY TO RESPONSIBILITY FOR NEGLIGENCE

TOPIC 1. CAUSAL RELATION NECESSARY TO THE
EXISTENCE OF LIABILITY FOR ANOTHER'S HARM

TITLE A. GENERAL PRINCIPLES

***

***

CHAPTER 17
CONTRIBUTORY NEGLIGENCE

TOPIC 1. GENERAL PRINCIPLES

TOPIC 2. WHEN BAR TO ACTION

TOPIC 3. WHEN NO BAR TO ACTION

TOPIC 4. CONTRIBUTORY NEGLIGENCE OF THIRD PERSONS; IMPUTED NEGLIGENCE

CHAPTER 17A
ASSUMPTION OF RISK

CHAPTER 18
NEGLIGENT INVASIONS OF INTERESTS IN THE PHYSI-CAL CONDITION OF LAND AND CHATTELS

CHAPTER 19
RECKLESS DISREGARD OF SAFETY

DIVISION THREE
STRICT LIABILITY

CHAPTER 20
LIABILITY OF POSSESSORS AND HARBORERS OF ANIMALS

TOPIC 1. TRESPASS BY LIVESTOCK

TOPIC 2. HARM CAUSED BY ANIMALS OTHERWISE THAN BY TRESPASS BY LIVESTOCK

287

DIVISION FIVE
DEFAMATION

CHAPTER 24
INVASIONS OF INTEREST IN REPUTATION

CHAPTER 25

DEFENSES TO ACTIONS FOR DEFAMATION

***

DIVISION SIX
INJURIOUS FALSEHOOD

CHAPTER 28
INJURIOUS FALSEHOOD
(Including Slander of Title and Trade Libel)

TOPIC 1. GENERAL PRINCIPLE

TOPIC 2. DISPARAGEMENT OF PROPERTY IN OR QUALITY OF LAND, CHATTELS AND INTANGIBLE THINGS

TOPIC 3. RULES APPLICABLE TO ALL PUBLICATION OF INJURIOUS FALSEHOOD

TOPIC 4. PRIVILEGES TO PUBLISH INJURIOUS FALSEHOOD

TOPIC 5. BURDEN OF PROOF AND FUNCTIONS OF COURT AND JURY

DIVISION SIX-A
PRIVACY

CHAPTER 28A
INVASION OF PRIVACY

DIVISION SEVEN
UNJUSTIFIABLE LITIGATION

CHAPTER 29
WRONGFUL PROSECUTION OF CRIMINAL PROCEEDINGS
(Malicious Prosecution)

TOPIC 1. GENERAL PRINCIPLES

TOPIC 2. TERMINATION OF PROCEEDINGS

TOPIC 3. PROBABLE CAUSE

TOPIC 4. PURPOSE

CHAPTER 33
RELATION OF PARENT AND CHILD

TOPIC 1. DIRECT INTERFERENCE WITH RELATION

TOPIC 2. INDIRECT INTERFERENCE WITH RELATION

DIVISION NINE
INTERFERENCE WITH ADVANTAGEOUS ECONOMIC RELATIONS

***

CHAPTER 37
INTERFERENCE WITH CONTRACT OR PROSPECTIVE CONTRACTUAL RELATION

***

CHAPTER 37A
INTERFERENCE WITH OTHER FORMS OF ADVANTAGEOUS ECONOMIC RELATIONS

***

DIVISION TEN
INVASIONS OF INTERESTS IN LAND OTHER THAN BY TRESPASS

CHAPTER 39
INTERESTS IN THE SUPPORT OF LAND

TOPIC 1. WITHDRAWING LATERAL SUPPORT

TOPIC 2. WITHDRAWING SUBJACENT SUPPORT

CHAPTER 40
NUISANCE

TOPIC 1. TYPES OF NUISANCE

CHAPTER 41

INTERFERENCE WITH THE USE OF WATER ("RIPARIAN RIGHTS")

Introductory Note and Scope Note to Chapter

TOPIC 1. DEFINITIONS

DIVISION ELEVEN
MISCELLANEOUS RULES

CHAPTER 42
INTERFERENCE WITH VARIOUS PROTECTED INTERESTS

CHAPTER 45A
IMMUNITIES

CHAPTER 46
DISCHARGE

DIVISION THIRTEEN
REMEDIES

CHAPTER 47
DAMAGES

TOPIC 1. GENERAL STATEMENTS

CHAPTER 48
INJUNCTION

TOPIC 1 . APPROPRIATENESS OF INJUNCTION

APPENDIX B

RESTATEMENT THIRD, TORTS (PRODUCTS LIABILITY)

CHAPTER 1
LIABILITY OF COMMERCIAL PRODUCT SELLERS BASED ON PRODUCT DEFECTS AT TIME OF SALE

TOPIC 1. LIABILITY RULES APPLICABLE TO PRODUCTS GENERALLY

TOPIC 2. LIABILITY RULES APPLICABLE TO SPECIAL PRODUCTS OR PRODUCT MARKETS

CHAPTER 2
LIABILITY OF COMMERCIAL PRODUCT SELLERS NOT BASED ON PRODUCT DEFECTS AT TIME OF SALE

CHAPTER 3
LIABILITY OF SUCCESSORS AND APPARENT MANUFACTURERS

APPENDIX C

RESTATEMENT THIRD, TORTS (APPORTIONMENT OF LIABILITY)

TOPIC 1
BASIC RULES OF COMPARATIVE RESPONSIBILITY

TOPIC 2
LIABILITY OF MULTIPLE TORTFEASORS
FOR INDIVISIBLE HARM

TRACK A
JOINT AND SEVERAL LIABILITY

INDEX

Most of the entries in this index refer to sections of *Restatement Second*, whose text dominates this compendium. References to *Restatement Third, Torts: Products Liability*, are denoted PL; references to *Restatement, Third Torts: Apportionment of Liability*, are designated APP. Within a section, "Com" refers to material in a Comment.

A

ABNORMALLY DANGEROUS ACTIVITIES
Generally, **Chapter 21, §§ 519–524A**
Abnormally sensitive activity, plaintiff's, **§ 524A**
Aircraft, ground damage from, **§ 520A**
Assumption of risk, **§ 523**
Contributory actions of third persons, animals and forces of nature, **§ 522**
Contributory negligence, **§ 524**
Factors, determining, **§ 520**
Strict liability, general principle, **§ 519**

ABNORMALLY DANGEROUS ANIMALS
Domestic animals, harm by abnormally dangerous, **§ 509**

ABNORMALLY SENSITIVE ACTIVITIES
Abnormally dangerous activities, strict liability for, **§ 524A**

ABSOLUTE PRIVILEGES
Invasion of privacy, **§ 652F**

ACTIONABLE PER SE
See Defamation

ACTOR'S DUTY TO RETREAT
See Duty To Retreat

ACTS OR OMISSIONS
Animals, acts of. See Animals and Livestock
Inadequate instructions or warnings, product defect categories, **PL § 2**
Negligence, act or failure to act, **§ 284**

ADMINISTRATIVE OFFICERS
Defenses to defamation actions, privileges, **§ 591**

ADMINISTRATIVE REGULATIONS
See Statutes, Rules, and Regulations

ADMISSION OF PUBLIC
Land leased for purpose involving admission of public, lessor's liability to persons on, **§ 359**

ADULT ACTIVITIES
Child engaging in adult activity, standard for, **§ 283A Com.** *c*

INDEX

AFFIRMATIVE ACTION
Duties of affirmative action, generally, §§ 314–323

AFFIRMATIVE DEFENSES
Products liability, apportionment of responsibility, **PL § 17**

AGENCIES, PUBLIC
Public nuisance, parties who can recover for, § 821C

AGREEMENTS
See Contracts and Agreements

AIRCRAFT
Ground damage from aircraft, abnormally dangerous activities, § 520A

ALLERGIC REACTIONS
Adequacy of warnings, product defect categories, **PL § 2 Com. *k***

ALTERATION
Adequacy of instructions or warnings, product defect categories, **PL § 2 Com. *p***

AMELIORATION DOCTRINES
Apportionment of liability, **APP § 3**

ANIMALS AND LIVESTOCK
Abnormally dangerous activities, contributing actions of animals, § 522
Domestic animals
    Harm by abnormally dangerous, § 509
    Liability for harm by, § 518
Land possessor's liability to invitees for harmful acts of, § 344
Trespass by livestock, § 504
Wild animals, possessor's liability, § 507

APPORTIONMENT OF LIABILITY
    Generally, **APP §§ 1–8, 10–17, 26, 33**
Amelioration doctrines for defining plaintiff's negligence abolished, **APP § 3**
Assigning shares of responsibility, factors for, **APP § 8**
Causation
    Divided by causation, when damages can be, **APP § 26**
    Proof of plaintiff's negligence and legal causation, **APP § 4**
Comparative responsibility, basic rules of, **APP §§ 1–8**
Concert, persons acting in, **APP § 15**
Contractual limitations on liability, **APP § 2**
Contribution, **APP § 23**
Independent tortfeasors, joint and several or several liability for, **APP § 17**
Indivisible injury of plaintiff, effect of plaintiff's negligence upon, **APP § 7**
Intentional tortfeasors, **APP § 1 Com. *c*; APP § 12**
Intentional torts, failure to protect plaintiff from specific risk of, **APP § 14**
Joint and several liability
    Effect on apportionment, **APP § 10**
    Partial settlement, effect of, **APP § 16**
Multiple tortfeasors' liability for indivisible harm, generally, **APP §§ 10–17**
Partial settlement, effect on jointly and severally liable tortfeasors' liability of, **APP § 16**
Plaintiff's negligence, proof of, **APP § 4**
Proof of plaintiff's negligence and legal causation, **APP § 4**
Several liability, effect of, **APP § 11**

APPORTIONMENT OF RESPONSIBILITY
Products liability, apportionment of responsibility, **PL § 17**

APPREHENSION OF HARMFUL CONTACT
See Assault

308

INDEX

APPROPRIATION OF NAME OR LIKENESS
Invasion of privacy, § 652C

ASSAULT
Generally, § 21, § 22, § 30, § 31
Conditional threat, § 30
Words, threat by, § 31

ASSUMPTION OF RISK
Abnormally dangerous activities, § 523; § 524 Com. *b*

ASSUMPTION OF RISK
Apportionment of liability, relationship to, **APP** § 3 Com. *c*

ATTORNEY FEES

Damages, § 914

ATTORNEYS AT LAW
Defenses to defamation actions, § 586

ATTRACTIVE NUISANCE
Artificial conditions highly dangerous to trespassing children, liability for, § 339 Com. *e*

AVOIDABLE CONSEQUENCES
Apportionment of liability, **APP** § 3 Com. *b*
Diminution of damages, § 918

AWARENESS
See Notice or Knowledge

B

BARBED WIRE
Defense of property, using mechanical devices for, § 84 **Com.** *c*

BATTERY
Bodily contact, interest in freedom from offensive, § 13
Harmful bodily contact, generally, § 13, § 16
Intent
    Harmful bodily contact, § 13(a), § 16, § 16 Com. *a*
    Offensive bodily contact, § 20
Offensive bodily contact, generally, §§ 18–20

BELIEF
Fraudulent misrepresentation, conditions of, § 526

BENEFIT OF THE BARGAIN
Fraudulent misrepresentation, damages for, § 549 Com. *l*

BODILY HARM
Defamation, damages in actions for, § 623
Nonpecuniary harm, compensatory damages for, § 905

BREACH OF CONTRACT
Intentional interference with contract, relation to, § 766 Com. *v*

BURDEN OF PROOF
Apportionment of liability, division of damages by causation, **APP** § 26 **Com.** *h*
Intentional interference with contract or prospective contractual relation, factors, § 767, § 767 **Com.** *k*
Negligence, proof of, generally, § 328A
Res ipsa loquitur, § 328D

BURDEN OF PROOF—Continued
Risk outweighing utility of act or manner of action, § **291 Com.** *b*

BUSINESS PREMISES OPEN TO THE PUBLIC
Third persons and animals, liability of possessor of land to invitees for harmful acts of, § **344**

BUSINESS
Slanderous imputations affecting, § **573**

C

CARETAKERS
Persons with dangerous propensities, duty of persons in charge of, § **319**

CAUSAL CONNECTION
Apportionment of liability, factors for assigning responsibility, **APP** § **8**

CAUSAL RELATION
See Negligence

CAUSATION
Apportionment of liability. See Apportionment of Liability
Intentional interference with contract, § **766 Com.** *l*
Superseding cause. See Negligence

CHANGE
Adequacy of instructions or warnings, product defect categories, **PL** § **2 Com.** *p*

CHATTELS
Conversion, generally, § **222A**, § **229**
Defenses of person, land, and chattels, generally, **Chapter 4**
Possession of land and chattels, defense of interest in, § **77**, § **84**, § **85**
Trespass to chattels, Generally, § **217**, § **218**

CHILDREN AND MINORS
Artificial conditions highly dangerous to trespassing children, § **339**
Mental deficiency, standard for negligent conduct, § **283B, Com.** *a*
Negligence, standard of conduct for children, § **283A**
Parent's duty to control conduct of child, § **316**

CIRCUMSTANTIAL EVIDENCE
Product defect, inference of, **PL** § **3**
Res ipsa loquitur, § **328D, Com.** *b*

CLASS
Defamation of group or class, § **564A**

COMING TO THE NUISANCE
Defenses, § **840D**

COMMERCIAL SELLER OR DISTRIBUTOR
Liability for harm caused by defective products. See Products Liability

COMMON CARRIERS
Abnormally dangerous activities, assumption of risk, § **523 Com.** *g*
Negligence, special relations giving rise to duty to aid or protect, § **314A(1)**

COMMUNICATIONS, DEFAMATORY
See Defamation

COMMUNITY
Abnormally dangerous activities, community value of, § **520 Com.** *k*
Customs of community, determining whether conduct is negligent, § **295A**

INDEX

311

INDEX

CONTRACTUAL RELATIONS, PROSPECTIVE
Interference with. See Interference with Contract or Prospective Contractual Relations

CONTRIBUTION
Apportionment of liability, **APP § 23**

CONTRIBUTORY NEGLIGENCE
Abnormally dangerous activities, **§ 524**
Misrepresentations. See Misrepresentation
Strict liability of product seller for physical harm to user or consumer, **§ 402A Com.** *n*

CONVERSION
Generally, **§ 222A, § 229**

COURTS AND JUDGES
Abnormally dangerous activities, functions of court, **§ 520 Com.** *l*
Defamation actions, **§ 614**
Legislative or regulatory standards for conduct, adoption of, **§ 286**
Negligence, court functions, **§ 328B**
Nondisclosure, liability for, **§ 551 Com.** *m*

CRIMINAL CONDUCT
Negligence, risk of criminal conduct, **§ 302B**
Slanderous imputations of, **§ 571**
Superseding cause, tortious or criminal acts the probability of which makes actor's conduct negligent, **§ 449**

CUSTODY OF PERSONS
Special relations giving rise to duty to aid or protect, **§ 314A(4)**

CUSTOMS
Standard of conduct, determining, **§ 295A**

D

DAMAGES
Generally, **§§ 904–920A**
Avoidable consequences, **§ 918**
Benefit to plaintiff resulting from defendant's tort, **§ 920**
Compensatory damages, generally, **§§ 905–906**
Defamation actions, generally, **§§ 620–623**
Diminution of damages, generally, **§§ 918–920A**
General damages. See General Damages
Intentional interference with contract, **§ 766 Com.** *t*
Litigation expense, **§ 914**
Mitigation. See Mitigation of Damages
Nominal damages, defamation actions, **§ 620**
Nonpecuniary harm, compensatory damages for, **§ 905**
Past, present, and prospective harms, **§ 910**
Payments to injured party, effect of, **§ 920A**
Pecuniary harm, compensatory damages for, **§ 906**
Punitive damages, **§ 908**
Special damages, **§ 904(2)**
Taxation, effect of, **§ 914A**

DANGEROUS ACTIVITIES
Abnormally dangerous. See Abnormally Dangerous Activities
Trespassers, land possessor's liability to constant, **§ 334**

INDEX

INDEX

DEFAMATION—Continued
Slander. See Slander
Special harm, communications causing, §§ **575–576**
True statements, § **581A**
Witnesses. See Privileges, *supra* this group

DEFECTIVE CONDITION
Strict liability of product seller for physical harm to user or consumer, § **402A**

DEFECTS, DESIGN
Product defect categories, **PL** § **2**

DEFENSES
Assumption of risk. See Assumption of Risk
Contributory negligence. See Contributory Negligence
Defamation actions. See Defamation
Nuisance, coming to the, § **840D**
Person, land, and chattels, Generally, **Chapter 4**

DESIGN DEFECTS
Product defect categories, **PL** § **2**

DIRECTIONS
Strict liability of product seller for physical harm to user or consumer, § **402A Com.**
  j

DISABILITIES, PHYSICAL
Negligence, standard of conduct, § **283C**

DISCLAIMERS
Defenses to products liability claims for harm to persons, **PL** § **18**

DISEASES
Slanderous imputations of loathsome disease, § **572**

DISTRESS, EMOTIONAL
See Emotional Distress

DISTRIBUTORS OF PRODUCTS
Apportionment of responsibility among plaintiff, sellers and distributors of defective
  products, **PL** § **17**
Liability of. See Products Liability

DOMESTIC ANIMALS
See Animals and Livestock

DROPPED OBJECTS
Ground damage from aircraft, § **520A**

DRUGS, PRESCRIPTION
Defective products, harm caused by, **PL** § **6**

DURATION OF INVASION
Nuisance liability, § **821F Com.** *g*

DURESS
False imprisonment, confinement by duress, § **40A**

DUTY TO RETREAT
Force not threatening death or serious bodily harm, § **63 Com.** *m*
Force threatening death or serious bodily harm, § **65(2)(a), (3); § 65 Com.** *g*
Negligent conduct, § **64(2)**

E

EMERGENCIES
Entries on land, belief in necessity, §§ **196–197**

314

EMERGENCIES—Continued
Legislation or regulation, excused violations of, § **288A**
Negligence, standard of reasonable conduct, § **296**

EMOTIONAL DISTRESS
Damages in defamation actions, § **623**

EMOTIONAL DISTRESS
Nonpecuniary harm, compensatory damages for, § **905**
Outrageous conduct causing severe distress, § **46**

EMOTIONAL DISTURBANCE
Physical harm resulting from, negligent, § **436**

EQUITABLE RELIEF
Intentional interference with contract, § **766 Com. *u***

ESCAPE
Means of escape from confinement, knowledge of, § **36(2)**, § **36 Com. *a***

ESTOPPEL
Defenses to products liability claims for harm to persons, **PL** § **18**, **PL** § **18 Com. *b***

EVIDENCE
Apportionment of liability, proof of plaintiff's negligence and legal causation, **APP**
  § **4**
Burden of proof. See Burden of Proof
Circumstantial. See Circumstantial Evidence
Legislation or regulation, unexcused violations of, § **288B**
Proof of negligence, generally, §§ **328A–328D**
Res ipsa loquitur, § **328D**
Witnesses. See Defamation

EXCULPATION
Defenses to products liability claims for harm to persons, **PL** § **18**

EXCUSED VIOLATIONS
Legislation or regulation, § **288A**

EXECUTIVE OFFICERS
Defenses to defamation actions, privilege, § **591**

EXISTING CONDITIONS
Land leased for purpose involving admission of public, lessor's liability to persons on,
  § **359**

EXPECTATIONS, CONSUMER
Inadequate instructions or warnings, product defect categories, **PL** § **2 Com. *g***

EXTREME CONDUCT
Severe emotional distress, intentional infliction of, § **46**

F

FACT
Fraudulent misrepresentation of fact, liability for, § **525**, § **525 Com. *d***
Mistaken belief of fact, trespass on land under, § **164**
Questions of fact. See Questions of Law and Fact

FALLING OBJECTS
Ground damage from aircraft, § **520A**

FALSE IMPRISONMENT
  Generally, § **35**, § **36**, §§ **39–42**

INDEX

H

HARM, SIGNIFICANT
Nuisance, liability for, § 821F

HARMFUL CONTACT
Interest in freedom from. See Assault; Battery

HEALTH CARE PROVIDERS
Manufacturers' failure to instruct or warn prescribing and other health care providers, **PL § 6 Com.** *d*

HOUSEHOLD MEMBERS
Licensees, as, **§ 330 Com.** *h*

HUSBAND AND WIFE
Defenses to defamation actions, privilege, § 592

HYPERSENSITIVE PERSONS OR PROPERTY
Nuisance liability, **§ 821F Com.** *d*

I

IDIOSYNCRATIC REACTIONS
Adequacy of warnings, product defect categories, **PL § 2 Com.** *k*

ILL WILL
Intentional interference with contract, **§ 766 Com.** *r*

ILLNESS
Negligence, standard of conduct, **§ 283C**

IMAGE
Appropriation of likeness, invasion of privacy, **§ 652C**

IMMUNITIES
See Privileges and Immunities

IMPLIED ASSUMPTION OF RISK
Apportionment of liability, relationship to, **APP § 3 Com.** *c*

IMPLIED REPRESENTATIONS
Fraudulent misrepresentations, **§ 525 Com.** *e, f*

IMPRISONMENT, FALSE
See False Imprisonment

INCAPACITY
Legislation or regulation, excused violations of, **§ 288A**

INDEPENDENT TORTFEASORS
Apportionment of liability, joint and several or several liability for independent tortfeasors, **APP § 17**

INDIFFERENCE
Apportionment of liability, factors for assigning responsibility, **APP § 8**

INDIVISIBLE INJURY
Apportionment of liability, effect of plaintiff's negligence on, **APP § 7**

INFANTS
See Children and Minors

INFERENCES
See Presumptions and Inferences

317

INDEX

318

INVASION OF PRIVACY—Continued
Absolute privileges, § **652F**
Appropriation of name or likeness, § **652C**
Conditional privileges, § **652G**
Intrusion upon seclusion, § **652B**
Personal character of right of privacy, § **652I**
Publicity given to private life, § **652D**
Publicity placing person in false light, § **652E**

INVASIONS OF INTEREST IN PERSONALITY, INTENTIONAL
Generally, **Chapter 2**

INVITEES
Activities dangerous to, land possessor's liability for, § **341A**
Definition, § **332**, § **332 Com.** *a*
Special liability of possessors of land to, § **344**

J

JOINT AND SEVERAL LIABILITY
See Apportionment of Liability

JUDGES
See Courts and Judges

JUDICIAL OFFICERS
Defenses to defamation actions, privilege, § **585**

JURORS
Defenses to defamation actions, privilege, § **589**

JURY FUNCTIONS
Negligence, § **328C**

JURY QUESTIONS
See Questions of Law and Fact
Defamation actions, § **614**
Negligence, standard of conduct, § **285 Com.** *g*
Nondisclosure, liability for, § **551 Com.** *m*
Severe emotional distress, intentional infliction of, § **46 Com.** *h*

JUSTIFIABLE RELIANCE
Fraudulent misrepresentation, §§ **537–538**, § **545A**

K

KNOWLEDGE
See Notice or Knowledge

L

LAND
Invasions of interest in exclusive possession of, generally, § **158**, § **163**, § **164**
Liability for condition and use of, generally, **Chapter 13**
Liability of possessors to persons on, generally, §§ **329–344**
Trespass on land, intentional intrusions, generally, § **158**, § **163**, § **164**

LANDLORD AND TENANT
Lessor's liability to persons on land, § **359**

M

N

INDEX

NEGLIGENCE—Continued
Superseding cause—Continued
    Defined, § 440
    Intervening acts, § 447
    Intervening cause as, § 442
    Intervening force
        Causing same harm as that risked by actor's conduct, § 442B
        Normal, § 443
        Risked by actor's conduct, § 442A
    Tortious or criminal acts the probability of which makes actor's conduct negligent, § 449
Third persons, duty to control conduct of, § 315, § 316, § 319
Unreasonable conduct, determining, § 291
Utility of actor's conduct, factors in determining, § 292
Warning, effect of, § 301

NEGLIGENCE PER SE
Legislation or regulation, unexcused violations of, § 288B

NEGLIGENT CONDUCT
Self-defense against, § 64

NEGLIGENT MISREPRESENTATION
Generally, §§ 552–552B

NOMINAL DAMAGES
Defamation actions, § 620

NON-CONSUMERS
Strict liability of product seller for physical harm to, § 402A Com. *o*

NONDISCLOSURE AND CONCEALMENT
Generally, §§ 550–551

NONFEASANCE
See Acts or Omissions

NONMANUFACTURING SELLERS
Adequacy of instructions or warnings, product defect categories, **PL § 2 Com.** *o*

NON-USERS
Strict liability of product seller for physical harm, § 402A Com. *o*

NOTICE OR KNOWLEDGE
Apportionment of liability, factors for assigning responsibility, **APP § 8**
Assault, attempt unknown to other, § 22
Avoidable consequences, diminution of damages for, § 918(2)
Defense of property, using mechanical devices for, § 84 Com. *f*
Defenses to defamation actions, knowledge of falsity or reckless disregard as to truth, § 600
False imprisonment, knowledge of confinement, § 42
Fraudulent misrepresentation, conditions of, § 526
Intentional interference with contract, § 766 Com. *i*
Legislation or regulation, excused violations of, § 288A
Means of escape, § 36 Com. *a*
Negligence, duties. See Negligence
Obvious and generally known risks, Adequacy of warnings, **PL § 2 Com.** *j*
Offensive bodily contact, § 18 Com. *d*

NUISANCE
    Generally, §§ 821A–822, § 826, § 840D
Abnormally dangerous activities distinguished, § 520 Com. *c*
Defenses, coming to the nuisance, § 840D

NUISANCE—Continued
Harm, significant, **§ 821F**
Private nuisance, generally, **§ 821D**
 General liability rule, **§ 822**
Private nuisance, unreasonableness of intentional invasion, **§ 826**
Public nuisance
  Generally, **§ 821B**
 Parties who can recover for, **§ 821C**
Types, **§ 821A**

NURSES
Manufacturers' failure to instruct or warn prescribing and other health care providers, **PL § 6 Com.** *d*

O

OBVIOUS AND GENERALLY KNOWN RISKS
Adequacy of warnings, product defect categories, **PL § 2 Com.** *j*

OFFENSIVE BODILY CONTACT
Defined, **§ 19**

OFFER OF BETTER TERMS
Intentional interference with contract, **§ 766 Com.** *m*

OFFICE
Slanderous imputations affecting, **§ 573**

OFFICERS, EXECUTIVE AND ADMINISTRATIVE
Defenses to defamation actions, privileges, **§ 591**

OFFICERS, INFERIOR STATE
Defenses to defamation actions, privilege, **§ 598A**

OFFICIALS, PUBLIC
See Public Officials

OMISSIONS
See Acts or Omissions

OPINION
Defamatory communications, expressions of opinion, **§ 559**
Fraudulent misrepresentation, liability for, **§ 525, § 525 Com.** *d*

ORAL THREATS
Assault by, **§ 31**

ORDINANCES
See Statutes, Rules, and Regulations

OUTRAGEOUS CONDUCT
Severe emotional distress, intentional infliction of, **§ 46**

P

PARENT AND CHILD
 See also Children and Minors
Negligence, Parent's duty to control conduct of child, **§ 316**

PARTIAL SETTLEMENTS
Apportionment of liability, effect on jointly and several liability of tortfeasors, **APP**
 § 16

INDEX

PARTIES
Judicial proceedings, privilege of parties to, § **587**
Public nuisance, parties who can recover for, § **821C**

PAST HARMS
Damages, § **910**

PATIENTS, DIRECT WARNINGS TO
Manufacturers' failure to instruct or warn, **PL** § **6 Com.** *e*

PAYMENTS TO INJURED PARTY
Damages, effect on, § **920A**

PERSONAL CHARACTER OF RIGHT OF PRIVACY
Invasion of privacy, § **652I**

PERSONALITY, INTENTIONAL INVASIONS OF INTERESTS IN
   Generally, **Chapter 2**
Assault. See Assault
Battery. See Battery

PERSONS, DEFENSES OF
Generally, §§ **63–65,** § **76**

PHYSICAL CONDITION
Negligence, harm increased in extent by other's unforeseeable physical condition,
   § **461**

PHYSICAL DISABILITY
Negligence, standard of conduct, § **283C**

PHYSICAL FORCE
Confinement by. See False Imprisonment

PHYSICAL HARM
Defined, § **7(3)**
Negligence. See Negligence

PHYSICIANS
Manufacturers' failure to instruct or warn prescribing and other health care providers, **PL** § **6 Com.** *d*

PLACE
Abnormally dangerous activities, § **520 Com.** *j*

PLAINTIFFS
Apportionment of liability, effect of plaintiff's negligence upon, **APP** § **7**
Apportionment of responsibility among plaintiff, sellers and distributors of defective
   products, and others, **PL** § **17**

POLITICAL SUBDIVISIONS
Public nuisance, parties who can recover for, § **821C**

POSSESSION OF LAND AND CHATTELS
Defense of interest in possession, § **77,** § **84,** § **85**
Possessor of land, special relations giving rise to duty to aid or protect, § **314A(3)**
Trespass to chattels, liability to possessor for, § **218**

PRESCRIPTION DRUGS
Defective products, harm caused by, **PL** § **6**

PRESENT HARMS
Damages, § **910**

PRESUMPTIONS AND INFERENCES
Product defect, inference of, **PL** § **3**

PUBLIC INTEREST
Defenses to defamation actions, privileged communication to one who may act in public interest, § **598**

PUBLIC NECESSITY
Land, privileged entry on, § **196**

PUBLIC NUISANCE
See Nuisance

PUBLIC OFFICIALS
Defamation, § **580A**
Public nuisance, parties who can recover for, § **821C**

PUBLIC, PREMISES OPEN TO
Land leased for purpose involving admission of public, lessor's liability to persons on, § **359**
Negligence, special relations giving rise to duty to aid or protect, § **314A(3)**
Third persons and animals, land possessor's liability to invitees for acts of, § **344**

PUBLICATIONS
Libel. See Defamation

PUBLICITY
False light, publicity placing person in, § **652E**
Private life, invasion of privacy, § **652D**

PUBLISHERS
Defenses to defamation actions, privileged protection of publisher's interest, § **594**

Q

QUESTIONS OF LAW AND FACT
Abnormally dangerous activities, court functions, § **520 Com.** *l*
Apportionment of liability, divisibility of damages, **APP** § **260 Com.** *f*
Defamation actions, § **614**
Intentional interference with contract, causation, § **766 Com.** *o*
Liability for negligence, § **328B Com.** *b, g*; § **328C Com.** *a*
Negligence
    Court functions, § **328B**
    Jury functions, § **328C**
Nondisclosure, liability for, § **551 Com.** *m*
Product safety statutes or regulations, noncompliance and compliance with, **PL** § **4**
Severe emotional distress, intentional infliction of, § **46 Com.** *h*

R

RADIO
Defamation, § **568A**

RAILINGS, SPIKED
Defense of property, using mechanical devices for, § **84 Com.** *c*

REAL PROPERTY
See Land

REASONABLE CARE
Abnormally dangerous activities, risk not eliminated by reasonable care, § **520 Com.** *g*

S

THREATS—Continued
Offensive bodily contact. See Assault

TIME OR DATE
Nuisance liability, duration of invasion, § 821F Com. *g*

TORTIOUS ACTS
Superseding cause, tortious or criminal acts the probability of which makes actor's conduct negligent, § 449

TRADE
Negligence, undertaking in profession or trade, § 299A
Slanderous imputations affecting, § 573

TRESPASS ON LAND
Intentional intrusions on, generally, § 158, § 163, § 164

TRESPASS TO CHATTELS
Generally, § 217, § 218

TRESPASSERS
Definition, § 329
Possessors of land, liability to trespassers by, §§ 333–335, § 339

TRUTH
Defamation, true statements, § 581A
Privilege defenses to defamation actions, reckless disregard as to truth, § 600

U

UNREASONABLE RISK
Determining unreasonable risk, § 291

UNREASONABLY DANGEROUS CONDITIONS
Strict liability of product seller for physical harm to user or consumer, § 402A

USE OF FORCE
See Privileges and Immunities

USERS
Strict liability of product seller for physical harm to user or consumer, § 402A

W

WAIVER
Defenses to products liability claims for harm to persons, PL § 18, PL § 18 Com. *b*

WARNINGS
Defense of property, using mechanical devices for, § 84 Com. *f*
Highly dangerous activities, failure to warn of artificial, § 335
Inadequate warnings, product defect categories, PL § 2, PL § 2 Com. *i, j*
Licensees, activities dangerous to, § 341 Com. *c*
Negligence, effect of warning, § 301
Strict liability of product seller for physical harm to user or consumer, § 402A Com. *j*
Trespassers, effect on land possessor's liability for dangerous activities to, § 334 Com. *f*

WARRANTY
Product defect categories, PL § 2 Com. *r*
Strict liability of product seller for physical harm to user or consumer, § 402A Com. *m*

INDEX

WEAPONS
Defense of property, using mechanical devices for, § **84 Com.** *d*, § **85**

WIFE AND HUSBAND
Defenses to defamation actions, privilege, § **592**

WILD ANIMALS
Possessor's liability, § **507**

WITNESSES
See Defamation

WORDS AND PHRASES
Abnormally dangerous, § **520 Com.** *f*
Actual injury, § **621 Com.** *b*
Basic fact, § **551 Com.** *j*
Basic, § **551 Com.** *j*
Battery, § **13**, § **18**
Bodily contact, offensive, § **19**
Burden of proof, § **328A Com.** *a*
Business visitor, § **332(3)**
Care, § **519 Com.** *c*
Children, standard of conduct, § **464(2)**
Common usage, § **520 Com.** *i*
Confinement, § **36**
Consent, § **10A**
Consumers, § **402A Com.** *l*
Contact with another's person, § **18 Com.** *c*
Contractual limitations on liability, **APP** § **2 Com.** *a*
Contributory negligence, § **463**, § **463 Com.** *b*
Conversion, § **222A**
Culpability, **APP** § **8 Com.** *a*
Defamatory communication, § **559**
Defective because of inadequate instructions or warnings, **PL** § **2**
Defective in design, **PL** § **2**
Domestic animal, § **506(2)**
Duty, § **4**
Express assumption of risk, **APP** § **2 Com.** *a*
Fact, § **525 Com.** *d*
Facts basic to the transaction, § **551 Com.** *j*
Fraudulent misrepresentation, § **526**
Further harm, § **322 Com.** *b*
General damages, § **621 Com.** *a*; § **904(1)**
Harm, § **7(2)**
Has reason to know, § **339 Com.** *g*
Inducing, § **766 Com.** *h*
Injury, § **7(1)**
Intent, § **8A**, § **8A Com.** *a*
Interest, § **1**
Invitee, § **332**, § **332 Com.** *a*
Learned intermediary rule, **PL** § **6 Com.** *b*
Legal cause, § **9**; § **431**
Legally protected interests, § **1 Com.** *d*
Licensee, § **330**
Manufacturing defect, **PL** § **2**, **PL** § **2 Com.** *c*
Misfeasance, § **314 Com.** *c*
Negligence "per se," § **288B Com.** *a*
Negligence, § **463 Com.** *b*
"No duty" rules, **APP** § **1 Com.** *c*
Non-feasance, § **314 Com.** *c*
Nuisance *per accidens*, § **821A Com.** *b*

INDEX

†